Th

19
97

17.
22. APR.

-6. JUN. 1

-1. D

24.

14.

PRENTICE-HALL
HISTORY OF MUSIC SERIES
H. WILEY HITCHCOCK, editor

second edition

NINETEENTH-CENTURY ROMANTICISM IN MUSIC

REY M. LONGYEAR

Department of Music
University of Kentucky

PRENTICE-HALL, INC., ENGLEWOOD CLIFFS, NEW JERSEY

Library of Congress Cataloging in Publication Data

Longyear, Rey Morgan.
    Nineteenth-century romanticism in music.

    (Prentice-Hall history of music series)
    Includes bibliographies.
    1. Music—History and criticism—19th century.
2. Romanticism in music.   I. Title.
ML196.L65 1973   780'.9034   72-3962
    ISBN 0-13-622670-1
    ISBN 0-13-622647-7 (pbk.)

Printed in the United States of America

10 9 8 7 6 5 4 3 2 1

© 1973, 1969 by Prentice-Hall, Inc.
Englewood Cliffs, New Jersey

PRENTICE-HALL INTERNATIONAL, INC., *London*
PRENTICE-HALL OF AUSTRALIA, PTY. LTD., *Sydney*
PRENTICE-HALL OF CANADA, LTD., *Toronto*
PRENTICE-HALL OF INDIA PRIVATE LIMITED, *New Delhi*
PRENTICE-HALL OF JAPAN, INC., *Tokyo*

TO DON, GORDON, ADELLE, AND NORMA JEAN

Music is the most Romantic of all the arts, as its subject is only the Infinite, the secret Sanskrit of Nature expressed in tones which fill the human heart with endless longing, and only in music does one understand the songs of the trees, flowers, animals, stones, floods!

E. T. A. HOFFMANN, *Kreisleriana*

[A Romantic work is] that kind of composition in which the artist freely gives himself up to the dominion of the imagination, considering all means as good, provided they produce effect. The grand requisite, therefore, in the romantic, is virtually to declare that the writer is not deficient in this quality, and that he has produced something piquant and new. It is to be doubted that many composers would venture to employ so dangerous a term, if they knew its true value.

The Harmonicon, 1830

What is Classic? What is Romantic? Two categories which, perhaps, are estranged only through exaggeration.

J. A. DELAIRE, "Des Innovations en musique,"
Revue musicale, 1830

FOREWORD

Students and informed amateurs of the history of music have long needed a series of books that are comprehensive, authoritative, and engagingly written. They have needed books written by specialists—but specialists interested in communicating vividly. The Prentice-Hall History of Music Series aims at filling these needs.

Six books in the series present a panoramic view of the history of Western music, divided among the major historical periods—Medieval, Renaissance, Baroque, Classic, Romantic, and Contemporary. The musical cultures of the United States, Latin America, and Russia, viewed historically as independent developments within the larger western tradition, are discussed in three other books. In yet another pair, the rich yet neglected folk and traditional music of both hemispheres is treated. Taken together, the eleven volumes of the series are a distinctive and,

Foreword continued

we hope, distinguished contribution to the history of the music of the world's peoples. Each volume, moreover, may be read singly as a substantial account of the music of its period or area.

The authors of the series are scholars of national and international repute—musicologists, critics, and teachers of acknowledged stature in their respective fields of specialization. In their contributions to the Prentice-Hall History of Music Series their goal has been to present works of solid scholarship that are eminently readable, with significant insights into music as a part of the general intellectual and cultural life of man.

H. WILEY HITCHCOCK, *Editor*

PREFACE

The spectrum of nineteenth-century music is characterized by a number of familiar and even overly-familiar compositions, a larger number of worthy works that have fallen into neglect, and an enormous mass of music still awaiting classification and evaluation. To the general observer, the history of nineteenth-century music resembles a panorama of mountains, some in shadow, separated by mist-shrouded valleys; in the limited space of this volume, an author describing this period can only direct the reader's attention to various aspects of the peaks, tell him something about their shadowy portions, and point out some of the salient features of the valleys.

In the few years that have elapsed since the writing of the first edition there has been a great upsurge of interest in the music of the nineteenth century, especially in that of its neglected composers. Festivals of Romantic music have given listeners an opportunity to hear works in live performance that are mentioned in histories of music but had been unperformed for several decades. Unfamiliar operas of the period have been revived, and recording companies have shown a new interest in the lesser-known works of a musically prolific and vital century. Much formerly unavailable music has been reprinted or has appeared in new editions prepared by enterprising publishers. Younger scholars are increasingly investigating the buried treasures of musical Romanticism. The nineteenth century is no longer an era to be rejected and disdained, but is now a frontier for investigation by enterprising scholars and performers.

Some of the procedures I have followed and some of the priorities I have assigned require explanation. The bibliographical notes at the end of each chapter are highly selective and emphasize works in English; those who desire additional references should consult the bibliographies for the pertinent articles in *Grove's Dictionary of Music and Musicians, Die Musik in Geschichte und Gegenwart, Music Index,* and, for studies from 1967 onwards, *RILM Abstracts.* Wherever feasible, I have used the English titles of compositions where they have common currency, even at the risk of such incongruities as "Siegfried's Rhine Journey" from *Die Götterdämmerung,* or have translated generally unfamiliar titles into English, such as *Wallenstein's Camp* for *Valdštynuv Tábor.* I have endeavored to follow current practices in transliterating Russian proper names rather than to perpetuate the antiquated French or German versions that still clutter concert programs and to use, as far as current practice permits, the original rather than the German spellings of the names of Czech composers.

Though this volume has been substantially expanded from its original form, it is still a survey rather than a comprehensive history of nineteenth-century music; approximately 150 composers are discussed in this study as contrasted with the 629 in William S. Newman's magisterial *The Sonata Since Beethoven.* I have found it particularly necessary to exclude those composers whose influence did not significantly extend beyond the single medium in which they were active; I thus apologize to cellists, violinists, and organists for omitting Sebastian Lee and Grützmacher, Vieuxtemps and Wieniawski, Boëly and Karg-Elert. Chapter 10 presented a special problem since by 1900 virtually every European people had its own "national" art music, and my approach was limited to those national schools and their composers with an international significance. The volumes in this series dealing with Russia, Latin America, and the United States should more than compensate for the limited treatment I have given the music of these countries. Chapter 11 posed another problem because of the number of post-Romantic composers whose careers began with many important works written during the nineteenth century yet whose active musical lives continued well into the twentieth; for those who may consider my discussions of d'Indy, Puccini, Mahler, and Richard Strauss to be too brief, I must point out that in this volume I have considered only their nineteenth-century careers and refer the reader to the subsequent volume in the Prentice-Hall series for coverage of their twentieth-century works. Finally, there are several important subsidiary aspects of nineteenth-century music—aesthetics, musical journalism, musical historiography, the composer's creative process, and the various "subcultures" of musical Romanticism—that I have had to mention only in passing or omit altogether.

Space does not permit my extending a personal acknowledgment to all those whose comments and suggestions were so valuable in preparing the second edition. I would like, however, to express my special gratitude to Mosco Carner, John Clapham, Jorge Mester, Donald Mintz, William S. Newman, and Abraham Schwadron, to my students, and to several of my colleagues at the University of Kentucky, especially Clifford Amyx, Lois Campbell, Mischa Fayer, Arthur Graham, W. S. Krogdahl, and Wesley Thomas. Stuart Forth, director of libraries at the University of Kentucky, and Adelle Dailey, Norma Jean Gibson, and Ronald Lloyd of his staff provided highly professional and unfailingly cheerful and valuable assistance. Jean-Marie Martin of Hollogne-aux-Pierres, Belgium, and Blackwell's Music Shop of Oxford, England, were of great assistance in procuring music, especially from eastern Europe, for this study. Through the kindness of M. François Lesure of the Bibliothèque nationale in Paris, I was enabled to participate in a week-long colloquium on nineteenth-century music in France (the results described in *Acta Musicologica*, XLIII [1971]) and thereby had the opportunity to encounter the most recent ideas on this period from an international coterie of colleagues. A sabbatical leave from the University of Kentucky and a grant from the John Simon Guggenheim Memorial Foundation provided time and funds for travel and study abroad during the spring of 1972; though the results of this study period are too specialized and detailed for inclusion in this volume, I was nevertheless enabled to hear many of the works discussed here in live performance before native audiences and to see many of the works of art described in the first chapter. Finally, I wish to acknowledge the editorial assistance of H. Wiley Hitchcock, the patience of Carole Richardson of Prentice-Hall, the encouragement of research among my superiors at the University of Kentucky, and the help of my wife in so many wonderful ways.

R. M. L.

CONTENTS

ONE

ROMANTICISM
AND MUSIC

narrowest

1828 – 1880

1789 – 1914

broadest

The very term "Romanticism" has conjured up, as Arthur Lovejoy has remarked, "one of the most complicated, fascinating, and instructive of all problems in semantics." Some writers have called for the abolition of this overly elastic term, yet what word could replace it?

Any period term, like Baroque, or Romantic, can be used pejoratively, neutrally, or as a term of praise; as a convenient substitute for citing dates; or to mean what its users intend it to mean. To writers on music, Romanticism means music between 1828 and 1880 in its narrowest and 1789 to 1914 in its broadest sense. Some consider Romanticism, in opposition to Classicism, a phenomenon which recurs throughout artistic and intellectual history: J. S. Bach, Monteverdi, the troubadours, St. Paul, and Plato have been called "Romantics" by various writers. Others wish to limit the term drastically to those German writers of the 1790's and those French writers of the 1830's who called themselves Romantics. The present fashion is to consider Classicism and Romanticism as oppo-

1

site sides of the same coin current between 1740 and 1830 (at its most limited) and 1910 (at its broadest); this eliminates searches for precursors or survivals or a jumble of "pre-," "post-," and "neo-" prefixes, but on the other hand does not fully take into account the changing clusters of musical and other ideas during the 90 to 170 years included in this period. A period term is simply a convenient way of implying that certain norms exist which at least tenuously link the personages and ideas subsumed under this heading, that other persons and configurations of thought are excluded, and also that a certain chronology exists even though the terminal dates at each end cannot be fixed with much precision and considerable overlapping occurs with adjacent periods.

CAN ROMANTICISM BE DEFINED?

Romanticism is a difficult period term to define because its protagonists, as opposed to their rationalistic predecessors, were so wary of definitions. Victor Hugo's statement that Romanticism was "a certain vague and indefinable fantasy" is as close to the mark as any attempt at a concrete definition; examination of salient characteristics will serve us better.

First of all, this movement was an international manifestation, strongest in Germany, quite influential in England, France, and Russia, but also evident in Bohemia, Poland, Spain, and Italy. Secondly, the nineteenth century was a period of extreme contrasts, and any idea expressed was certain to elicit its exact opposite. In religious thought, for example, one may compare the diverse ideas of Joseph Smith, Pope Pius IX, Ernst Haeckel, and Mary Baker Eddy and recall that religious martyrdom occurred not only in Uganda and Indo-China during this period but also in Paris under the Commune of 1871. This diversity explains why we can subsume under the heading of Romanticism such contradictory composers as Bruckner and Offenbach, Donizetti and Brahms, Chopin and Sousa. Thirdly, Romanticism repudiated Classic emphases on harmonious adjustment, discipline, moderation, and adaptation whereas it valued striving rather than achieving, becoming rather than being, emotional and inspired rather than rational expression, Classic "uniformitarianism," on the other hand, considered differences in opinion and taste to be evidences of erroneous deviation from the "rationalist collectivism" which taught that the artist should try to communicate not the unique but the views and sentiments common to an idealized mankind. Finally, none of the past seven centuries has ended without a significant change in musical style during its last decade. In the 1790's a new musical language became evident, albeit well-prepared by significant forerunners, and it existed side by side with the old musical language (Haydn, Pleyel, Rossini) for a few decades; a similar co-existence took place during the period from 1890 to 1914 (Debussy, Stravinsky, and subsequently Schoenberg as opposed to d'Indy, Elgar, and Mahler), the new idiom becoming, around 1910, what is loosely called "contemporary" music.

Are we justified in calling the musical language which became discernible as a new idiom around 1790 and declined during the first decade of the twentieth century Romantic? Ernst Theodor Amadeus Hoffmann (1776–1822), a writer with unimpeachable Romantic credentials, considered J. S. Bach, Haydn, Mozart, and especially Beethoven to be Romantics, and Théophile Gautier (1811–1872), a charter member of the Romantic movement, bestowed a similar accolade on Berlioz and Chopin. Hoffmann remarked on several occasions that music, particularly instrumental music, was the most Romantic of the arts, and instrumental music was at least intellectually dominant between 1790 and 1910; it may also be noted that during the nineteenth century both opera and art-song had increasingly active instrumental accompaniments. Parallels, some more tenuous than others, can be drawn between the new expressive melody, the rhythmic experimentation, the coloristic use of harmony and instrumental timbres, the relaxation of and uncertainty about formal canons, the veneration and occasional misuse of the legacy of the past mingled with a sense of writing for the future, and the new tendencies in poetry, the drama, the novel, the pictorial arts, and architecture which are customarily called Romantic. A few of the external themes common to Romanticism in general that are reflected in the music of the nineteenth century deserve closer examination.

Individualism. The intense individualism and subjectivity of the Romantic composer, paralleling that of the Romantic poet, artist, or even ruler, have dictated the very organization of this volume by composers rather than by musical genres. There is no "typical" Romantic symphony, art-song, piano piece, or composer, much as there is no typical Romantic novel, poem, painting, or artist. What musical period can show such intense individualists as Beethoven and Wagner, or such deeply subjective composers as Chopin, Schumann, Chaikovsky, and Mahler? This individuality is reflected in the number of popular biographies of Romantic composers (to say nothing of the fictional novels or films about them) in which information about their lives overwhelms facts about their work. And in studying the lives of these composers one is amazed at the number of highly complex personages, from Beethoven and Weber to Mahler and Skryabin, with such relatively uncomplicated figures as Spohr, Verdi, Dvořák, and Fauré in the minority. The lives, letters, and memoirs of most of the preceding and succeeding generations of composers seem almost prosaic in comparison.

Intensity of feeling, which is better sensed through hearing the music itself rather than reading a verbal description of it, separates Romantic music from its eighteenth- and twentieth-century counterparts much as this same intensity divides Classic and "Modern" from Romantic in the other arts.

One form of this Romantic intensity of feeling has been given the name *Weltschmerz*, best understood as a feeling of world-weariness with overtones of frustration and as a melancholy which at its extreme can lead to pathological states of nihilism, insanity, and suicide. Goethe's *Werther* (1774), in which the protagonist kills himself over unrequited love, is a prototype of this pathological despair in literature. In music such Romantic pathology transpires most often on the operatic stage, with the "mad scenes" of such works as Bellini's *I Puritani*, Donizetti's *Lucia di Lammermoor*, and Thomas' *Hamlet*, or the suicides in Donizetti's *Lucia di Lammermoor*, Verdi's *Luisa Miller* (based on Schiller's *Kabale und Liebe*, one of the most powerful "*Sturm und Drang*" dramas), Wagner's *Flying Dutchman* and *Die Götterdämmerung*, and Puccini's *Madame Butterfly*.

There is a sweetly gloomy tone (*morbidezza*) in much Romantic music. This had occasionally surfaced during the Classic period in such works as Mozart's A minor Rondo, K. 511, and G minor String Quintet, K. 516, but it appears more strongly in some piano works by Field, Chopin, Glinka, Balakirev, and Skryabin, or in the *Weltschmerz* of Schubert, Chaikovsky, and Mahler. A counterpart to the morbidness that parallels the irrationalism and demonism of E. T. A. Hoffmann and Lenau in literature or the *Caprichos* (1790–1800) of Francisco Goya (1746–1828) and the nightmare paintings of Henry Fuseli (1741–1825) in art is the macabre diabolism of Berlioz, Liszt, and Mahler.

In contrast, and also as an example of one of many illustrations of the diversities and contradictions in Romanticism, there is a determined optimism in much Romantic music, best seen in the finales of many of the symphonies from Beethoven through Dvořák or in the apotheoses of the Lisztian symphonic poem—an optimism comparable to that of Victor Hugo (1802–1885) and Alfred Lord Tennyson (1809–1892).

Changes in this intensity of feeling mark the transition from Romanticism to post-Romanticism. The muting of this intensity through understatement in many of the works of Saint-Saëns, Chabrier, Fauré, Puccini, and Debussy constitutes one of the principal reactions against Romanticism and should also serve as a warning against lumping too many late-nineteenth-century composers under the heading "neoclassic." On the other hand, an exaggeration of intensity can be seen in the negation of the optimistic finale, from Chopin's B-flat minor Sonata through the suicidal despair of the last movement of Chaikovsky's Sixth Symphony and the concluding song of Mahler's *Das Lied von der Erde,* the forced optimism of the finales of Glazunov's Fourth and Mahler's Seventh Symphonies, and the ending of Richard Strauss' *Also sprach Zarathustra,* at first nostalgic and then cryptic.

Romanticism as escape. The two principal historical trends of the nineteenth century, industrialization and nationalism, both provoked Romantic reactions. The Industrial Revolution, prominent only in England by 1800, had by the close of the century spread all over Europe and even to Japan and the United States. Though the Romantics appreciated the economic growth that provided financial support for the arts, the urban public that could be more easily reached, the expansion of education (many Romantics, like Rousseau, Pestalozzi, Macaulay, and Froebel, provided impetus for educational reform), and creature comforts like steamship and rail travel or the electric light, most Romantics rebelled against the ugliness of the "dark Satanic mills," the dehumanization of factory life in which workers were regarded as things, the exaggeration of materialism into a cult of progress, and the glorification of a mechanistic science. A new view of art took shape: whereas in the eighteenth century art was often degraded to an entertainment and diversion (accounting for the pretty superficiality of much art and music of the time), now it was ennobled as an escape, even as a substitute for religion. The feeling of a private world into which the composer would lead his audience is discernible in Beethoven's late sonatas and quartets and reaches peaks in Wagner's *Ring, Tristan,* and *Parsifal,* Mahler's idea of the symphony as an entire world, and the twentieth-century exaggeration by Skryabin of an orchestral work as an entire synaesthesic universe.

The love of an unspoiled pre-industrial nature that characterizes much pre- and early Romantic poetry and painting (from Goethe, Wordsworth, Thoreau, and Constable to Ruskin, Corot, and the Barbizon school of painters) had a strong and powerful counterpart in music. Although Haydn was the only "nature-lover" of the Classic period, the number of such Romantic composers is legion, headed by Beethoven, whose "Pastoral" Symphony, almost contemporaneous with Wordsworth's *The Prelude,* bore the warning "With more of an expression of feeling than painting" to contrast with the naive musical imitations of Handel and Haydn. Space permits the mention of only the most conspicuous portrayals of nature by Romantic composers: the forest paintings in Weber's *Der Freischütz* or Wagner's *Siegfried;* the landscapes and seascapes of Mendelssohn and Gade; the Alpine pictures in Schumann's or Chaikovsky's *Manfred;* the love of wandering that permeates the music of Schumann and Brahms; the moods of the sea as depicted in Wagner's *Flying Dutchman* or Rimsky-Korsakov's *Sadko, Scheherazade,* and *Tsar Saltan.* And just as the attempts to portray nature impressionistically rather than realistically by such painters as J. M. W. Turner (1775–1851), Claude Monet (1840–1926), and Paul Cézanne (1839–1906) gave birth to twentieth-century styles of painting, so did a similar musical aesthetic, with nature as the dominant theme of his program music, cause Debussy to strike out along a new musical path and Schoenberg to evolve an entirely new kind of orchestral writing in his coloristic portrayal of "Summer Morning by a Lake" in his *Five Orchestral Pieces*, Op. 16 (1909).

Whether Romanticism was an escape from the political systems of the nineteenth century is a moot, if not meaningless, question. The variety, contradictions, and simultaneities of Romanticism at any particular time are reflected in the divergent political systems of the period; one need but recall that the regimes of Andrew Jackson in America, Tsar Nikolai I in Russia, Prince Metternich in Austria, and Louis Philippe in France all overlapped. As a general rule, the Romantic musician tended to support political stability, since this was necessary for the support of the arts, though welcoming and supporting changes that led to a more open society and the mitigation of censorship, repression, and the suppression of ethnic minorities. If we view the political spectrum from "left" to "right," the two extremes are seen in France, with the Saint-Simonian Félicien David at one pole and the monarchist anti-Dreyfusard Vincent d'Indy at the other. From the overt or implied political sentiments of the composers of the century one can distinguish, apart from nationalist ideas, a majority sentiment for what we would call a moderate bourgeois urban liberalism by nineteenth-century standards that would have been repelled by extremes of either democracy or reaction.

Romanticism and nationalism. Romanticism as a movement was international, yet it appeared at different times in different places and spoke with different voices and accents. When we speak of Classicism, in music or any other art, we refer to an all-embracing movement unified by its cultural uniformity and its practitioners who crossed national boundaries with ease: Hasse, Gluck, Haydn, and Mozart in music, Voltaire, Thorwaldsen, Casanova, and Benjamin Franklin in other spheres of eighteenth-century activity. Romanticism, on the other hand, is always given a nationally qualifying adjective (German, Russian, French) despite the "family likenesses," as Barzun has called them, among the manifestations of this movement in all lands. And as nineteenth-century nationalism is characterized by the spread of national consciousness, identities, and artistic achievements to formerly suppressed or ignored ethnic and linguistic groups, musical nationalism is exemplified by the emergence of major voices with their own national as well as personal identities: the lands that produced Pushkin, Mickiewicz, Palacký, and Ibsen also produced Glinka, Chopin, Smetana, and Grieg.

There are two kinds of nationalisms, defending and aggressive.

Defending nationalism is characterized by dedication to achieving a cultural identity and by a strong emphasis on the arts; aggressive nationalism seeks to impose a cultural identity on others. Defending nationalism has a strong streak of idealism in it and can be international as well as national (as witness the careers of Verdi and Dvořák in music or the comparable careers of Walter Scott, Mazzini, Aleksandr Herzen, and Theodor Herzl), whereas an aggressive nationalism is closely identified with *Realpolitik*, xenophobia, and the suppression of counter-national tendencies. One can best see defending nationalism in the plots of the eastern European "national" operas, for their settings deal with times of troubles rather than national aggrandizement: Glinka's *A Life for the Tsar*, Erkel's *Hunyádi Lászlo*, and Smetana's *The Brandenburgers in Bohemia* are representative illustrations.

In the course of the century nationalism became aggressive in many lands and thus lost its Romantic connotations. In music the change is not as much in content as it is in context and in its associations. Wagner's aggressive nationalism after 1860 is less evident in *Die Meistersinger* and the *Ring* than in his venomous literary attacks on the French and the Jews, and even the most rhapsodic admirer of Brahms passes in silence over his *Triumphlied,* written to celebrate the German victory over the French in the Franco-Prussian War of 1871, which can be considered a watershed date in western Europe for the change from defending to aggressive nationalism. A subtle shift from defending to aggressive nationalism can be seen in several works in various countries written after this date: Bizet's *Patrie* overture, d'Indy's *Symphonie cévenole*, Chaikovsky's *Marche slave* and *1812 Overture,* Elgar's "Pomp and Circumstance" marches (paralleling the imperialist poetry of Rudyard Kipling), Dudley Buck's overture on "The Star-Spangled Banner," and the marches of John Philip Sousa which accompanied America's aggressive entry as a world power in 1898. Yet no musical compositions contain the bitter chauvinist venom that bubbles to the surface in some of the writings on music, not only of Wagner, but also of Saint-Saëns, d'Indy, and Pfitzner, and these make a shabby contrast to the friendly and cosmopolitan openness of the composers of the first half of the century like Beethoven, Schumann, Berlioz, Glinka, and Liszt.

Minor themes. Even in some of Romanticism's minor themes, and in the contradictions within them, one can discern close parallels between music and the other arts. Romantic hedonism, especially in amatory matters (Shelley, Byron, Victor Hugo) is paralleled not only in the lives of Glinka, Liszt, and Skryabin but also in the operas of Massenet and Puccini; yet in Wagner's operas the love interest has a happy outcome only in *Die Meistersinger,* and one may note the immense number of nineteenth-century composers who died unmarried: Beethoven, Schubert, Chopin, Liszt, Bruckner, Musorgsky, Hugo Wolf. An early death terminating a meteoric career of intense creativity is a hallmark of the Romanticism of the first half of the century (Wackenroder, Novalis, Shelley, Keats, Byron, Géricault, the painter Philipp Otto Runge, Leopardi, Pushkin, Lermontov, Poe); it is paralleled not only by the short lives of Schubert, Bellini, Weber, Mendelssohn, and Chopin but also by the Romanticized views of the brief careers of Pergolesi and Mozart. Significantly, the idolization of the Romantic prodigy-composer who died young belongs to the first half of the nineteenth century. This is indicative of another trend; during the first half of the century Romanticism is characterized by youth, as witness the amount and quality of music produced by Beethoven, Rossini, Mendelssohn, Chopin, and Schumann before their thirtieth birthdays, whereas after 1850 (with Richard Strauss as the solitary exception) virtually every composer had but barely embarked on his career by the time he was thirty.

ROMANTIC WRITERS AND MUSIC

The seeds for the interpenetration of the arts which was such a salient characteristic of the nineteenth century were sown by Jean-Jacques Rousseau (1712–1778), known chiefly as a social and educational philosopher and novelist but also gifted in music, musical criticism, and sketching. To him, and to a lesser extent the writers of the French *Encyclopédie* (28 vols., 1751–1772), can be credited the virtual mania for writing about music that arose around 1770.

During most of the eighteenth century, writings about music were by musicians for musicians, and the musical interests of the nonprofessional authors of the time were directed to such practical topics as the use of incidental music in the drama. After 1770 a greater interest in music is a hallmark of German literature, as seen, for example, in the frequent use of music as a literary effect, such as the expressive clavichord playing by Lotte in Goethe's *Werther* or Lady Caroline in Klinger's drama *Sturm und Drang* (1776), which gave its name to an entire if brief literary epoch. "Romantic" musicians as literary figures begin to appear in the mid-1770's and culminate in the incarnation of the Romantic musician, Kreisler, in the stories and novels of E. T. A. Hoffmann.

The writers associated with the movement known as Weimar Classicism—Christoph Martin Wieland (1733–1813), Johann Wolfgang von Goethe (1749–1832), Johann Gottfried Herder (1744–1803), and Friedrich Schiller (1759–1805)—had a lively and often Romantic interest in music. Herder collaborated with J. C. F. Bach, one of J. S. Bach's sons, translated the texts of Handel's *Messiah* and *Alexander's Feast,* and collected folk songs. Schiller distrusted the effect of music because of its appeal to sensuous natures, yet precisely because of its power he used incidental music extensively in most of his dramas, musical metaphors and characterizations in many of his literary works, and musical ideas as an ancillary but not insignificant part of his aesthetic system. Among Goethe's many other activities in Weimar, he also wrote texts for *Singspiele* for amateur court productions and later served as director of the court theatre, where most of the significant operas of the 1780's and 1790's were performed. Yet the musical tastes of these writers were inherently conservative: Schiller ranked Gluck above Haydn and Mozart, Herder considered vocal music superior to "empty" instrumental music and disliked the dominance of music over text in Mozart's operas, and Goethe, though a champion of Mozart's music, rejected the settings of his songs by Beethoven and especially Schubert, preferring the simple tunes of Carl Friedrich Zelter (1758–1832).

Other interesting personages of the time with intense musical activities were C. D. F. Schubart (1739–1791), an organist and composer as well as a poet, aesthetician, and journalist who was imprisoned for his libertarian ideas, and Johann Friedrich Reichardt (1752–1814), a composer and journalist whose activities on behalf of the French Revolution involved him in a celebrated literary feud with Goethe and Schiller.

The role of music in the thought of the German Romantics who came to maturity in the 1790's remains fully to be investigated. One can credit the increasing interest in music partially to the novels of J. J. W. Heinse (1746–1803), but the most influential of the early Romantic writers on music seems to have been Wilhelm Heinrich Wackenroder (1773–1798), who influenced both Hoffmann and Ludwig Tieck (1773–1853). With both Wackenroder and Jean Paul (J. P. Friedrich Richter, 1763–1825), one senses the idea of music as a drug or balm; Wackenroder could listen to music attentively for only an hour, but found that music, apart from the particular mood created by a given composition, would stimulate his thought and imagination (Schiller similarly liked to have music played in an adjoining room while he wrote). "In the mirror of tones the human heart learns to know itself; it is how we learn to feel feelings," Wackenroder wrote, and his fictional musician Josef Berglinger heard "sounds that seem to be words" in music. Jean Paul's ideas on music were Romantic in their contradictions: he once compared music's effect to a lion's tongue licking at the heart "which tickles and scratches until the blood flows," yet later called music, rather than poetry, the "happy art." He preferred the "simple souls" of Haydn and Mozart to composers with great self-possession like Reichardt, and his description of Walt's hearing a Haydn symphony is so rhapsodic, colorful, and impassioned that one would suspect that Beethoven or Schumann had been the composer.

Though Tieck was a musical amateur, Hoffmann spent five years as Kapellmeister (musical director) in Bamberg and directed an opera troupe for a year; composed sonatas, chamber music, and several operas of which *Undine* (1816) is considered a landmark in German Romantic opera; wrote reviews for the *Allgemeine musikalische Zeitung*, the leading musical journal of the time; and created in Kreisler one of the greatest fictional musicians.

Tieck and Hoffmann both agreed that instrumental music was superior to vocal music. In his essay "Symphonien," published in 1814, Tieck regarded the "symphony," as he understood it, as the highest form of art and considered sonatas and chamber music merely as preliminary studies for it, yet he seems to be discussing Reichardt's music for *Macbeth* and Beethoven's music to *Egmont.* Despite his activity as an opera composer and conductor, Hoffmann gave instrumental, and particularly orchestral, music the palm. His statement "Music is the most Romantic of all the arts" recurs constantly throughout his writings, but in his essay "Beethoven's Instrumental-Musik" he qualified it to refer to instrumental music alone. Other Romantic writers placed a primary emphasis on music; among them, Jean Paul stated that "no color is as Romantic as a tone," and Heinrich von Kleist (1777–1811) considered music the root of all the other arts.

Hoffmann tended to view all his musical heroes—Beethoven, Mozart, Haydn, even J. S. Bach and Palestrina—as Romantics. Though he esteemed Haydn for perceiving "the human in human life Romantically," he was among the first to appreciate the daemonic element in Mozart's music and compared Bach's eight-part motets to the "daring, wonderful, Romantic" construction of the Strasbourg cathedral. Hoffmann mocked the shallow appeal of virtuosos and repeatedly portrayed the dualism between the Romantic artist and the pseudo-cultured "Philistine," a favorite topic of later Romantic writers on music like Berlioz and Schumann.

All of the German Romantic writers, as well as such later poets as Baudelaire (1821–1867) and Verlaine (1844–1896) and musicians like Skryabin and Ciurlionis, and even the historian Oswald Spengler (1880–1936), perceived music as part of a glorious synaesthesia, *audition colorée,* in which words were tones and tones colors. Heinse called music a "speech without consonants." Tieck asked, "Isn't it permitted and possible to think in tones and to make music in words and thoughts?" and Hoffmann described how, after hearing much music, he experienced a delirium preceding sleep in which he felt a synaesthesia of colors, tones, and odors.

Music played a less significant role in the writings of the French Romantics; it was not a major force until the 1880's, with the symbolist poets and the *Révue Wagnerienne*. French Romanticism was later than its German counterpart and, except for Rousseau and Chateaubriand (1768–1848), did not fully develop until 1830. Henri Beyle (1783–1842), writing under the pen name of Stendhal, was the French writer most interested in music; although his biographies of Mozart and Haydn were at least partially plagiarized, his *Life of Rossini* (1824) is still a valuable document. Yet Stendhal disliked Weber's music. Although Honoré de Balzac (1799–1850) gave lip service to Beethoven and Alfred de Musset (1810–1857) to Schubert, their chief delights were Italian opera and French Grand Opera; Balzac's two musical novellas, *Massimilla Doni* and *Gambara,* are rhapsodic analyses of, respectively, Rossini's *Mosé in Egitto* and Meyerbeer's *Robert le Diable.* The lady writers of the French Romantic period found the musicians of the time most interesting as amatory partners. Théophile Gautier discussed only three composers in his *History of Romanticism* (1874): Berlioz, Chopin, and the insignificant Hippolyte Monpou (1804–1841). Though he jokingly confessed to the Goncourt brothers that he preferred silence to music, he publicly supported Berlioz and was one of the first Frenchmen to come to Wagner's defense. The French Romantic novelists chiefly used music to portray social milieux, and their works are excellent sources for a sociological history of music.

In conclusion, the influence of Romantic writers on composers was greater than the influence of composers, even in Germany, on the writers. Romantic literature is echoed through the music of the nineteenth century far more than Romantic music is discussed or even mentioned in the writings of the time. It is also important to recall that most nineteenth-century musicians had strong interests and capabilities in other fields, in contrast to the preceding century when such versatile figures as Rousseau, Schubart, and Reichardt were rarities. Berlioz and Wagner were significant literary figures apart from their music; Weber, Schumann, and d'Indy had more than a common competence as authors; and many composers wrote their memoirs or a series of essays on music. Spohr, Mendelssohn, and especially Mikolajus Ciurlionis (1875–1911) were gifted painters, and the latter's paintings with musical titles, e.g., "Serpent Sonata," represent a high point of Romantic synaesthesia. Many Romantic musicians were musical journalists, and such composers as Brahms, Chaikovsky, Saint-Saëns, and d'Indy edited early music. Most Romantic composers were well-read and literarily sensitive to a degree unprecedented in the history of music, and only a few musical figures, like Bruckner and Dvořák, displayed the exclusive concentration on music characteristic of most eighteenth-century composers.

THE END OF ROMANTICISM

Literary historians date the end of Romanticism between 1843, when Victor Hugo's drama *Les Burgraves* failed, and 1849, when the last of the unsuccessful revolutions which had convulsed continental Europe was suppressed. Historians of the visual arts usually end Romanticism at about 1863, with the death of Delacroix and the revolt against French academic painting shown in the *Salon des Refusés*. The movements that followed—Realism, Naturalism, and Symbolism—represent the continuation of Romanticism, but along various lines, much as a river spreads out various arms to form a delta. Parallels between these movements and Romanticism in music can be drawn in only limited instances. For whereas Realism and Naturalism represented a seeking to portray real life and were often supported by a strong social conscience, music showed a tendency after 1850 either to withdraw into its own autonomous realms (the private world of the Wagnerian music drama, a return to absolute music, a "defending" musical nationalism) or to intensifying previous Romantic trends to a final point of exaggeration or disintegration.

The socially conscious aspects of Realism and Naturalism had little place in music, not even on the operatic stage where parallels between musical and literary trends are most obvious. There were no musical equivalents of Charles Dickens (1812–1870), Gustave Courbet (1819–1877), or Gerhard Hauptmann (1862–1946). The collaboration of late Romantic French composers like Alfred Bruneau (1857–1934) and Gustave Charpentier (1860–1956) with Naturalist authors like Émile Zola (1840–1902) had little effect on musical Romanticism. The operatic movement known as *verismo* in Italy at the end of the century was a degradation of Naturalism, employing its shock techniques for melodramatic purposes rather than for rousing an audience to seeking social reform and ending injustice. Musorgsky is the only nineteenth-century composer of major stature to be thoroughly influenced by Realism and Naturalism.

Realism takes a different turn in the music of Wagner and Liszt. Though Wagner had created his private operatic worlds as a retreat from real life, he depicted their internal details with great literalness through his meticulous stage directions and liberal reiteration of leitmotives, especially in the *Ring*. The eroticism of Wagner's *Tristan* and Liszt's "Vallée d'Obermann" from Book I (Suisse) of his *Années de Pèlerinage* is almost tangibly palpable (which can account for the swooning in the audience that often occurred during performances of *Tristan*), in contrast to the sublimated eroticism of Brahms, the perfumed eroticism of Skryabin's later works, or the theatrical sensuality of the heroines of Massenet and Puccini.

Symbolism is Romanticism at its least tangible and palpable and essentially consists of the use of often familiar ideas and symbols in new, unfamiliar, and even disorienting contexts. The early stages of Symbolism in music are best seen in Wagner's frequent association of leitmotives and tangible objects in the *Ring* and *Parsifal*, in which he thereby endowed spears, swords, gold, and other material objects with a considerably enhanced significance. However, not until Debussy's new pianistic and orchestral timbres, melodies, and non-functional harmonic progressions can we speak of a musical language of Symbolism. This is best seen in his setting of one of the leading Symbolist dramas, *Pelléas et Mélisande* by Maurice Maeterlinck (1862–1949), which had also inspired such diverse composers as Fauré, Sibelius, and Schoenberg. Musical Symbolism is another dividing line between the nineteenth and twentieth centuries, whether practiced by the Frenchman Debussy, the German Franz Schreker (1878–1934), the Russian Skryabin, or the Englishman Cyril Scott (1879–1971), a Theosophist like Skryabin.

Neoclassicism, parallel to Romanticism especially in music and painting, can be best viewed as a kind of constant existing from 1800 to the near-present. In Chapters 3 and 9 the musical criteria of neoclassicism will be discussed; for now it is sufficient to say that the Romantic composers inherited virtually all their forms from their Classic predecessors, and that the clarity and logically balanced structures which the Romantics considered the hallmarks of Classic music fascinated nearly every composer from Beethoven through Richard Strauss. Only in part was neoclassicism an escape to a Romantically perceived eighteenth century with its order, stability, clarity, and balance, and a corresponding rejection of the irregularity and grandiloquence of Romanticism, the literalness of Realism, the gritty seaminess of Naturalism, and the vagueness of Symbolism. It is preferable, in describing the music of either the nineteenth or the twentieth centuries, to speak of neoclassicisms in the plural, indicating that neoclassicism was no more uniform than Romanticism. The constants of these artistic neoclassicisms include simplicity, renewed emphases on form (which, however, take some surprisingly innovative turns), and selective retention and modification of all devices from the past: neoclassicism did not eschew elements from the Baroque or Renaissance. Fauré, Ravel, and Max Reger represent the same kind of division between the nineteenth and twentieth centuries in music, from the standpoint of a revival of Classicism that looks forward to modern times, that Georges Seurat (1859–1891) and the post-Impressionistic works of Paul Cézanne (1839–1906) do in painting, although this movement occasioned changes in painting far earlier than the comparable shifts in music.

Cultural primitivism, in the later years of the nineteenth century, assumed a large number of forms and a wide variety of manifestations. One aspect of cultural primitivism is a simplification that exceeds the bounds of neoclassicism by focusing on the deliberately trivial. A second aspect is the impact of music and art from outside the Romantic cultural heartland. The International Exposition of 1889 was a high point of Western colonialism, and the "primitive" arts and music of Africa and Southeast Asia were introduced for the first time to the general public, creating an impact felt well into the twentieth century. Exotic and folk arts and music provided new stimuli to jaded tastes.

Cultural primitivism is the one constant in the art historians' catchall term "post-Impressionism," which includes the Tahitian figures of Paul Gauguin (1848–1903), the sunflowers of Vincent van Gogh (1853–1900), the jungle scenes of Henri Rousseau (1844–1910), and such artistic schools as Futurism, Cubism, Vorticism, and Expressionism. Under the influence of cultural primitivism, Naturalism became grittier and more shocking, best illustrated by the scatological expletive with which Alfred Jarry's play *Ubu Roi* (1908) opens. In contrast, Symbolism either withdrew into a world of virtual incomprehensibility to the general public or entered a realm of hothouse decadence with sophisticated perversions and malaises: the genesis of this "decadence" lies in the works of Baudelaire, Verlaine, Arthur Rimbaud (1854–1891), and Algernon Swinburne (1837–1909), and its peaks are represented in the works of Joris-Karl Huysmans (1848–1907), Marcel Proust (1871–1922), Oscar Wilde (1854–1900), and Aubrey Beardsley (1872–1898). Two cities, Vienna and Paris, were the locales of *fin de siècle* decadence, played against a backdrop of impending violence that was to culminate in World War I.

Earlier in this chapter an analogy of Romanticism's branching out around 1850 with a river's spreading out arms to form a delta was presented. A delta is formed at the mouth of some rivers, e.g., the Mississippi; it is made up of swamps, marshes, occasional hummocks covered with jungle or scrub vegetation, intermixtures of fresh and salt water among isolated brackish pools, and offshore islands formed by silt deposits, with the central channel of the river lost among meanders, bayous, tributaries, and cut-off oxbow lakes. Thus was post-Romanticism between 1900 and 1914. There is no "center" in music or any of the other arts, none of the culmination and summary that we associate with the names of Michelangelo, Shakespeare, Pope, J. S. Bach, Mozart, or Haydn.

Even before World War I new changes were to terminate the intellectual outlook of the nineteenth century, not in the arts but in the sciences. Science was to change from applied technology, invention, and engineering into a pure science that was to become increasingly incomprehensible to the layman, who could understand Darwin but not the work of Albert Einstein (1879–1955) and Lord Rutherford (1871–1937) in atomic physics or Max Planck (1858–1947) in quantum physics, except that their theories shattered the orderly cosmology of the Newtonian universe much as Darwin's hypotheses shattered Protestant theology. Studies in psychological aberration and pathology culminated in the theories of the unconscious as elaborated in Vienna by Sigmund Freud (1856–1939); these had a strong impact on literature and art, for the unconscious became a new aspect of cultural primitivism. World War I simply swept away all remaining illusions: the year 1914 is a far more critical watershed date in history than even 1789, yet its terminal character was anticipated in the arts some years before Gavrilo Princip's first pistol shots at Sarajevo.

BIBLIOGRAPHICAL NOTES

The literature on the nineteenth century is extremely copious with a vast amount of material available. The following bibliography can only serve as a guide, with an emphasis on recent publications, to further reading and investigation.

The Century in General. The best short general overview of the history of the century is still R. R. Palmer's *A History of the Modern World* (New York, 1954), pp. 387–657; pertinent sections in Crane Brinton, J. B. Christopher, and R. L. Wolff's *A History of Civilization* (Englewood Cliffs, N.J., 3rd ed., 1967) are also well worth study. For more detailed investigations of the century, consult separate volumes in individual historical series. The best American series, *The Rise of Modern Europe*, contains only one recent volume, William L. Langer's *Political and Social Upheaval 1832–1852;* the other volumes, some more than thirty years old, badly need updating. A more recent English series, published by Longmans, covers the century in three volumes: Franklin L. Ford, *Europe 1780–1830;* H. Hearder's *Europe in the Nineteenth Century* [1830–1880]; and John Roberts' *Europe 1880–1945.* The intellectual history of the period is strikingly and synoptically presented in Crane Brinton's *The Shaping of Modern Thought* (Englewood Cliffs, N.J., 1963), a revision of his earlier *Ideas and Man;* the economic history is given a readable and stimulating overview by Walt W. Rostow in his *The Stages of Economic Growth* (Cambridge, 1960). A handsome and sumptuously illustrated volume, with essays on various topics by different writers, is Asa Briggs' *The Nineteenth Century* (London, 1970), providing more detail than Kenneth Clark's *Civilisation* (New York, 1969), which nevertheless contains some striking insights. Florian Znaniecki's *Modern Nationalities* (Urbana, 1952) is an excellent short nonpejorative discussion of cultural nationalism, though in music he includes Chopin and Moniuszko but omits Verdi. The artistic currents of the period are brilliantly and systematically covered, with well-chosen illustrations, in John Canaday's *Mainstreams of Modern Art* (New York, 1959). Among the most stimulating overviews of the period are Lewis Namier's *Vanished Supremacies* (1958; reprint, New York, 1963) and a synoptic social history of the world by a French historian, Charles Morazé's *The Triumph of the Middle Classes* (1957; English translation, New York, 1968), though its musical information should be used with caution.

Romanticism in general. The literature on Romanticism is extremely copious; I have found the following to be valuable because of their divergent ideas: Frederick B. Artz, *From the Renaissance to Romanticism* (Chicago, 1962); Irving Babbitt, *Rousseau and Romanticism* (New York, 1919); Arthur O. Lovejoy, "On the Discrimination of Romanticisms" in *Essays in the History of Ideas* (Baltimore, 1948); and René Wellek's articles on Romanticism in his *Concepts of Criticism* (New Haven, 1962), which includes a survey of recent writings on this topic. The methodology of W. T. Jones' *The Romantic Syndrome* (The Hague, 1961) is not readily applicable to music. Anthony Thorlby's *The Romantic Movement* (London, 1966) contains a wide selection of critical comments on Romanticism as well as many short documents.

Collections of writings by major Romantic figures in English translation are contained in Howard E. Hugo (ed.), *The Viking Portable Romantic Reader* (New York, 1957), John C. Cairns, *The Nineteenth Century 1815–1914* (New York, 1965), and John B. Halsted, *Romanticism* (London, 1969).

Of the discussions of music in connection with other currents of Romantic thought, the best is H. G. Schenk's *The Mind of the European Romantics* (Garden City, 1969). Jacques Barzun's *Classic, Romantic, and Modern* (New York, 1961, a revision of his earlier *Romanticism and the Modern Ego*) is more speculative in its discussion of music, whereas Lilian R. Furst treats music in a very cursory manner in her *Romanticism in Perspective* (London and New York, 1969). Friedrich Blume's *Classic and Romantic Music* (New York, 1970), an English translation of his articles "Klassik" and "Romantik" in *Die Musik in Geschichte und Gegenwart*, relates musical Romanticism chiefly to its German literary counterparts.

More specialized studies of the relationship of literary Romanticism and music are: Wilhelm Bode, *Die Tonkunst in Goethes Leben* (Berlin,

1912); R. M. Longyear, *Schiller and Music* (Chapel Hill, 1966); Willi Reich, *Musik in romantischer Schau* (2 vols., Basel, 1946), a selection of excerpts from Romantic writers; Ronald Taylor, *Hoffmann* (New York, 1963); Julien Tiersot, *La Musique aux temps romantiques* (Paris, 1930); Walter Wiora, "Herders und Heinses Beiträge zum Thema 'Was ist Musik?'" *Die Musikforschung* XIII (1960), 385–95; and Michael Spencer, "Théophile Gautier, Music Critic," *Music and Letters,* XLIX (1968), 4–17. Oliver Strunk's *Source Readings in Music History* (New York, 1950) contains excerpts, translated into English, from the writings on music by Jean Paul, Wackenroder, and Hoffmann.

TWO

ROMANTIC MUSICAL STYLES

Several of the tendencies of Romanticism in general which have been discussed in the preceding chapter also apply to Romantic musical styles. The Romantic era in music is a period of contrast and antithesis, discernible not only between generations or among different composers living at the same time, but even within the works of individual composers. Romantic musical style is also fluid rather than stable; in describing it one can speak only in terms of trends and tendencies rather than norms. Especially in the second half of the century, several differing styles existed at the same time and developed independently, and apparent "regressions," like the avoidance of chromatic harmony by Brahms, Saint-Saëns, and Fauré, proved to be "advances" in a different direction.

There is no sharp dividing line between Classic and Romantic styles, for most Romantic style-traits are based on the transformation and intensification of ideas present before 1800. Although Romantic composers, like Romantic writers and artists, were extreme individualists and sought to proclaim their uniqueness in their music, there are some discernible tendencies common to musical Romanticism that separate this movement from Classic or Modern musical styles. Some writers have objected to the use of Romanticism as a virtual synonym for nineteenth-century music, yet one can justifiably ask, "Who were the composers active between 1785 and 1905 who entirely escaped or avoided Romanticism?"

In the first chapter we saw that it is virtually impossible to find a simple definition of Romanticism in general, and that examining some themes common to Romanticism—individualism, nationalism, interpenetration of the arts, escape into nature or a vaguely identifiable past—is the more serviceable approach. A study of the writings of nineteenth-century composers or critics discloses equally thorny problems in defining musical Romanticism, for the composers were as vague and contradictory as were their literary counterparts. Although one can find in the musical writings of the nineteenth century almost any definition of Romanticism, there are a few common themes that suggest the integrity of this period as a separate epoch in the history of music.

In the preceding chapter our discussion centered around the elements common to Romantic composers and their literary and artistic contemporaries. Now the main task is to delimit musical Romanticism in terms of its musical styles: how do Romantic and Classic musical styles differ, how do the individual elements of musical style change in the course of the nineteenth century, and what happens to these stylistic elements at the end of the century so that they can no longer be called Romantic? Our discussion, couched in the most general terms from the standpoint of style in general, is planned as an overview rather than as a series of detailed investigations.

ELEMENTS OF ROMANTIC MUSICAL STYLE

Melody and periodicity. As in the Classic period, most Romantic melody is phrase-dominated, with the prevalent texture describable as "melody with accompaniment." Increased individualism is a hallmark of Romantic melody, and if one asks a layman to list ten "immortal" melodies, the chances are overwhelming that all those he cites will be from nineteenth-century works.

Two typical eighteenth-century melodies are cited in Example 2-1. Mozart's theme is concise whereas Haydn's theme is longer, but both are well balanced, closed rather than open, and with easily perceived inner relationships between the contrasting sections. Stepwise motion is dominant, and the skips and leaps are balanced by opposite stepwise motion.

EXAMPLE 2-1. (a) Mozart, String Quartet in C major, K. 465 (1784), first movement; (b) Haydn, Symphony No. 30 (1765), second movement.

In contrast, most Romantic composers sought to write long melodic lines, whether constructed from phrases (Examples 2-2a and 2-2d), motives (Example 2-2b), or, rarest of all, from a virtually seamless, unperiodic, exuberant melodic line (Example 2-2c). Instrumental themes especially tend to increase in length. The melodies of Examples 2-1a and 2-2c have similar functions: the opening allegro theme of a first movement in sonata form with the initial phrases repeated and spun out to lead the transition to the second theme group. Yet whereas Mozart's theme is nine measures long, Schumann's is thirty-two measures in length.

EXAMPLE 2-2. (a) Brahms, Symphony No. 2 (1877), second movement; (b) Richard Strauss, *Ein Heldenleben* (1899), opening; (c) Schumann, String Quartet in F major, Op. 41, No. 2 (1842), first movement; (d) Chaikovsky, Symphony No. 5 (1888), second movement.

Other devices characteristic of Romantic melody include wide leaps for expressive purposes, often leaps of sixths, sevenths, and other intervals, diminished or augmented; this tendency becomes exaggerated in late-Romantic composers, as in Example 2-2b, which also shows, in its ambitus of four octaves, the tendency toward increasing the melodic range. One may compare the relative irregularity of Brahms' melody (Example 2-2a) with the regular periodicity of Chaikovsky's (Example 2-2d); both are slow movement symphonic themes and can be considered each composer's epitome of melody *qua* melody.

Other Romantic melodies that do not correspond to the illustrations in Example 2-2 can be cited. The finely arched Classic melody, symmetrical, closed (*i.e.*, cadencing at its end) rather than open, phrase-dominated, vocally oriented, and with a stanzaic construction equivalent to that of poetry, can be found chiefly in the German Lied from Reichardt through Robert Franz; Italian opera from Rossini through middle-period Verdi; French operatic genres, including the operetta; and the short piano piece, whether abstract (Brahms' A major Intermezzo, Op. 118, No. 2) or based on dance forms (Chopin's mazurkas). Non-stanzaic melodies with loosely related phrases are one of the harbingers of musical Romanticism. A stanzaic melody and a non-stanzaic melody are shown in Example 2-3.

EXAMPLE 2-3. (a) Stanzaic melody: Beethoven, Symphony No. 4 (1807), trio of third movement; (b) Non-stanzaic melody: Koželuch, Piano Sonata in D minor, Op. 20, No. 3 (ca. 1787), first movement.

Instrumental color is often closely associated with Romantic melodies: Example 2-2a with the cello section, for example, and Example 2-2d with the solo horn. One coloristic procedure has been given the German name *Durchbrochene Arbeit* to describe a melody that is divided among various instruments; Example 2-4 is the epitome of this type. This may be compared with a late-Romantic exaggeration that

EXAMPLE 2-4. Beethoven, Symphony No. 3 (1804), first movement.

is too long to cite here, the opening of the allegro moderato section of the first movement of Glazunov's Fourth Symphony (1893), in which the theme is divided among several registers as well as instrumental colors, from high violins and flutes to the lowest strings and woodwinds. Although the melody itself is longer than Beethoven's example, there is less contrast between motives because of the composer's trying to write as effusively lyrical an idea as possible. Another late-Romantic device, seen in such disparate works as Bruckner's symphonies and Puccini's operas, is the intense, pregnant, soaring melodic climax (Example 11-2).

One type of Romantic melody, adaptable to a variety of transformations rather than just to ornamental variation, has its roots in the motivically oriented thematic work of C. P. E. Bach and Haydn. Even in the Classic period one can sense an underlying philosophical program behind the thematic transformation that occurs in minor-mode sonata-form movements, where second- and closing-group thematic material is stated in mediant major in the exposition and tonic minor in the recapitulation. A melody or motive that can undergo a wide variety of transformations is the underlying basis of Romantic cyclic form.

Associated with Romantic musical nationalism are melodies which are either borrowed folk tunes or original themes utilizing piquant char-

acteristics of folk melodies, usually irregular phrase structures or alterations of the major or minor scales. Rarely can these melodies be
subjected to development or transformation; variation, ornamentation,
re-harmonization, or fragmentation are the only possible treatments.
Several such melodies are cited in Chapter 10.

  Rhythm. Freedom and flexibility are the chief elements that separate Romantic from Classic treatments of rhythm. Although Haydn had
made occasional rhythmic experiments, as in the trio of the minuet of his
"Oxford" Symphony (No. 92), it was Beethoven who overcame what he
called the "tyranny of the bar-line" as early as 1800, as Example 2-5

EXAMPLE 2-5. Beethoven, String Quartet in B-flat major, Op. 18, No. 6 (ca.
1800), third movement.

demonstrates in its syncopations, rhythmic counterpoint, and unprecedented cross-accents. The liberation of the musical macrorhythm from
its underlying metric structure was continued throughout the century;
one need but cite such diverse orchestral scherzos as those of Schumann's First Symphony, Brahms' Second Symphony, Dvořák's Seventh
Symphony, and Chabrier's *España*.

  Cross-rhythms are of three types in the Romantic period. The first
and most common, duplets against triplets or other permutations of the
concept of two beats in one part against three in another, occurs in some
Classic music (the slow movement of Mozart's C major Piano Concerto,
K. 467); though considered a hallmark of Brahms' style, it frequently
occurs in the music of E. A. Förster, Berlioz, Chopin, Liszt, Bruckner,
and many others. A second type of cross-rhythm, consisting of silvery
washes of pianistic color with rapid, irregularly grouped notes in the
right hand against a steady beat in the left hand, is considered typical of
Hummel and Chopin but can be found as far back as C. P. E. Bach and
as far ahead as Balakirev. The most complex type of cross-rhythm, the
intersection of two or more rhythmic planes, usually a macrorhythmic
plane enhanced with syncopation against a metric microrhythm, has been
described in the preceding paragraph.

  One typically Romantic rhythmic device may be compared with
what the English Jesuit poet Gerard Manley Hopkins (1844–1889) called

"sprung rhythm," based on word stress rather than syllabic count. In music this was most frequently achieved by substituting occasional measures of meters different from the prevailing rhythmic organization (a measure of 3/4 or 6/8 in rapid 2/2 meter), syncopations, sforzando accents in the "wrong" places, and syncopated harmonic rhythms giving the effect of "misplaced" bar-lines, as in Example 9-3c.

Irregular and complex meters are sometimes present in Romantic music. Eastern European music, from Glinka to Rimsky-Korsakov, has been cited as the principal source of these meters, yet there are some curious and interesting Western counterparts in such diverse works as Boieldieu's *La Dame blanche,* Liszt's *Faust Symphony,* Cornelius' *The Barber of Bagdad,* Sullivan's *The Yeomen of the Guard,* and the finale of d'Indy's Second Symphony. By 1900 the most radical form of metric change consisted of changing beat-units as well as meters (Example 2-6).

EXAMPLE 2-6. Rimsky-Korsakov, *Tsar Saltan* (1900), Act I.

Rhythmic complications are one of the leading characteristics of late- to post-Romantic music. A thread of such complexities runs from Berlioz through Liszt to Chaikovsky, Richard Strauss, and (with Russian folk influences) Glière. Permutations of compound meters (especially 9/8), half-note triplets in 4/4 meter, constantly shifting meters, and interactions of rhythmic planes of increasingly great complexity all contribute to the establishment of twentieth-century rhythmic styles.

An apparently contrary and antithetical development in the nineteenth century is the close interpenetration of dance and art music. The idealized, stylized dance is as important to Romantic composers as it was to the writers of keyboard and orchestral suites in the Baroque. One need but cite the use of the waltz in Schubert, Schumann, Chopin, Brahms, and Richard Strauss; the quadrille in French *opéra comique,* the galop in Offenbach, the operatic processional march, or the numerous eastern European dances with their piquant rhythmic effects. Fascinating collections of Romantic dance-types are the ballet, especially among French or Russian composers, and the multitudinous collections of national or "exotic" dances for piano duet. One striking example of Romantic dance stylization is the steady dance-beat in the accompaniment with cross-rhythms in the melody.

A major failing of many of the lesser Romantic composers is that they rely on one rhythmic pattern to sustain interest throughout a major portion of a composition or symphonic movement. Another failing, often acute among late Romantics, is that they lack rhythmic imagination, and therefore their music "sags"; this is an even more acute problem when combined with frequent repetition of melodic material.

Expression. Tempo and other expression markings increase in complexity and verbosity during the Romantic period; not for the Romantics such simple terms as "allegro" and "forte"! Yet the frequent clusters of modifying adverbs are not meant to restrict the performer, but to give him more freedom and interpretative license. Not until the close of the century, with such composers as Debussy and Mahler, did composers meticulously mark each effect and nuance, doubtlessly in a reaction against some of the overly subjective interpretations by performers and conductors. Extremes of dynamic gradations from the Classic outer limits of *pp* and *ff* began with the French "rescue opera" composers of the 1790's and reached, with late Romantic composers, extremes from *ppppp* to *ffff,* or even greater.

Harmony. Separate volumes would be needed to do proper justice to the concepts of harmony and tonality in the nineteenth century. Harmony was one of the greatest pre-occupations of Romantic composers, as seen by the proliferation of treatises or textbooks on harmony between 1800 and 1914. Especially among German, German-influenced, or most late- or post-Romantic composers, harmony was the chief vehicle for musical individuality.

From the standpoint of harmony, the chief difference between Classic and Romantic composers is that the former used dissonant chords relatively infrequently and then in a functional manner, usually to enhance or intensify the progression of a dominant to a tonic or as a pivot in modulation, but Romantic composers frequently used the same chords in a coloristic sense and progressively elevated the milder dissonant chords, usually dominant or diminished sevenths, to the level of consonances. Throughout the century there is a steadily rising "dissonance threshold," especially among German and Russian composers or Franck and his disciples; a counter-reaction was the rejection of chromatic harmony for its own sake by the various kinds of "neoclassic" composers who often used diatonic harmonies in radically different ways from those of their Classic models.

Only a few general typologies of chromatic microharmony (chords and their progressions) from the Romantic period can be cited. The chord of the *diminished seventh* (F-sharp–A–C–E-flat, for example), usually an enhancement of the dominant in works in the minor mode during the Baroque and Classic periods, became elevated in the "rescue operas" of the 1790's to an all-purpose coloristic effect to depict emotional tension or storms. Early Romantic composers perceived that this chord, with its four equally possible resolutions, could open new vistas for modulation, need not be resolved if used for coloristic purposes, and could even be the first chord in a composition. Two of the many coloristic uses of this chord, one early and one late Romantic, are cited in Example 2-7: the first, from Schubert, is a coloristic expansion of tonic

EXAMPLE 2-7. (a) Schubert, String Quintet in C major, D. 956 (1828), first movement; (b) Chaikovsky, *Francesca da Rimini* (1876), opening.

harmony that permits a major-minor interchange; the second, from Chaikovsky, is a programmatic use of this chord, unprepared and unresolved, to create an atmosphere of unsatisfied yearning.

Among the other chords of the seventh, the *half-diminished seventh* (D–F–A-flat–C, for example) had been used during the Classic period in the minor mode as a cadential progression (ii°$\frac{6}{5}$6–V–i), but Romantic composers found it an effective color harmony because it had a different "flavor" in each of its four inversions. Chords of the *minor seventh* (C–E-flat–G–B-flat) and *major seventh* (C–E–G–B) were not fully discovered until the closing years of the century; with the post-Romantics they were treated as dissonant climaxes, whereas the French neoclassicists used them as passing chords in inversions, since they could fit without alteration into the minor or major scales respectively.

Altered chords represent one of the most ambiguous terminologies in the theorists' vocabularies. One must exclude from this category the so-called "borrowed" chords, whether taken from minor to major or major to minor, and the so-called "applied," "secondary," or "tonicizing" dominants, the most important means of harmonic sequence and modulation from Corelli to Schumann. Borrowed chords, chiefly diminished sevenths as enhancers of dominants, minor subdominant harmony, or the supertonic half-diminished seventh chord, all transferred from the minor to the major mode, are among the favorite harmonic devices of Beethoven's contemporaries, and their abuse (as early as Spohr) led to an insufferably cloying sentimentality that is one of the major ingredients of musical *kitsch* (see Chap. 12). Altered chords proper can be subsumed under the following headings:

1. *Chromatically altered triads, usually with the raised fifth* (the augmented triad). Whereas with Classic and even early Romantic composers this was a passing harmony from tonic to subdominant, from about 1850 onward it became a coloristic harmony for its own sake. Example 2-8 contains four highly varied, but all coloristic, uses of this

EXAMPLE 2-8. (a) Liszt, Faust Symphony (1854), first movement; (b) Liszt, "Unstern" (ca. 1883); (c) Ethelbert Nevin, "Mighty Lak' a Rose" (1901); (d) Puccini, *Madame Butterfly* (1904), Act I.

(a)

harmony: 2-8a as a harmonization of a melody containing all twelve tones of the chromatic scale; 2-8b as a coloristic device to blur a traditional feeling of tonality; (see Example 10-6b for its use as a percussive dissonance); 2-8c, an augmented triad with an added seventh, to flavor a piece of musical *kitsch;* and 2-8d, unprepared and unresolved augmented triads leading to a musical and dramatic climax.

2. *Chromatic or enharmonic alteration of a chord containing a minor seventh,* the most frequently encountered such chord being the augmented sixth. Functionally, this harmony has enhanced dominant harmonies as far back as the mid-Baroque, but during the Romantic period it was often used coloristically, often with irregular or no preparation or resolution; it is a chief constituent of the lushness of Romantic

harmony. The normal treatment of the two most critical members of this chord is to regard one as a leading-tone resolving upward, another as a seventh resolving downward, and to re-spell individual notes enharmonically in order to alter their basic tendencies of resolution; most familiar is the so-called "German sixth," an enharmonically re-spelled dominant-seventh chord. Examples 9-5 (Franck), 10-3c (Grieg), and 10-3d (Delius) show some of the varied late-Romantic uses of the chord of the augmented sixth. On a more popular level, borrowed and altered chords are the essential ingredients of "barbershop" harmony for male voices.

Non-harmonic tones in the Baroque and Classic period were mostly passing dissonances; when used on the beat they often intensified cadences, particularly a 7–8 melodic movement in a cadence in minor, or served as expressive "sighs." Although Beethoven as a rule eschewed non-harmonic tones occurring with chromatic alteration on the beat, his younger contemporaries delighted in them, even doubling them at the third or sixth below to enhance their effect. A prevalent tendency during the Romantic period was the delaying of the resolution of these accented non-harmonic tones in order to heighten the effect of yearning and longing which occurs, even in diatonic harmony, when the resolution of these tones is delayed (see Examples 8-5b, 8-5c, 8-5d).

Higher discords, a late-Romantic term, resulted from building chords upward by thirds. Whereas during the Classic and early Romantic period the upper level was the minor or major ninth, late-Romantic composers built their chords farther upward to the point where ambiguity resulted between, for example, chords of the minor thirteenth and augmented triads with an added minor seventh (see Example 2-8c).

Chord progressions during the Romantic period tend to differ from their Classic equivalents through the passage from functional to coloristic harmony, the increasing freedom in part-writing, and resolutions that are often enharmonic, delayed, or even non-existent. Precedents for nearly all of these devices can be found in the music of C. P. E. Bach. Among the late Romantics from Wagner and Liszt onward, many chords can be explained only in terms of their contexts. Any given note could be harmonized as a leading-tone, or as a seventh with a tendency to resolve downward, or the natural tendencies of given notes could be changed through enharmonic spellings. Principles of functional harmonic analysis (the "Roman numeral" system) gradually cease to be applicable because of microharmonic ambiguity and macroharmonic modulation; often only a descriptive analysis is possible. The dividing line between the nineteenth and twentieth centuries, from the standpoint of harmony, comes when chords can no longer be described in tertian terms (Skryabin's famous "mystic chord" or the quartal chords, built by fourths, in the early songs of Alban Berg); when unresolved chromatic harmonies, often further complicated by enharmonic spellings and clustered non-harmonic tones, are a pervasive fabric and lack diatonic anchors as points of reference; when diatonic or chromatic harmonies pass from one to another in a kind of side-slipping in parallel or contrary motion; or when dissonant chords are used not as functional or coloristic harmonies, but as percussive sounds in the context of a musical "cultural primitivism."

Harmonic rhythm (the rate of chord change, expressed in terms of duration) is one of the subtlest aspects of a composer's musical style. Although a fast harmonic rhythm is typical of Baroque music and a slow harmonic rhythm is characteristic of Classic music, no such generalization is possible in the Romantic period. During this era a slow harmonic rhythm is often used to create an atmosphere of repose (for example, the first movement of Beethoven's Sixth Symphony), and Brahms and Dvořák frequently used syncopated harmonic rhythms to reinforce the effect of an interaction of rhythmic planes. On the other hand, the *longueurs* of much of the extended music of late Romantic composers arise from an insufficient control or understanding of harmonic rhythm, especially when coupled with the harmonic ambiguity and pervasive tonal flux of much post-Romantic music; this weakened the principle of harmonic rhythm as a structural device.

Reactions against chromatic harmony took place in the course of the nineteenth century. One was a return to functional diatonicism with the emphasis on widening the spectrum of tonality to include various mediant and submediant harmonies, in their major and minor forms, as well as the traditional tonic, dominant, and subdominant; rooted in Beethoven's music, this "diatonic reaction" became the essential resource of nearly every composer who has been termed "neoclassic." Another reaction was to introduce a so-called "modal" harmony, with a strong emphasis on secondary triads (ii, iii, and vi in major; III, v, VI, and VII in minor) in the diatonic scales, treated in non-functional ways. Although this harmonic fabric is considered typical of Russian music (see Examples 10-1 and 10-5b), modal-type harmonies were applied to many melodies by Western composers as well, from Berlioz onward; it became a means of widening tonal spectra among various types of neoclassic composers, especially Brahms (Example 9-4) and Saint-Saëns (Example 11-4b). A further influence on modal harmony was the revival of Gregorian chant, with its new organ accompaniments contrived to remove the earlier major-minor straitjacket into which the modes had previously been forced; this kind of modal harmony is evident in the music of Fauré and Puccini.

Example 2-9 shows a late example of the "diatonic reaction" in

EXAMPLE 2-9. Saint-Saëns, Piano Concerto No. 5 (1896), first movement.

which the roots of twentieth-century "pan-diatonicism" are clearly visible. It represents a reaction against the "leading-tone" or dominant-seventh-oriented chromaticism of the century. Note (1) the leading tones that do not lead upward but are harmonized with mediants and descend, (2) the purely diatonic nature of the theme and its harmony, and (3) the composer's reliance on secondary triads that weakens the feeling of dominant or subdominant harmonies as essential structural elements.

Among the composers who relied on the diatonic reaction against Wagnerian chromaticism were Brahms, Raff, Saint-Saëns, Fauré, Chausson, and Rimsky-Korsakov, to list the few whose examples are cited in the text; all have strikingly different harmonic palettes. The dividing line between nineteenth- and twentieth-century diatonicism is most strikingly crossed in the music of Debussy and Ravel, with their use of parallel diatonic triads, sometimes with sevenths and ninths added in a kind of organum; extended non-functional sequences of diatonic triads; displacements of one diatonic scale by another; and the blurring of tonal centers by superposing unrelated tones or even other triads on the original chord, especially in final cadences, and often for coloristic or programmatic purposes.

Tonality. The expansion of the tonal frame of reference is one of the most crucial elements of Romantic musical style. In simple terms, the definition of a given key was substantially widened. The dominant as well as the tonic was a determining factor, with the mediant and sub-mediant degrees (often the flatted degrees of the scale) assuming an importance close to that which the dominant and subdominant had held in the Classic period. Many harmonies, when chromatically altered, could assume an even stronger functional character. There were new vistas in modulation through the use of the deceptive cadence (V–vi or V–♭VI), enharmonically spelled chords of the diminished seventh or augmented sixth, or "borrowed chords" (the flatted mediant or sub-mediant the most frequent) as pivots from one tonal center to another. Unprepared shifts, sudden and dramatic, from one key to another were increasingly tolerated. All these provided an enhanced and enlarged feeling of tonality that permitted a dramatic expansion of musical space itself.

Keys themselves were treated with greater freedom. Whereas during the Classic period the normative limitation was between E and E-flat in major and between F minor and E minor, any key could be and was used by the Romantics, and several composers, from Hummel and Chopin to Busoni and Skryabin, wrote sets of preludes or etudes in all the major and minor keys. Music for the piano was the first to be written outside the Classic key limitations, but the improvement of brass and wind instruments enabled chamber and especially orchestral music to be written in keys that were highly unusual by Classic standards. The key of F-sharp minor can almost be called *the* Romantic key, especially in piano music.

The minor mode's increasing popularity between 1780 and 1800 is a major harbinger of Romanticism, a mode that rose to a position of near-dominance in Romantic music. Whereas approximately 5% of Classic symphonies are in the minor mode, during the second half of the nineteenth century approximately 70% of the symphonies are in minor, with Glazunov the only symphonist of consequence who strongly preferred the major mode. The natural instability of the minor mode permitted the admission of more chromaticism and altered harmonies; this can already be seen among some Classic composers, with most of the harmonic originalities of C. P. E. Bach, Haydn, and Mozart appearing in their works in minor. The intrusion of harmonies "borrowed" from minor into works in the major mode, an ingredient of early Romantic chromaticism, increased to the point where, in 1904, d'Indy could simply state that his Second Symphony was in B-flat since the major-minor question was no longer operative (see Example 11-8a).

The expansion of tonality can be seen principally in the following areas:

1. Extended introductions that usually begin outside the key and eventually settle on the dominant (dominant preparations).

2. Definition of a key by writing "around its dominant," as it were, with the key defined not by emphasizing its tonic but by enhancing its dominant (see Example 6-3 and Figure 8-1).

3. Tonal parentheses (sometimes called "transient modulations") separating the tonal cells that unify the work; Example 7-9 is an illustration of a simple tonal parenthesis.

4. A freer treatment of modulation, anticipated in many of the sonatas and especially the fantasias of C. P. E. Bach, with a wider spectrum of related tonal areas than in the Classic period.

5. Entire sections of a late-Romantic composition in purely non-functional harmony, with the key defined only by occasional tonal cells, and with a statement of the tonic in root position either as a signal that the key is to be quitted or as the final chord. Example 2-10 illustrates non-functional harmony with occasional tonal cells, and it is a representative example of late-Romantic practice, with its altered chords, irregular progressions, and clustered or single non-harmonic tones.

EXAMPLE 2-10. MacDowell, "Starlight," from *Sea Pieces,* Op. 55 (1898).

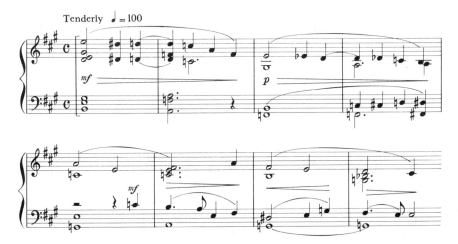

6. On the grandest scale, the expansion of tonality through the use of unrelated keys as contrasting movements in instrumental cycles, seen as early as Haydn's late sonata in E-flat (E flat–E–E flat); the use of third-related or step-related keys for the second theme-groups of instrumental cycles; and the architectonic design of given acts of Wagner's operas (see Figure 8-2).

The dissolution of tonality is a topic that belongs to a study of twentieth-century music, with the reservation that many twentieth-century composers have relied on tonality, but in a greatly widened sense. It should be mentioned here, however, that the dissolution of the

strong tonal anchors that had characterized musical composition from
Corelli through Mahler began during the nineteenth century through the
exaggeration of all the tendencies of harmony and tonality that have
been cited in this chapter. Chromatic harmony led eventually to the
serializing of pitches with a deliberate avoidance of triadic implications;
modulation became so frequent and far-reaching as to vitiate the structural role of tonality entirely; diatonic harmony led to pan-diatonicism,
with all the diatonic notes treated equally, or to polytonality; and composers strove to create new harmonic sonorities by constructing their
chords from fourths rather than thirds.

Counterpoint. Although both the Classic and Romantic periods are
regarded as dominated by homophonic musical textures, counterpoint
played a subsidiary yet important role. The historicism that impelled
Romantic composers to study the music of the past led them to explore
the techniques of Renaissance and Baroque counterpoint and to regard
this device as a legacy of the past, to be passed on with interest. *Canons*
by Romantic composers are almost invariably accompanied, in order to
provide euphony and enhanced sonority. *Fugues,* obligatory for Classic
and Romantic composers of church music and oratorio, sometimes appeared in Classic finales. Romantic composers soon found the fugue to be
an important means of expanding the development of a large sonata-form
movement, and later Romantic composers found the fugal treatment of a
previously homophonic theme to be a striking element of dramatic
rhetoric, best seen in the finales of Liszt's *Faust Symphony* and Chaikovsky's *Manfred.* Yet, among all the composers who continued Baroque
contrapuntal techniques into the Classic and Romantic period, one has
the feeling that only Mozart and Brahms were genuinely able to incorporate these techniques smoothly into their musical language; even with
Haydn and Beethoven one senses a certain self-conscious parading of the
ability to handle contrapuntal artifice, and often a deliberate archaism.

Linear counterpoint, often complicated by chromatic harmonies
and non-harmonic tones, developed during the Romantic period. This
kind of writing has been called "Meistersinger counterpoint" because of
its most striking epitome, the prelude to Wagner's *Die Meistersinger*
(Example 2-11). There are several precedents for this type of linear writing: the irregularly resolving non-harmonic tones and independent lines
of the slow movement of Mozart's E-flat Quartet, K. 428; Beethoven's
contrary motion at the expense of euphony; Berlioz' combination of
themes for programmatic purposes; and the active inner parts of Glinka,
Chopin, and Liszt. Linear counterpoint, harmonically extended to include a free use of dissonance, is frequently found among late- or post-
Romantic composers (Example 11-10). The use of a stark and open
linear counterpoint (e.g., after 1904, Strauss, Mahler, d'Indy) marks an-

EXAMPLE 2-11. Wagner, *Die Meistersinger* (1862), prelude.

etc.

other dividing line between nineteenth- and twentieth-century musical styles.

Sonority. The attitude toward sheer sound in Romantic music is one of the main constants in style that binds the Romantic era together and sets it apart from the Classic and Modern periods. Romantic sonority may be divided into two elements: (1) euphony, the Romantics' concept of "sweet and pleasing sound," and (2) color, the exploitation of instrumental and vocal timbres.

Euphony, for the Romantics, meant the avoidance of the relatively lean and spare sonorities of Classic writing by achieving a greater fullness of sound. This is seen at its extreme in the re-writings of earlier music, like the second piano parts that Grieg added to some of Mozart's sonatas. Even some early Romantic piano music by Weber and Schubert was re-worked, mainly by adding octave doublings and fuller chords, to provide richer sonorities. Media that could provide the ultimate in rich, full, euphonious sound—the male chorus, the string quintet or sextet in chamber music, the brass section of the German orchestra—reached a peak in Romantic music. The full, lush, rich euphony of Romantic music, whether seen in the multiplicity of eight-foot stops on the organ, the sustaining pedal to create fuller sounds in the piano, or the expansion of middle-register sonorities in the orchestra, is one of the chief strands binding together the Romantic movement in music, from Dussek, Weber, and Schubert through the epigones of Romanticism like Skryabin, Rakhmaninov, and Dohnányi.

Yet reactions against Romantic euphony arose during the nineteenth century. The astringent sonorities in Beethoven's late sonatas and quartets, so often attributed to the deafness which precluded his hearing how the music sounded, is an early example. Musorgsky's "anti-Romanticism" is shown not only by the sharp and empirical dissonances in his piano writing but also in their frequently percussive treatment, blunted when his piano music is given orchestral garb. The "open" scoring of so many works with orchestra written toward the close of the century, including Saint-Saëns' last two piano concertos, Verdi's *Falstaff*, and Rimsky-Korsakov's *Sadko*, implies a rejection of the full sonorities of Wagner, Franck, Chaikovsky, and Brahms. Not only Debussy, but subsequently Mahler and Strauss, substantially lightened their orchestral textures, and a striking feature of most orchestral music written between 1900 and 1914 is not a reduction of the size of the orchestra but a reversal of the trend to fill as much of the page as possible; an often stark and anti-euphonious (and linear) writing, quite typical of Mahler; and a search for more astringent orchestral sounds.

Color, whether on the piano or in orchestral writing, is such an individual property of each composer, even more so than his harmony, that it is difficult to sort out tendencies. The new resources of instrumental color would have been impossible without the technological improvements in all musical instruments. The principal vehicles for Romantic color were the clarinet, bass clarinet, French and English horns, and harp; the expanded string sections with the individual sections often divided to achieve richer sonorities; comparable expansion of the woodwind and brass choirs to extend their colors over a wide range; and the improved piano, particularly the Bösendorfer "Imperial Concert Grand" with its extra octave and non-percussive sound. Between 1800 and 1914 the orchestra nearly trebled in size, not for the purpose of expanding its volume but for enhancing sonority: more winds to achieve homogeneous tone colors on a given chord, more strings to balance the number of winds, more percussion instruments for new colors or increasingly dramatic climaxes.

Perhaps the most succinct contrast, in terms of color, between Classic and Romantic can be summed up as follows: few critics would attempt to differentiate, in performance style, between Haydn and Mozart, yet each performer must adapt his style not just from Classic to Romantic music but among each Romantic composer; the oboist, for example, must make subtle differences in his tone for Beethoven, Weber, Berlioz, Schumann, Wagner, Brahms, Chaikovsky, Saint-Saëns, Mahler, and Delius. During the period of overlap between Romantic and Modern music, the problem is characterized by the great variety of styles needed to play the music of each of the current composers between 1890 and 1914—even for the cymbal player!

Vocal timbres underwent equally far-reaching changes. Although the bulk of nineteenth-century operas were written with certain singers in mind, the operatic repertoire became increasingly varied and internationalized with a literally world-wide audience by 1914. Tenors, in particular, became increasingly specialized: one need but cite the light, agile tenor of *opera buffa* or *opéra comique;* the soulful light tenor of

French *opéra lyrique;* the powerful dramatic tenor, with elements of the forced-up baritone, in Verdi's operas; the Wagnerian *Heldentenor* with his problems of sheer endurance; the sobbing tenor of Italian *verismo* opera; the smooth, sentimental, and even oily tenor of Russian opera. Mezzo-sopranos, contraltos, baritones, and basses were given increasing prominence on the operatic stage. The proliferation of opera houses and the immense quantitative expansion of oratorio and the art-song written for professional singers permitted this increased specialization.

THE CONTINUITY OF ROMANTICISM IN MUSIC

Some writers have attacked the idea that Romanticism was a continuing phenomenon during the nineteenth century. Among their concepts are: Romanticism as an essentially Germanic phenomenon running through Wagner or, at the latest, Brahms, with the French version terminating in the middle of Berlioz' career; Italian opera or the various neo-classicisms as anti-Romantic movements; or musical Romanticism as short-lived as its literary or pictorial counterparts. Yet eight elements provide the same continuity in Romanticism from its eighteenth-century beginnings to its twentieth-century dissolution that the recitative, thoroughbass, and *concertato* styles provide for Baroque music.

1. *Tonality.* Increasingly bent, masked, and blurred in the course of the century, it nevertheless constitutes the most vital motive and architectonic force of Romantic music. The basic element is a system of tonal hierarchy, considerably widened over that of the High Baroque and Classic periods, yet still rooted in tonic-dominant relationships.

2. *Tertian harmony.* Though more coloristically and less functionally treated in the course of the century, with more blurring through non-harmonic tones, it remains the essential harmonic fabric.

3. *Sonority.* With its emphasis on euphony and color, it avoids the spareness of Classicism and the astringency of Modern music.

4. *Music as a vehicle for personal and individual communication.* This applies to composer and performer alike. The audience might be the "happy few" that understood Beethoven's late quartets or as much a mass audience as possible—whether reached for idealistic purposes (Berlioz, Wagner) or for commercial reasons (Meyerbeer, Puccini, touring virtuosi)—but musical esotericism *per se* was absolutely contrary to the Romantic temperament. Yet the communication was that of an individual who is purveying himself rather than a product.

5. *Rhythmic predictability.* This is a norm from which deviations

can be expected. When complication and unpredictability are normative elements in themselves, the music ceases to be Romantic.

6. *Euphonious treatment of musical instruments and voices.* The growing technological improvements and the progressive escalation of orchestral technique had as a principal aim the enhancement of euphonious sonority. Percussive writing for piano or strings, extension of the extreme ranges of the instrument for strange rather than euphonious colors, and unusual combinations of instruments in chamber-music works to achieve astringent sounds are all counter to Romantic concepts of euphony, though a main basis of these effects (and especially affecting vocal timbres) lies in the Naturalistic side of Romanticism.

7. *Reliance by composers on Romantic literature* (including the works of Shakespeare, the author most esteemed by Romantics) as a stimulus for opera, song, or program music. The rejection of Romantic literature between 1890 and 1914 by many composers provides a break in the musical continuity; it is a topic deserving further exploration but can only be mentioned here.

8. *Acceptance of the legacy of musical form from the Classic period,* a topic so extensive that it must be considered separately in the next chapter.

BIBLIOGRAPHICAL NOTES

See bibliographical notes in Chapters 1 and 3.

Among general histories of music, the best treatments of the nineteenth century are in Donald J. Grout, *A History of Western Music* (New York, 1960); Albert Smijers, *Algemeene Muziekgeschiedenis* (Amsterdam, 1940); Karl H. Wörner, *Geschichte der Musik* (3rd ed., Göttingen, 1961), Jules Combarieu, *Histoire de la musique* (3 vols., Paris, 1913–1919), and the nineteenth-century sections in Guido Adler (ed.), *Handbuch der Musikgeschichte* (1924; reprint, Tutzing, 1961). Of the books wholly devoted to nineteenth-century music, the best is Ernst Bücken's *Die Musik des XIX. Jahrhunderts bis zur Moderne* (Potsdam, 1932), which follows a chronological approach. Gerald Abraham's *A Hundred Years of Music* (3rd ed., Chicago, 1964), the best in English, is particularly strong in its sections on opera and musical nationalism; several additional points are covered in his essays *Slavonic and Romantic Music* (New York, 1968). The strongest features of Alfred Einstein's *Music in the Romantic Era* (New York, 1947) and Friedrich Blume's *Classic and Romantic Music* (English translation, New York, 1970) are their treatments of the cultural context of Romantic music. Georg Knepler's *Musikgeschichte des XIX. Jahrhunderts* (2 vols., Berlin, 1961) is limited to France, England, Germany, and Austria; in addition to its musical discussions, it stresses the sociological background of nineteenth-century music from a Marxist standpoint. A third volume, embracing approximately 1870 to 1920, is in preparation. The recent study by Kenneth Klaus, *The Romantic Period in Music* (Boston, 1970), is loosely organized by style-traits and genres. The two nineteenth-century volumes in the French series *Histoire de musique* (Paris, 1966) by Romain Goldron, *Les Débuts de romantisme* and *Du Romantisme à l'expressionisme,* are very brief and most valuable in their pictorial illustrations; English translations of these volumes have been announced. Though Irving Kolodin's *The Continuity of Music* (New York, 1969) consists in great part of searches for echoes "past, present, and to come," which the Germans call *Reminiscenz-Jagd,* his basic thesis is highly viable. Still worth reading, though in its final chapters tending to be more catalog than history, is Hugo Riemann's *Geschichte der Musik seit Beethoven* (Berlin, 1901). Short but stimulating studies of the topic "Romanticism in Music" are Edward J. Dent's "The Romantic Spirit in Music," *Proceedings of the Royal Musical Association,* LIX (1933), Hans Tischler's "Classicism, Romanticism, and Music," *Music Review,* XIV (1953), and Leon Plantinga's essay on Romanticism in his *Schumann as Critic* (New Haven, 1967). Hans Mersmann's *Moderne Musik* (Potsdam, 1928) and William Austin's *Music in the 20th Century* (New York, 1966) provide the best survey of twentieth-century post-Romanticism, a topic that still awaits in-depth coverage.

The German series *19. Jahrhundert,* with a large number of volumes of monographs, gives detailed coverage of several topics of nineteenth-century music that are beyond the scope of this book, especially musical journalism, aesthetics, and historiography. A counterpart series having the same title, containing much unpublished or hitherto-unobtainable music, has been begun by Bärenreiter-Verlag in Germany. The *Norton Critical Scores,* a series of individual works from the standard repertory, include not only the score of the composition but also analyses and essays on the work by various writers.

One can spend fascinating hours in examining the musical periodicals of the nineteenth century. Space does not permit a complete listing of these, but those most significant for the reader are the *Allgemeine musikalische Zeitung* (begun in 1798), *The Harmonicon* (1823), *Berliner allgemeine musikalische Zeitung* (1824), *Cäcilia* (1824), *La Révue musicale* (1827), *Le Ménestrel* (Paris, 1833), *Neue Zeitschrift für Musik* (1834), *The Musical Times* (1844), *Dwight's Journal of Music* (1852), *La Guide musicale* (1855), *Signale für die musikalische Welt* (1843), *The Musical Standard* (1862), *The Monthly Musical Record* (1871), *Proceedings of the Royal Musical Association* (1874), *The Etude* (1883), and *Music* (1891). The periodicals of the time that were addressed to the general educated reader contain numerous articles on music: examples are the *Illustrated London News, Revue des deux mondes,* and *Deutsche*

Rundschau. Nineteenth-century newspapers include contemporaneous musical criticism, reports of performances, and necrologies of composers.

Among the histories of musical style traits, those with significant sections on the nineteenth century are Bence Szabolcsi's *A History of Melody* (English translation, New York, 1965); Curt Sachs' *Rhythm and Tempo* (New York, 1953); Ernst Kurth's *Romantische Harmonie und ihre Krise in Wagners Tristan* (1920; reprint, Tutzing, 1968); Graham George's *Tonality and Musical Structure* (New York, 1970); and Adam Carse's *A History of Orchestration* (1925; reprint New York, 1964). Highly valuable, though more condensed, studies of individual style traits may be found in such standard musical encyclopaedias and dictionaries as *Die Musik in Geschichte und Gegenwart* (Kassel, 1949–), *Grove's Dictionary of Music and Musicians* (6th ed., 1973), and *The Harvard Dictionary of Music* (2nd ed., 1969).

THREE

FORM IN ROMANTIC MUSIC

Discussions of the elements of musical style—melody, rhythm, harmony, tonality, sonority—converge in the study of musical forms.

No new instrumental forms *per se* were created during the Romantic period: even the double-function one-movement form of Liszt represents a synthesis of elements of sonata form with the three- or four-movement instrumental cycle. The musical structures of the Classic period—sonata form,[1] the various kinds of rondos, binary and ternary forms, the symphony, concerto, overture, and chamber-music work—are the principal legacy of the eighteenth century to the Romantics. In vocal music the change from Classic to Romantic is more striking: the new vehicles are the German lied and its offshoot, the French *mélodie,* with

---

[1] Throughout this volume I use the term "sonata form" since the old terms "sonata-allegro" or "first-movement" form describe poorly a large number of musical structures that are neither in fast tempo nor initial movements.

the through-composed opera gradually replacing the Classic "number" opera with its self-contained set-numbers separated by recitative or spoken dialogue.

ROMANTIC INSTRUMENTAL FORMS

The expansion of instrumental forms continued from the Classic throughout the Romantic period; one can trace a direct line of expansion from the operatic overtures of Alessandro Scarlatti (1660–1725), the principal "proto-Classic" composer, to the symphonies of Mahler. Beethoven must be credited with bringing the large instrumental forms to their peak (see the conclusion of Chapter 4), and his influence dominated virtually all instrumental composition until the early years of the twentieth century.

Instrumental cycles. Whether these be symphonies, sonatas, concertos, or chamber works, they are the principal vehicles in the instrumental sphere for the major musical statement during the Romantic period, as well as the best vantage points for viewing the change from Classic to Romantic or the turn from late- to post-Romanticism.

The instrumental cycle, and to a lesser extent the Italianate "number" opera, during the High Classic period represents a peak of equilibrium, whether regarded as a whole or in their individual movements, between form and content; this is the real reason why the word "Classic" is applied to these works of Haydn's and Mozart's maturity. Only once before in the history of music had a comparable equilibrium been attained, in the High Renaissance mass and motet from Josquin to Palestrina.

This High Classic equilibrium implied at one end of the scale a certain invisible "floor" which maintained a certain minimum level of competence and interest, but also an equally palpable yet invisible "ceiling" at which Mozart particularly chafed, a ceiling which restricted the amount of individual expression and the extent of the emotions which could be represented, especially the heroic, the colossal, the tragic, and the pathetic. Within these limits an enormous amount of music could be and was written, as attested by the existence of at least 10,000 orchestral symphonies from the Classic period. It is the absence of this sense of equilibrium, balance, and control that makes the music of C. P. E. Bach, interesting as it is in individual details or innovations, seem somehow flawed; it is the presence of this equilibrium that permitted an immense amount of instrumental cycles to be created, almost as if by formula, all of which meet a certain minimum standard. That this equilibrium is palpable though intangible and not susceptible to quantitative measurement in detail can be seen in various attacks on the High Classic style by those who *dislike* this music: the music, they say, lacks the strikingly obvious characteristics, signatures, and "fingerprints" of the individual composer; Classic composers produced their instrumental cycles not in individual births but in litters of six as if they were puppies or kittens; the Classic composer regarded his work not as an achievement of his inner spirit but as a *product,* as if it were a piece of furniture; or "all Classic music sounds alike."

Many composers strained against the limitations of the Classic equilibrium betwen 1780 and 1800. Mozart's struggles against the upper boundaries of these limitations resulted in some of his greatest achievements, and not only the young Beethoven, but also his contemporaries or even predecessors like Clementi, Dussek, Koželuch, and Viotti, pushed against the Classic equilibrium, with Spohr, Weber, Kuhlau, and Schubert working in parallel paths. By 1820 at the latest the Classic equilibrium had been irretrievably shattered, with the composer now freer to communicate his individuality to his audience and to express a wider range of emotion. Yet while freeing himself from the limitations that the Classic equilibrium had imposed, he in turn forfeited its support by destroying the grooves in which his musical imagination could coast, as it were, with a minimum of personal involvement. The Romantic composer was free to build a musical edifice which would soar into the clouds, but this edifice could also fall with a resounding crash. The principal structures most prone to soaring or toppling were the instrumental cycle, the opera, and the extended choral work, and these problems are all evident in Beethoven's *oeuvre.*

Virtually every nineteenth-century treatment of the instrumental cycle appears in Beethoven's works: (1) the cyclic idea, with recapitulation of themes from preceding movements; (2) contraction of the cycle to as few as two movements or expansion to as many as six real movements; (3) the performance of the cycle without pauses between movements; (4) drastic contraction or great expansion of individual movements, especially those in sonata form; (5) programs, whether expressly stated or internally implied, for the cycle; and (6) expansion of the overture to the level of a self-sustaining instrumental composition, emancipating it from its operatic or dramatic origins: a direct stage in the evolution of the symphonic poem. Precedents for almost all these devices can be found in the music of our "proto-Romantic," C. P. E. Bach, but it was Beethoven who decisively imposed them on the nineteenth century.

First Movements. Slow introductions frequently occur during the High Classic period, especially in Haydn's later symphonies, with Koželuch expanding his introductions to the dimensions of a short slow movement, and with both Haydn and Clementi using their introductions to state motivic material later to be heard as an integral part of the first movement proper. These practices continued throughout the Romantic period, with an opposite tendency to reduce a slow introduction to merely a gesture of a few measures. Yet whereas Classic composers opened their introductions with clear-cut statements of the tonic, many Romantic works, beginning with Beethoven's String Quartet, Op. 59, No. 3, have introductions with non-tonic beginnings, their main purpose being the preparation of the dominant so that the tonic's appearance will be a major event. Extensive introductions to variation sets or to large-scale piano works are Romantic developments. Even a few operatic preludes (Verdi's *Rigoletto* and Wagner's *Das Rheingold* and *Siegfried*, for example) resemble sonata-movement introductions rather than self-contained independent operatic overtures. Slow introductions for finales also appear in the Classic period and continue in the nineteenth century.

The first movement proper, as in the Classic period, is overwhelmingly fast in tempo and is in sonata form. Two kinds of sonata form had been prevalent in the Classic period: the kind exemplified by Mozart, with the form clear-cut, the themes phrase-dominated, and the different theme-groups[2] and sections clearly demarcated; and the kind favored by Haydn, with the form a vehicle for experimentation and surprise, based on motivic expansion and contrast. Two distinct theme-groups, usually separated by a clear articulation or even a pause, and an arietta-like closing group are typical of Mozart's expositions; in the movement as a whole, all sections are very clearly perceivable, with a generally short development, sometimes incorporating entirely new musical material, separating exposition from recapitulation. In contrast, Haydn's themes are usually highly motivic, the second theme-group is often more distinguishable by tonal shift rather than by thematic contrast as with Mozart, and a folk-like closing theme is strongly emphasized; the developments are longer and more intricate than Mozart's, and a sometimes truncated recapitulation is likely to contain several surprises.

Beethoven's sonata-form movements, which served as models for the entire nineteenth century and for much of the twentieth century as well, represent a certain coalescence between these two kinds, with considerable extremes in approach: the first movement of the B-flat major Piano Sonata, Op. 22, as clear-cut as any sonata-form movement by Mozart, that of the Seventh Symphony as monothematic as any work by

---

[2] "Theme-group," rather than "theme," is the proper term, since often two or more separate themes occur. "Subject," the British term, is most applicable to the fugue and causes confusion in describing forms that are reconciliations of sonata form and fugal textures. Theme-groups are identified by position (first, second) and function (closing); the terms "principal" and "subordinate" to identify theme-groups apply to some but hardly to all sonata-form movements, and the usefulness of these terms collapses completely when one must speak of recapitulations that consist entirely of "subordinate" themes!

Haydn, that of the E-flat String Quartet, Op. 74, extremely motivic and athematic. Beethoven's sonata-form movements range between extremes of compression (F minor Quartet, Op. 95) and expansion ("Eroica" and Ninth Symphonies, "Hammerklavier" Piano Sonata). The areas of expansion, with parallels and even anticipations in sonata-form movements by Clementi and Dussek, are the transitions between the first and second theme-groups, the development sections, and the codas. Figure 3-1 is an

SECTION	FUNCTION	KEY-CENTER
Introduction (optional)	Prepares first appearance of tonic	May fluctuate widely; usually enhances the dominant
Exposition	Statement of thematic material	
First theme-group		Tonic
Transition	Modulation from tonic to related key	Modulatory
Second theme-group		Normally V in major, III in minor. Quite often (major) III, ♭VI, vi, iii, ♭III. At end of century may be in quite distant keys
Closing group	Concludes exposition	Usually in same key as second group
Development	"Working-over" of some or all the previously stated thematic material; sometimes new themes introduced	Tonally fluctuating; in longer developments a series of tonal plateaux
Retransition	Return to tonic	
Recapitulation	Restatement of thematic material	
First theme-group		Tonic
Transition (modified)	Balances comparable section in exposition; sometimes drastically curtailed	Starts and ends in tonic, often with excursion to IV
Second theme-group		Tonic
Closing group		Tonic
Coda (optional)	Summary of movement; sometimes a "second development"	Tonic, often with excursions to other keys

FIGURE 3-1. Normative Sonata-Form Movement in the Nineteenth Century

illustration of the normative sonata-form movement current in the nineteenth century.

The breakdown of the Classic equilibrium in the sonata-form movement was anticipated in the works of C. P. E. Bach and his successors. The Romantic sonata form showed several lines of development: (1) the "academic" kind, which followed Mozart's example and resulted in a near-"textbook" sonata form; (2) the kind containing extremes of contrast between the theme-groups, sometimes expressed as a "masculine" first theme and a "feminine" second theme, providing a problem of reconciling opposites; (3) the opposite of (2), in which a lack of differentiation between the theme-groups is perceivable, seen either in highly lyrical late-Romantic compositions where all the themes "must sing," or in late- and post-Romantic sonata-form movements where the composer tried to use as few motives as possible or even, following Haydn's example, tried to make one thematic idea serve a variety of functions. Development sections were the greatest problem for many composers because lyrical or folk-like themes were unamenable to contrapuntal treatments and could only be repeated sequentially or artificially fragmented. The development sections of the outer movements of Dvořák's "New World" Symphony show nearly all the developmental problems of the Romantic sonata form.

The expansion of tonality provided the main structural anchors for the enlarged sonata-form movement, and it is the strong feeling of tonal directionality that provides the greatest element of success for such large-scale movements. In their individual ways, the major sonata-form movements of the century, from Clementi and Beethoven to d'Indy and Mahler, represent as much a triumph of structural engineering as do their contemporaneous counterparts in the Crystal Palace or the transcontinental railroads. Yet within this expanding tonality lurked the seeds of danger; themes which in themselves lacked a clear tonal definition, and were separated by stretches of pervasive tonal flux, weakened the architectonic nature of sonata form itself. One may legitimately entertain the complaints about many post-Romantic sonata-form movements that they were "all development," with unclearly defined themes embedded in a slithering mass of modulation.

Some of the more interesting developments in sonata form occur in the recapitulations. Among the variants of the traditional recapitulations are: (1) omission of part or even all of the first theme-group, especially when motives from this group are extensively treated in the development (Chopin, Brahms); (2) symphonic recapitulations in which the themes are presented in entirely new guises through changes in orchestration and dynamics (Dvořák); (3) recapitulations in which new material is inserted (Beethoven); (4) substitution of new thematic materials in place of ideas belonging to the exposition proper, seen as early as the first movement of Rutini's sonata, Op. 3, No. 5, around 1755; these new materials may come from the development (Schumann's Fourth Symphony, first movement) or from the introduction (Glazunov's Fourth Symphony, first movement).

The coda, from Beethoven onward, often was the climactic summary of the movement itself. Although extensive codas are not too frequent in the Classic period (the outer movements of Haydn's Symphony No. 44 or of Mozart's large works in C major are among the few Classic examples), they assume major importance in the Romantic period. Lesser composers found the applause-catching cabalettas and strettos from the Rossinian opera, with cumulatively faster tempos, effective in symphonic music, especially in overtures.

Slow movements in Classic music are of three basic kinds: (1) the aria-like movement, typical of Mozart, often an abridged sonata-form without a development; (2) the hymn-like slow movement, often an expanded ternary form or some kind of successive variation principle, typical of Haydn; (3) the romanza-like movement, often folk-like in character (see Example 2-1b), sometimes the locus of a set of variations, used by both composers.

Among the Romantics, Beethoven preferred the aria and especially the hymn, with his contemporaries often using the romanza-type movement. Schubert developed a slow movement analogous to the art-song, either ternary in form or a set of variations. The late Romantics exaggerated all these tendencies: Bruckner the hymn, Chaikovsky the aria and romanza, Brahms and Mahler the song. Toward the end of the century the slow movement was sometimes "telescoped" with a scherzo-type movement.

By 1800 *scherzo- or intermezzo-type movements* replaced the minuet as the normative third movement of the instrumental cycle (see Example 2-5); when the minuet was used in the nineteenth century, it was generally as a nostalgic retrospection toward the bygone Classic era (Schubert, Mendelssohn, Brahms).

A bumptious scherzo in a very fast tempo, with one beat to the measure, was often necessary relief to the deep emotional profundity of the slow movement, and a line of development of such scherzos extends from Beethoven and late Schubert through Bruckner. A wide variety of scherzos developed during the nineteenth century, many quite extensive in length with two trios and a coda. Among the different kinds are the elfin (Mendelssohn), the daemonic (Chopin), the stylized national dance (Dvořák), the mysteriously ghostly (Brahms), and the distorted and sardonic (Liszt, Mahler). Some composers even reverted to the early Classic three-movement form by occasionally "telescoping" the scherzo with the slow movement, as mentioned above.

A directly contrasting tendency to the fast scherzo is the slowing down of the third movement to create an intermezzo-type movement, sometimes a reflective romanza (Mendelssohn, Brahms, Dvořák). A wider variety of meters than in the Classic era was used for both scherzo and intermezzo: 2/4, 2/2, 6/8, or even an occasional quintuple meter replacing the traditional 3/4 of the minuet or early scherzo.

Final movements. The prevalent kinds of final movement in the Classic era, after the minuet had ceased to be the last movement, were usually of rondo character, often made more serious and complex as sonata-rondos in which the middle section was a true development, or sonata-form movements. Particularly intense finales were those incorporating fugal techniques or those in the minor mode. One senses in the finales of the High Classic instrumental cycle a feeling of balance and equilibrium which is disturbed by the developments in the finale during the nineteenth century.

Nearly every kind of Romantic finale—sets of variations, Hungarian-gypsy finales with some tonal ambiguity between tonic minor and a major mediant or submediant tonality, rondos, triumphant apotheoses, finales with "flashbacks" to earlier movements—occurs in Beethoven's instrumental cycles. Beethoven also firmly established the principal idea of the Romantic finale—that it be a conclusion on a note of triumph, thus reflecting the concept of Romantic optimism.

This is most clearly seen in finales in the major mode as conclusions to instrumental cycles in which the first movement is in minor. Some aestheticians, usually basing their conclusions on the most blatant example (Beethoven's Fifth Symphony), have concluded that such a finale represents the triumphant resolution or overcoming of a conflict that has been depicted in the minor-mode first movement. Most of the finales of instrumental cycles that begin in minor are in the major mode; even when the minor mode is used for the final movement, there is usually a triumphant coda in major (e.g., Mendelssohn's "Scotch" Symphony, Bruckner's Third Symphony), or at least an extended "tierce de Picardie" that provides the finale with prolonged tonic major harmony for its conclusion (e.g., Beethoven's String Quartet, Op. 131 and Dvořák's Seventh Symphony). The reverse process, a finale in minor for an instrumental cycle in the major mode (e.g., Brahms' Third Symphony, Bruckner's Sixth Symphony) almost invariably contains a coda or at least an extended close in major. Finales that are unmistakably in minor from beginning to end are usually in chamber music works (e.g., Schubert's "Death and the Maiden" Quartet, Brahms' Piano Quintet) or in compositions in which some kind of underlying pessimistic programs can be sensed (e.g., Chopin's B-flat minor Sonata, Chaikovsky's Sixth Symphony).

The idea of the triumphant finale led many composers to strive to make this movement the grand culmination of the instrumental cycle. The models for this idea were the finale of Mozart's "Jupiter" Symphony with its fugal coda and triumphant conclusion, and the last movements of Beethoven's Third, Fifth, Seventh, and Ninth Symphonies, "Hammerklavier" Sonata, and the original version of his B-flat String Quartet, Op. 130, which ended with the "Grosse Fuge." Although Beethoven's contemporaries and immediate successors shrank from this monumental kind of finale, the idea of the triumphant conclusion on the grand scale was revived by composers of the second half of the century. Liszt's apotheoses, Bruckner's chorales, and Mahler's choral endings are striking examples of these grand conclusions. Themes from previous movements, whether "flashbacks" to set the scene for the finale proper or as part of a rounded cyclic relationship (Brahms), intensified the summarizing quality of the finale. Extensive fugal sections in the finale contributed to its air of high seriousness. The last movement of d'Indy's Second Symphony almost epitomizes the triumphant, summarizing late Romantic finale: a slow introduction with reminiscences of themes from earlier movements, a massive fugue (see Example 11-10e), an animated sonata-form movement, and a triumphant chorale (see Example 11-10f).

A sharp contrast to these kinds of finales is seen in some of the concluding movements by composers of the first half of the nineteenth century who seemed to deliberately avoid the triumphal or monumental finale by writing a gay, light-hearted, and unpretentious movement: Dussek, Schubert, and Schumann are the principal composers of such finales, with the last movement of Schumann's First Symphony one of the best examples. Analogous to the lighter kind of finale are the Hungarian-gypsy finales, occasionally written by Haydn but reaching their peak with Beethoven, Schubert, and especially Brahms.

Yet the successful finale was the principal problem for even the best Romantic composers of instrumental cycles. To begin with, there are several "unfinished" Romantic cycles that end with slow movements, most notably Beethoven's Piano Sonatas, Op. 109 and Op. 111, Schubert's Eighth Symphony, and Bruckner's Ninth Symphony; note that three of these four works have first movements in the minor mode. Secondly, each of the three principal kinds of finale—the triumphal, the monumental, and the unpretentious—contained major pitfalls for the composer: bombast (Chaikovsky's Fifth Symphony), sprawl (many of Schubert's lengthy finales), or triviality (Dussek's Piano Sonata, Op. 25, No. 2). Finally, one subjectively senses that in a large number of Romantic instrumental cycles the final movements do not seem to be on an equal level with the other movements; it may be that the Romantic attitude of striving for the unattainable is best reflected in the finale of the extended instrumental cycle. Certainly the problem of the finale to the instrumental cycle has remained an equally difficult one for composers of the twentieth century.

Other instrumental cycles. Divertimento-type cycles, multi-movement forms sometimes called serenades, notturnos, or cassations, were frequently utilized for light music by Classic composers and were seemingly terminated by the early Romantics like Schubert, Hummel, and Field. Later in the nineteenth century, usually under the title of "Serenade," this cycle became the equivalent of an unpretentious symphony, often for a limited or unusual combination of instruments, and revealed several composers in their neoclassic phases (Volkmann, Brahms, Chaikovsky, Dvořák, Elgar). *Suites* after the Baroque model were revived as keyboard works as a vehicle for neoclassic or even neo-Baroque expression (Saint-Saëns, Raff); orchestral suites were usually either musical travelogues or were carpentered out of ballets or instrumental interludes from operas. After 1810 *groups of characteristic piano pieces* appeared as a favorite vehicle of Romantic expression; often the titles of the individual pieces have such vaguely indefinite connotations as Eclogue, Bagatelle, Impromptu, or Capriccio. Some of these groups of pieces, as seen from their succession of contrasting movements and their key-relationships, resemble the divertimento (Weber's four-hand piano pieces), are linked through cyclic thematic transformations (Schumann's *Carnaval*), or resemble sonata-type cycles (Brahms' Op. 119 piano pieces), sometimes with extra movements (see Figure 6-1, Schumann's *Kreisleriana*). The dimensions of the individual pieces range from the extremely short fragment, a short, pithy musical aphorism stated without any attempt at development, continuity, or narrative[3] like those in Schumann's *Papillons* or Fibich's *Souvenirs*), through the finely wrought musical miniature of one or two pages in length, to the substantial piece in a fairly complex rondo or sonata form.

Variation cycles in the Classic period were chiefly individual movements, usually slow movements and less often finales, of instrumental cycles or they were independent piano compositions. Both were based chiefly on the ornamentation of a familiar melody, usually an operatic air, or an original theme. During the nineteenth century the variation cycle took two directions. One direction was toward a debasement that consisted of technically brilliant piano variations on catchy operatic tunes or "national" airs; these became the stock-in-trade of the touring virtuoso. The other direction was toward an ennoblement of the variation cycle in which the structure and basic harmony of the theme were the "constants" and all the other elements, including the melody

---

[3] The "fragment" was also an important literary device of the Romantics and pre-Romantics; it was used in philosophy, criticism, and literature by Herder, Friedrich Schlegel, Novalis, Kierkegaard, and Machado de Assis, among others.

itself, were the "variables." Such "character variation" cycles were written as orchestral compositions in the second half of the century (see Figure 9-1). A late- and post-romantic development was the very free variation cycle based primarily on motivic reminiscences from the theme itself, as in Franck's *Variations symphoniques* or Delius' *Appalachia.*

ROMANTIC VOCAL FORMS

Although different kinds of vocal music are usually called genres rather than forms, the problem of musical form is inherent in all music. More innovations took place in the vocal than in the instrumental music of the nineteenth century, for Romantic vocal music had to keep pace in developing a musical language to correspond with the lyrical or dramatic literature of the time. Almost all the innovations in orchestration and many of the new harmonic developments took place in vocal music rather than in the more abstract instrumental forms of the nineteenth century. The major areas of change in vocal music during the period were opera, the art-song, and choral music.

Opera. Points of operatic equilibrium in the Classic period were attained in (1) the monumental tragedies of Gluck; (2) the *dramma giocoso,* wherein serious and comic elements were brought together in a realistic plot that closely parallels the development of the eighteenth-century novel, with Mozart's mature Italianate works like *The Marriage of Figaro* and *Don Giovanni* representing the culmination of this genre; and (3) the lighter operas, whether called *opera buffa, Singspiel, opéra comique,* or ballad opera, all but the first consisting of isolated musical numbers separated by spoken dialogue.

Operatic equilibrium was disturbed even before 1800, chiefly in France and largely (though not exclusively) in the "rescue opera," a genre that reached its peak in Beethoven's *Fidelio.* The main problem of equilibrium was the relationship of the singers to the orchestra, which was increasing in importance. Sometimes composers gave sections of prominence now for the instrumentalists and now for the singers, whether in the grand tableaux of the French opera from Salieri to Berlioz or in the Italianate operas with their ritornelli and interludes as showpieces for the solo instrumentalists and the arias proper, in which the singers were prominent or the soloist and instrumentalists competed on equal terms (Simon Mayr, Paër, Rossini). The role of the orchestra increased in providing a psychological underpinning for the action or in portraying landscapes, storms, forest scenes, and the like. All these developments began around 1790 and proceeded along parallel, though not ly exclusive lines, thanks to the increasing internationalization throughout the century.

The structure of opera in 1800 consisted of isolated set-numbers—arias, duets, larger ensembles—separated by recitatives or spoken dialogue. Closing each act was a highly organized finale held together by strong tonal relationships, often "tonal rondos," and recurrent thematic material. Sometimes operatic introductions were equally highly developed. The Romantic task was to fuse these separate elements together, often in "scene-complexes" which permitted stage action to be transacted in more musical terms than the previous "dry" recitative, often with the orchestra providing the musical continuity with the voices in a declamatory *parlando,* and with arias, ensembles, or choruses providing points of both dramatic and tonal stability. This resulted in fewer actual points of sharp articulation in each act, with individual set-numbers being fused together, and often the act itself shows a strong tonal organization. It is often difficult, however, to determine whether this organization was a "happy accident" or not, especially in Italian opera, owing to corrupt versions that have ben handed down as authentic; to transpositions of arias demanded by singers; to interpolations, substitutions, or extractions of individual vocal numbers; or to the various revisions made for performances at different opera houses. Not until the middle of the nineteenth century can there be any degree of certainty about the "authentic" versions of most popular operas.

The next step in operatic development was the creation of the continuous operatic act. This developed along parallel lines, with some regression, in various operatic media and among various composers after 1850: Verdi in Italy, Wagner in Swiss exile, Meyerbeer in France, Dargomÿzhsky in Russia, Erkel in Hungary. The pure number opera, though given its last lease on life in Bizet's *Carmen,* became increasingly relegated to lighter music, especially the operetta in which the spoken dialogue was still retained.

The continuous act provided more dramatic realism and more musical continuity to the opera, yet its rationale seemed to vitiate what many regarded as the *raison d'être* of opera: the points of dramatic rest where the emphasis could focus on the star singer. The aria and the set-number ensemble could not entirely be eliminated because singers and the general public wanted them retained. A compromise, used even by Wagner, was a kind of libretto in which the isolated set-piece could still be retained as dramatic monologue, love duet, or the response to an invitation to sing a song. Despite the attempts of composers to connect their numbers organically, nothing could prevent the audience's bursting into applause at the end of a favorite aria or the extraction out of the opera, for independent concert performance, of the more telling numbers, whether orchestral interludes by Wagner or arias by Puccini.

By the end of the century the continuous operatic act was the norm. The musical module at the opening of the century was the set-number, which expanded to the scene-complex and finally to the act itself at the hands of Wagner (see Figure 8–2).

Only a beginning has been made in the study of the general structure of nineteenth-century opera, and that chiefly from the standpoint of tonality. The coherence of an opera largely depends on its dramatic structure, yet purely musical factors may be tangible elements in this coherence: not just tonality, but points of tension and repose, spacing of climactic arias and ensembles, schemas of instrumentation, and recurrences of previously heard musical material seem to be of nearly equally essential import. Some operas of the time show themselves ingeniously linked internally through tonal organization, sometimes of two or more planes that have been called "interlocking tonalities": for instance, D-flat and to a lesser extent D, in their minor or major form, have been cited as the principal tonalities of Verdi's *Rigoletto,* with E major or minor (the keys of Gilda's two big arias) as points of intersection.

Choral music. In both Classic and Romantic choral works many Baroque elements, chiefly contrapuntal techniques, survived. Yet whereas the Classic composer retained these elements as conventions, Romantic composers, with their strong sense of historicism, actually intensified them, particularly Protestant composers who were influenced by J. S. Bach's choral music. Haydn's last two oratorios may be regarded as the immediate precursors of the Romantic oratorio, a genre which deserves far more detailed study than it has hitherto received.

The principal features of the oratorio in the nineteenth century are (1) the development of the "continuous" rather than the "number" oratorio of Handel and Haydn, a change that is parallel, if not exactly analogous, to the move from the "number" to the "continuous-act" opera; (2) settings of the Catholic Mass and Requiem intended for the concert hall rather than for the church; and (3) the immense proliferation of choral societies and music festivals, especially in Protestant countries, that resulted in a steady demand for oratorios and other large choral works.

A kind of ecumenicalism arose in the choices of texts. Although almost all Protestant composers based their oratorios on texts from the Bible and Catholic composers generally wrote musically expanded settings of the liturgy, Protestants and even unbelievers wrote Masses (Spohr, Schumann), and many Catholic composers of oratorio (Gounod, Dvořák, Elgar) wrote some of their finest works in this genre for the music festivals of Protestant England.

Solo song. Three principal kinds of solo song were present in the nineteenth century. The *Lied,* or German art-song, is one of the few genuinely new forms of the Romantic period; its Classic-era origins and early history are treated in Chapter 5, along with a discussion of Schubert as the one who gave the Lied its strongly Romantic cast. In the Lied the piano and singer are at least theoretically equal partners, with the resources of harmony and atmospheric effects in the accompaniment used to reinforce the word-painting or the psychological import of the text. In the course of the century the vocal part became increasingly declamatory.

A counterpart to the Lied is the French *Romance*. In contrast to the Lied, the Romance is strongly dominated by tuneful melodies in the voice with the piano merely providing support. Outside Germany the Romance was dominant.

Both Lied and Romance contained problems of equilibrium. The principal dangers faced by the Lied were overemphasis on the vocal melody with the accompaniment restricted to a mere supporting function, or, on the other hand, overemphasis on the accompaniment to the point of creating a piano piece with words. A further danger, during the second half of the century, was the creation of a song which would retain the partnership of voice and piano, but would focus so much attention on the music that the poem would seem to be merely a series of syllables to permit vocalization. The Romance's problems were its threat of lapsing into triviality or becoming an operatic aria with piano accompaniment. For the composer, the choice of text was a severe problem, for much poetry in itself is highly "musical" in its use of assonance, alliteration, rhyme, and broken lines, effects which are weakened or lost altogether in musical settings. Some composers, notably Brahms and Richard Strauss, simply seem not to have been able to tell a bad poem from a good one.

The Romance finally attained a musical equilibrium in the French *Mélodie*, a kind of chamber music for voice and piano that emphasized precise vocal declamation of the text with an increased importance of the piano part, chiefly for atmospheric effects. Schubert's songs in French translation, French *opéra lyrique*, and the revival of instrumental music all enriched the romance and led to the development of the *Mélodie*, which flourished in France between 1885 and 1915.

The principal developments of song in the course of the century were (1) the application of the new vistas of harmonic resources to the accompaniments; (2) a concomitant focus on musical declamation, occurring in parallel lines of achievement in the best songs of Musorgsky, Fauré, and Wolf; (3) songs with orchestral accompaniment. A kind of wrong turning took place in settings of ballads: except for a few highly concentrated examples by Schubert and Carl Loewe (1796–1869), the tendency was either to write a sprawling composition of considerable length or to create the equivalent of the operatic *scena ed aria*, until composers felt that the ballad deserved its proper setting in the dramatic cantata or reverted to strophic settings. Settings of folk songs with piano accompaniments were written in virtually every country. On the lighter level, the drawing-room song represents the popular counterpart of the Romance. Such songs, usually strophic, with mild chromatic harmonies accompanying a sentimental text, and published with an illustrative steel engraving, are multi-media presentations, literary, musical, and artistic, of nineteenth-century *kitsch*.

Between 1900 and 1914 the dividing line between the centuries became strongly evident in vocal music as well as in the instrumental sphere. The application of the aesthetic of the *Mélodie* to opera culminated in Debussy's *Pelléas et Mélisande;* the new resources of quartal harmony appear in the early songs of Schoenberg and Berg; the heightening of vocal declamation, coupled with the desire to portray the emotions of the subconscious, led to a kind of speech-song called *Sprechstimme*. One even encounters textless vocal compositions: the vocalise in the realm of solo song, or the textless choruses to create a kind of added tone color as in Ravel's *Daphnis et Chloë*.

SUMMARY

Musical form, whether in instrumental or vocal music, was the chief means of achieving equilibrium and balance during the High Classic period. The Romantics shattered this equilibrium and compelled each composer to find for himself the balance between musical shape and its individual components. The greatest composers, regarding form as a process rather than a mold, restored new vigor to the structures they had inherited from their Classic predecessors, particularly sonata form and the techniques of variation. Vocal music provided the chief areas for musical innovation, especially in the German Lied and the continuous opera, yet the Romantic use of form as a means of achieving musical equilibrium was highly individual rather than collective. Toward the very end of the century, however, one could discern that sonata, symphony, and opera were coming full circle to their origins in the early Baroque: sonata as "sound-piece" for a small group of instruments; symphony, though considerably inflated in length and resources, to a similar meaning; and opera, whether in the hands of Richard Strauss, Debussy, or Puccini, to resembling in structure and dramatic rationale Monteverdi's *Orfeo* rather than Mozart's "number" operas.

BIBLIOGRAPHICAL NOTES

See the bibliography for Chapter 2. Histories of various musical forms and genres, whether in English or any other language, vary drastically in both coverage and quality. Donald Grout's *A Short History of Opera* (2nd ed., New York, 1965), Adam Carse's *The Orchestra from Beethoven to Berlioz* (New York, 1949), and William S. Newman's *The Sonata in the Classic Era* (2d ed., Chapel Hill, 1972) and *The Sonata Since Beethoven* (2d ed., Chapel Hill, 1972) are by far the best, with detailed bibliographies, intensive coverage of the period, and set models for investigation of all other genres. General surveys of various genres with significant portions devoted to the nineteenth century include Homer Ulrich's *Symphonic Music* (New York, 1952) and *Chamber Music* (2nd ed., New York, 1966); Robert Simpson's *The Symphony* (Baltimore, 1966, 2 vols.); F. E. Kirby's *A Short History of Keyboard Music* (New York, 1966); Walter Georgii's *Klaviermusik* (3rd ed., Zürich, 1966); Fritz Egon Paner's "Das deutsche Lied im 19. Jahrhundert" in Guido Adler (ed.), *Handbuch der Musikgeschichte* (1924; reprint, Tutzing, 1961); Jack M. Stein's *Poetry and Music in the German Lied* (Cambridge, Mass., 1971); Frits Noske's *French Song from Berlioz to Duparc* (English trans., New York, 1970); Donald Ivey's *Song: Anatomy, Imagery, and Styles* (New York, 1970); and the prefaces of the genre volumes in *Anthology of Music*, the English translation of *Das Musikwerk*, a multi-volume collection prepared by German scholars.

The standard investigations of musical form are Donald Tovey's *Essays in Musical Analysis* (London, 1935–1945, 6 vols.) and *The Forms of Music* (1929; reprint, New York, 1956), and Wallace Berry's *Form in Music* (Englewood Cliffs, N.J., 1966). Jan LaRue's *Guidelines for Style Analysis* (New York, 1970) opens new vistas for the study of musical style and structure. Newman's previously cited volumes on the sonata include considerable discussions of musical form. Issues of the *Journal of Music Theory* and *The Music Forum* (2 volumes to date) include discussions of musical structure.

FOUR

BEETHOVEN
AND HIS PREDECESSORS

Whereas the *style galant* of the eighteenth century arose first in Paris and Naples, the ultimate source of musical Romanticism was the Venice of the seventeenth and early eighteenth centuries. Personal expression and subjective feeling make a work like Monteverdi's *L'Incoronazione di Poppea* (1642) sound surprisingly "modern," and the subsequent Venetian operas, with their expressive arias and highly organized ritornelli, led directly to the Venetian concertos of Tomaso Albinoni (1671–1750), Alessandro (ca. 1684–ca. 1750) and Benedetto (1686–1739) Marcello, and especially Antonio Vivaldi (ca. 1669–1741). In Vivaldi's music the future is discernible in such passages as the long melodic lines of his slow movements (Concerto for Three Violins, F major), the dotted unison ritornelli in other slow movements (C minor Violin Concerto, Fanna No. 92), and the dramatic syncopations, drumming basses, slow harmonic rhythm, and emotional turbulence of the Concerto for the Dresden Orchestra. The Vivaldian style was brought to Germany (especially

Saxony-Thuringia) by his pupil J. G. Pisendel (1687–1755), J. S. Bach, and finally G. B. Platti (1690–1763), one of the major keyboard composers of the early Classic period.

PRECURSORS OF ROMANTICISM

There are two basic styles in Classic music, the light, airy *style galant* and the emotional, subjective *empfindsamer Stil,* the latter best seen in the music of two of J. S. Bach's sons, Wilhelm Friedemann (1710–1784) and Carl Philipp Emanuel (1714–1788). Wilhelm Friedemann was an extremely expressive composer whose output was small, more from laziness than from a supposed fondness for the bottle, and his subsequent influence was slight. On the other hand, C. P. E. Bach can be justly called the most original and one of the most influential composers of the Classic period. Geiringer has admirably described his musical style as

> a daring harmonic language with incisive dissonances and stunning chord-combinations; dramatic pauses, unexpected rests, alterations in tempo, and sudden changes in major and minor modes, an effect often increased by varying dynamics and the use of different registers.[1]

C. P. E. Bach sincerely believed that music should touch the heart, which, as he said, could not be done through "running, rattling, drumming, or arpeggios." His music is surpassed during the eighteenth century only by the major works of Gluck, Haydn, and Mozart, and his yearning appoggiaturas and strange, distant modulations were only tentatively approached by his more timid successors. His Sinfonia in E minor (1756)[2] contains virtually all the effects of the so-called *Sturm und Drang* symphonies of the 1770's, and his use of instrumental recitative (first "Prussian" sonata, 1742) looks ahead to Beethoven, Spohr, and Weber. Some of the appoggiaturas and modulations of his later fantasias anticipate the harmonic practice of Liszt and Wagner (Example 4-1).

Although C. P. E. Bach may be called the first "Romantic" composer, his influence is most immediately important in its effect on Mozart and Haydn. As a young man, Haydn diligently studied Bach's "Prussian" and "Württemberg" sonatas, and their strong influence is the chief difference between Haydn's best sonatas and the more brilliant and fluent

---

[1] Karl Geiringer, *The Bach Family* (New York, 1954), p. 335.
[2] Published in Karl Geiringer (ed.), *Music of the Bach Family* (Cambridge, Mass., 1955), pp. 141–155.

EXAMPLE 4-1. C. P. E. Bach, Fantasia II from *Die sechs Sammlungen von Sonaten, freien Fantasien und Rondos für Kenner und Liebhaber, Fünfte Sammlung* (published 1785).

keyboard works of Mozart. Mozart knew Bach's sonatas and their imitations written by German composers residing in France, but was most affected by Bach's symphonies, which he heard at Baron van Swieten's academies in Vienna in the early 1780's and which brought about the increased depth and richness of his last five symphonies.

The terms *Sturm und Drang* (storm and stress, taken from Maximilian Klinger's drama of 1776) or *crise romantique* have been loosely used to designate a tense, terse, excited musical style, incorporating surprises in dynamic changes and modulations and an extensive use of the minor mode, that was employed by some composers around 1770, especially in Haydn's symphonies and sonatas. Yet most of these effects are found in operas around 1730 and in much of C. P. E. Bach's keyboard music of the 1740's, and the period of the 1770's contains fewer instrumental compositions in the minor mode than do the preceding or the following decades.[3]

[3] See my study "The Prevalence of the Minor Mode in the Classic Era," *Music Review*, XXXII (1971), 27–35.

Haydn seldom composed in the *Sturm und Drang* idiom after 1774, presumably because his patron, Prince Esterházy, disliked it,[4] and his attempts to recapture this mood in a few of his later works (e.g., Symphonies Nos. 78, 80, 83, 95) were not successful. The spirit of dawning Romanticism is most pronounced in Haydn's symphonic introductions, the slow movements of his later symphonies (especially that of No. 102) and string quartets (the "Fantasia" of his Op. 76, No. 6 quartet), and the "Representation of Chaos" in *The Creation* (1798). Mozart, on the other hand, more successfully sublimated and assimilated *Sturm und Drang;* even during what his biographers Wyzewa and Saint-Foix call his *crise romantique* of the early 1770's, Mozart balanced tragic works like his early G minor Symphony (K. 183) with sunny, *galant* works like the motet *Exsultate, Jubilate,* and in later years paired his intensely personal and tragic or daemonic works in the keys of C minor, G minor, and D minor with contrasting gayer compositions, often for the same or similar media. These contrasts are best seen in the opposition of D minor and D major in his opera *Don Giovanni* or in the second and closing theme-groups of his sonata-form movements in the minor mode, stated in mediant major in the exposition but given an air of poignancy and even high tragedy through their recapitulation in tonic minor. The sublimation and assimilation of the *Sturm und Drang* style by Mozart, Clementi, Kože-luch, and Dussek was to have greater influence on the future than Haydn's use of this idiom.

Mozart's influence on Beethoven was immense: one need only compare two of their C minor piano sonatas, Mozart's K. 457 and Beethoven's Op. 13, or "Pathétique." Mozart's ventures into chromatic harmony, most evident in his E-flat String Quartet, K. 428, and his *Requiem,* influenced Beethoven's contemporaries like Hummel and Spohr, who regarded themselves as Mozart's legitimate heirs.

LUDWIG VAN BEETHOVEN (1770–1827): HIS APPRENTICESHIP

Beethoven is the most important composer of the nineteenth century, for all his successors were influenced or even intimidated by his works, which became the touchstone for Romantic critics from E. T. A. Hoffmann onward. Beethoven's music is the culmination of the "Viennese Classic" tradition, yet it furnished the impetus for virtually all instru-

---

[4] Haydn's activity as an opera composer (especially of comic operas) also may have affected his musical style after 1772. See Charles Rosen, *The Classical Style* (New York, 1971), pp. 146–154.

mental and much vocal composition of the nineteenth century; not a single major composer of this period could wholly escape his influence.

Many writers have attempted to organize Beethoven's compositions according to "periods": from two to as many as five have been postulated, with three the most commonly agreed upon number. Beethoven's compositions written before the publication of his Opus 1 in 1795, however, constitute a separate period of apprenticeship, and groups of transitional works came between the first and second, and second and third, periods. Demarcations between periods can only be approximate, and there also is some chronological overlapping between periods, since Beethoven frequently had several compositions in progress at the same time.

Beethoven lived in Bonn until 1792 and during his stay there wrote works which reveal in embryo many of the salient traits of his style. The two most important of these early pieces, the 24 variations on the arietta "Vieni, amore" by Vincenzo Righini (1756–1812), WoO[5] (without opus number) 65, and the Cantata on the Death of the Emperor Joseph II (Example 4-2), were written in 1790, although the variations were revised in 1802.

The cantata is an excellent anticipation of Beethoven's "noble" style, seen at its best in his later hymn-like slow movements; it not only anticipates his *Missa Solemnis* but also Brahms' works for chorus and orchestra. The influence of the Mannheim symphonist and opera composer Ignaz Holzbauer (1711–1783) has been found in this work; equally important influences are the styles of Gluck and his most important successor, Luigi Cherubini. It was this cantata which induced Haydn to accept Beethoven as a pupil.

EXAMPLE 4-2. Beethoven, Cantata on the Death of Joseph II, WoO 87.

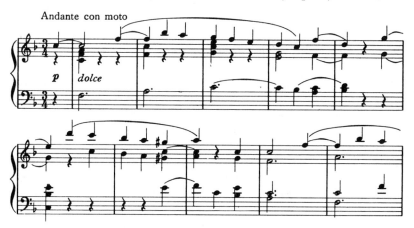

---

[5] *Werke ohne Opuszahl.*

The Righini variations display several characteristics of Beethoven's style: aggressive contrary motion (Var. I), sharp and unexpected
dynamic contrasts (Var. II), trills (Var. IV), tempo contrasts which anticipate the first movement of the Piano Sonata, Op. 109 (Var. XIV), hymn-
like writing (Var. XVII), and the long coda (final variation); variation
XXIII closely resembles the opening of the slow movement of his Piano
Sonata, Op. 2, No. 2. The frequent inversions of chords, especially of the
dominant seventh, provide both an interesting bass line and a harmonic
drive. Mozart's piano variations are an obvious model, as are those by
Beethoven's teacher in Bonn, Christoph Gottlob Neefe (1748–1798).

INFLUENCES ON BEETHOVEN'S FIRST PERIOD

Beethoven studied with Haydn for two years after arriving in
Vienna in 1792 and subsequently took lessons from the contrapuntist J. G.
Albrechtsberger (1736–1809) and Gluck's disciple Antonio Salieri (1750–
1825). Their influence, as well as those of Mozart and the French Revolutionary composers, has been extensively discussed in the Beethoven
literature, but three other composers also substantially affected his first-
period works: Muzio Clementi (1752–1832), Leopold Koželuch (1752–
1818), and Emanuel Aloys Förster (1748–1823).

A Roman by birth, Clementi was taken to England at the age of
fourteen and spent most his life there, except for concert tours and busi-
ness trips. In the early 1780's he concertized on the continent, competed
against Mozart (arousing his enmity) before the Emperor Joseph II, and
entered into a tragic love affair which drove him from France in 1784
after he wrote some of his finest sonatas. After his return to London he
wrote symphonies (now forgotten and mostly lost) in competition with
Haydn, and during his long lifetime served as composer, teacher, publisher, and piano manfacturer. The sonatas, his most important compositions, extend from 1765 to 1821.

Clementi was a direct musical descendant of Domenico Scarlatti
(1685–1757) and one of the great innovators in writing for the piano. He

was the first important composer who really thought in terms of the modern piano, and his conception of the instrument is evident as early as the sonatas of Op. 2, written around 1770. Such characteristic forward-looking devices as powerful octaves, fast repeated notes, rapid chains of parallel thirds and sixths, fast scales and arpeggios, and thick, full, quasi-orchestral chords are often blended with legacies of the past like murky (broken octave) basses, two-voiced textures, or Scarlattian turns and ornaments. The sonatas of 1782 and 1783 (Opp. 7, 9, and 10) had a particularly strong impact on Beethoven. The singing, ornamental melodies over a slow harmonic rhythm or the sonority and spacing of the slow movement of Op. 9, No. 3, could easily be mistaken for a first-period Beethoven work, as can the Trio of the second movement of Op. 10, No. 1 (Example 4-3) which so admirably exploits the singing tenor register of the piano.

After the Op. 14 sonatas, Clementi's compositions show less freshness of inspiration despite such magnificent exceptions as the sonatas in

EXAMPLE 4-3. Clementi, Sonata, Op. 10, No. 1, trio of second movement.

F-sharp minor (Op. 26, No. 2) and G minor (Op. 34, No. 2), since most of his sonatas between 1784 and 1804 were written for concert tours or other commercial purposes. His best late works, five sonatas and the *Gradus ad Parnassum,* were written between 1819 and 1826 and had a considerable influence on the second generation of Romantic piano composers.

Beethoven knew and esteemed Clementi's sonatas even though he did not meet him personally until 1807. Among Clementi's more discernible influences on the younger composer are the design of the first movement of the G minor Sonata (Op. 34, No. 2), in which the slow introduction is used in the development, a procedure which probably was a model for Beethoven's "Pathétique" Sonata; his use of rhythmic motives from his expositions in his development sections; and his explosive developments and finales, whose influence culminated in Beethoven's Sonata ("Appassionata"), Op. 57.

Many reasons have been advanced for the gross neglect of Clementi's compositions, among them Mozart's sarcastic personal comments ("a charlatan like all Italians") and incompetent editions of his music designed for pedagogical use rather than for musical merit; perhaps the chief reason is that aspiring pianists learn Clementi's sonatinas as youngsters and later regard them as representative of his *oeuvre,* which is like considering the "Minuet in G" and the *Album for the Young* typical specimens of Beethoven's or Schumann's music. Clementi at his best is a major composer of more than historical significance.

Leopold Anton Koželuch was one of the first Czech composers to migrate to Vienna toward the close of the eighteenth century. He was a prolific composer, and many of his works display Romantic traits, best seen in the slow introductions to his sonatas, which he sometimes repeats or echoes at the end of the first movement (a further influence on Beethoven's "Pathétique" Sonata), and in the slow movements of his works for piano and orchestra. There are also striking similarities between Koželuch's and Beethoven's rondo-type sonata finales, sequences, and thematic contrasts in sonata expositions. The sonata from which Example 4-4 is taken was most probably written in 1785.

EXAMPLE 4-4. Koželuch, Sonata, Op. 15, No. 1, first movement: (a) introduction; (b) opening of first theme-group; (c) portion of second theme-group.

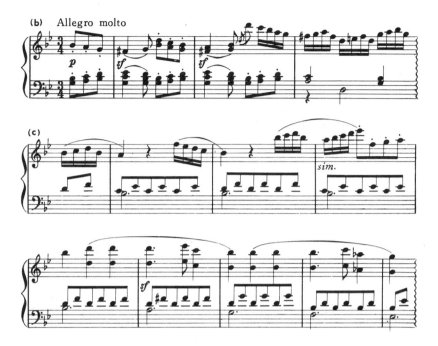

The chamber music of Emanuel Aloys Förster, whom Beethoven regarded highly and to whom he sent pupils who wanted to study composition, bears the same relationship to Beethoven's early string quartets as Clementi's and Koželuch's piano works do to his first-period sonatas. Mozart's "Haydn" quartets and late quintets are obviously Förster's points of departure. His style is quite contrapuntal (as could be expected of a composer who as a student arranged all the fugues from J. S. Bach's *Well-Tempered Clavier* for string quartet), and every member of the chamber ensemble has an important part to play. As Förster's String Quintet, Op. 19 (1802), shows, C minor meant to him what it did to Mozart and Beethoven. Such Beethovenian devices as a finale in minor with a fading-out coda ending in major, contrary motion in thirds even at the risk of dissonance, and a "bonus" recapitulation with more music than in the exposition can be encountered in Förster's works. He is not merely a forerunner and early contemporary of Beethoven but also a significant if underestimated member of the Viennese Classic school of instrumental composition (Example 4-5).

The direct influence that the music of the French Revolution and the Napoleonic Empire had on Beethoven's music is difficult to ascertain precisely. The dynamic and dramatic range of the heroic Gluckian opera had been greatly enlarged by Salieri and by the composer Beethoven

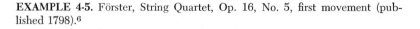

EXAMPLE 4-5. Förster, String Quartet, Op. 16, No. 5, first movement (published 1798).[6]

most highly esteemed among his contemporaries, the Italian-born but Paris-resident Luigi Cherubini (1760–1842), whose even greater and more skilled enhancement of the dramatic rhetoric of opera began with his *Demofoönte* of 1788. Yet a number of tendencies evident in Beethoven's music developed simultaneously in France along parallel but not intersecting lines: these are best seen in the symphonies and operatic overtures of Etienne-Nicolas Méhul (1763–1817). Though the expanded orchestral sonorities and dynamic levels of the French "rescue opera" are strongly evident in Beethoven's "Eroica" and Fifth Symphonies as well as in his "rescue opera" *Fidelio,* the most important influence on Beethoven from France was the extreme simplicity of so much of the Revolution's ceremonial music, intended for massed bands and choruses in open-air performance (Example 4-6). Beethoven's use of diatonic, triadic simplicity to depict an atmosphere of heroism is one of the most striking features of his music, and his reliance on unclouded diatonic harmony throughout his career is one of the principal style-traits that separates his music from that of his contemporaries (Dussek, Spohr, Weber) who were

[6] Published in *Denkmäler der Tonkunst in Oesterreich,* LXXVII.

EXAMPLE 4-6. Gossec, "Aux Mânes de la Gironde" (1795).[7]

[7] Published in Constant Pierre (ed.), *Musique des fêtes et cérémonies de la révolution française* (Paris, 1899), pp. 322–327.

experimenting with chromaticism and the effects possible from non-harmonic tones.

BEETHOVEN'S FIRST PERIOD

This period of composition extends from approximately 1794 to 1800, with the "Spring" Sonata for violin and piano, Op. 24, the First Symphony, and the D major Piano Sonata, Op. 28, as the major terminal works. The piano, either in a solo capacity or in a chamber ensemble, is the dominant instrument.

Formal experimentation, deriving from Haydn's examples, is typical of Beethoven's early piano sonatas, with their structures ranging from the quite free forms of Op. 2, No. 2 and Op. 10, No. 2 to the clarity of form of Op. 22. The moods of the sonatas range from the tempestuousness of the two C minor sonatas to the placid contemplativeness of Op. 28 (called "Pastoral") and the playfulness of Op. 10, No. 2. Many of these sonatas are technically easy, but only an accomplished pianist can do justice to Op. 10, No. 3, the finest sonata of this period. Many of these sonatas have four movements, with the third generally called "scherzo." Perhaps because of Clementi's influence, Beethoven's piano sonatas are the most original of his first-period compositions.

Beethoven's chamber music for or with winds need not detain us long save to mention that his classicism is strongest in these works and that he abandoned this medium after his Septet, Op. 20 (which he came to detest) and the Serenade, Op. 25. His chamber music for strings consists of several duet sonatas of which the Op. 24 violin sonata is the most popular, a group of trios of which Op. 3 is really a divertimento, and the six string quartets, Op. 18, of which the first, fourth, and sixth are the most interesting. The orchestral music includes two rather conventional piano concertos (Opp. 15 and 17, the latter composed first) and the First Symphony. The introduction of the latter was thought radical, for Beethoven omitted stating the customary unison tonic at the opening and began by going to the subdominant, establishing his tonic by circumscribing it. The second movement (as in the Op. 18, No. 4 Quartet) contains contrapuntal *tours de force*, a legacy of his study with Albrechtsberger; the third movement is a full-blown scherzo though entitled "menuetto," and the finale has the playfulness of Haydn's last movements.

The transitional works leading to Beethoven's second period were written during his progressive loss of hearing; in his own words he described the history of this catastrophe:

I have been feeling, I may say, stronger and better, but my ears continue to hum and buzz day and night. I must confess that I lead a miserable life. For almost two years I have ceased to attend any social functions, just because I find it impossible to say to people: I am deaf. If I had any other profession I might be able to cope with my infirmity. . . . In order to give you some idea of this strange deafness, let me tell you that in the theatre I have to place myself quite close to the orchestra in order to understand what the actor is saying, and that at a distance I cannot hear the high notes of instruments or voices. . . . Already I have often cursed my Creator and my existence. Plutarch has shown me the path of *resignation*. If it is at all possible, I will bid defiance to my fate, though I feel that as long as I live there will be moments when I shall be God's most unhappy creature. . . . Resignation, what a wretched resource! Yet it is all that is left to me. . . .[8]

Of the principal works of this transitional period, the piano sonatas between Op. 26 and Op. 31 show most clearly the dissolution of the composer's earlier style and his groping for new means of expression. An irregular order of movements, with a slow movement first and the "sonata-allegro" movement at the end, characterizes the Op. 26 and Op. 27 sonatas, the second of which is the popular "Moonlight"; novel, too, are the storminess of the "Tempest" Sonata, whose slow movement was partially influenced by the French funeral marches of the 1790's (but less so than the third movement of Op. 26), and the fine Op. 31, No. 3 sonata with its non-tonic opening, rich harmonies, and scherzo-like slow movement with sforzandi in unexpected places. Of the violin sonatas of Op. 30, the best is the second, a typical C minor work; also in this key is the powerful Op. 37 piano concerto, with a deeply expressive slow movement in the remote key of E major and an unusual finale. The most novel elements of the Second Symphony are the lengthy slow introduction to the first movement and the finale, whose capriciousness and playfulness exceed Haydn's. The "Kreutzer" Sonata for violin and piano (Op. 47), originally written for the Negro violinist George Bridgetower (1780–1860), is the terminal work of the first transitional period.

BEETHOVEN'S SECOND PERIOD

Most of Beethoven's popular works come from this period, which begins with the Third ("Eroica") Symphony and ends with such works

[8] Emily Anderson (ed. and trans.), *The Letters of Beethoven* (London, 1961, 3 vols.), I, pp. 59–60.

as the "Emperor" Concerto and the incidental music to Goethe's drama *Egmont*. To this group of works belong Beethoven's Fourth, Fifth, and Sixth symphonies; his most and least popular concertos; his only opera; some overtures; most of his songs; and the three string quartets of Op. 59; but only three piano sonatas.

The "Eroica" Symphony is the grandest and most grandiose specimen of the instrumental music of this time. Though the sonata had been gaining in length, the symphony had not, and Mozart's "Jupiter" Symphony (K. 551) and Haydn's last three symphonies (Nos. 102, 103, and 104) were the most monumental of the preceding works in this medium. Attempts have been made to trace the influence of the French Revolution in the "Eroica" Symphony, chiefly its prominent triadic themes; further investigation may show that the overtures to the "rescue operas" may have contributed to Beethoven's symphonic "breakthrough."

Those who have studied this symphony have frequently commented on Beethoven's introducing a new "theme" in the development section of the first movement; this was not a startling innovation, for Mozart had done this, but what is novel is the new theme's reappearance in the immense coda. The second movement is a funeral march on an unprecedented scale, though Beethoven had made preliminary essays in his Op. 26 and Op. 31, No. 2 sonatas. The scherzo begins the vein of "cosmic humor" that culminates in the scherzo of the Ninth Symphony; its prevalent stepwise motion is balanced by the difficult horn fanfares in the trio. The finale is a set of variations on a bass line with an accompanying melody which Beethoven had used as a contradanse and as a ballet movement in *The Creatures of Prometheus*, Op. 43; the Op. 35, or "Eroica" Variations, a piano work based on the bass line more than the theme, is complementary to, rather than a study for, the Third Symphony's finale. Beethoven is said to have preferred this symphony above all his others.

The Fourth Symphony is a contrasting and delightful (if unjustly neglected, like virtually all his works in B-flat major) interlude before the Fifth Symphony, in which Beethoven was trying to achieve a certain cyclic relationship, rhythmic as well as thematic, between some of the movements and within the first movement, which is noteworthy for its intense concentration and the rhythmic motive which unites all its sections; however, such interesting elements are absent from the repetitious second movement, a "double variation" in the style of Haydn. The third movement—anyone knowing the Beethovenian scherzo of the period will know why I hesitate to call it a scherzo—was considered the most "Romantic" of all the movements by contemporaneous critics and is bound to the noisy finale by a mysterious transition over a steady drumbeat. The triumphant finale in C major is an excellent specimen of the "optimistic" solution of the conflict inherent in the symphony in a minor mode (in the recapitulation of the first movement the second and closing theme-groups are stated in tonic major but are overwhelmed by the coda in minor); the return of a portion of the scherzo at the end of the development section is an inspired idea; but the coda is unequaled in sheer noise until the patriotic finales of the Russian nationalist composers later in the century. The exquisite Sixth, or "Pastoral," Symphony achieves its contemplative effects through light orchestration and slow harmonic rhythm.

These symphonies show Beethoven's increasing impatience with the limitations of the instrumental technique of his time. A virtuoso performer himself who had heard and composed music for the best living instrumentalists, he demanded a comparable facility from his orchestral musicians. One need but cite the demands on the horn players in the "Eroica" Symphony or *Fidelio,* or on the technique of the string bass players in the trio of the third movement of the Fifth Symphony; Beethoven had previously heard a string bass virtuoso playing his cello sonatas on this instrument. Beethoven even emancipated the trumpets and timpani from their previous noisemaking and rhythm-emphasizing functions, yet he was no "orchestrator," and several conductors, notably Felix Weingartner (1863–1942), have tried to revise his scoring.

Among the concertos, the G major Piano Concerto (No. 4) is one of Beethoven's most serene and contemplative works, whereas the Fifth ("Emperor") is one of his most triumphant compositions. The Violin Concerto (Beethoven also wrote an alternative version as a piano concerto) shows the influence of the "military" concertos of G. B. Viotti (1755–1824) and Pierre Rode (1774–1830), the most renowned violinists of the period. The "triple concerto," Op. 56, for piano, violin, and cello, is a minor work.

Before discussing the sonatas of the period, a digression is necessary to examine briefly the form that Beethoven had inherited. From Mozart he obtained clean craftsmanship and the idea that the violin in the duet sonata was an equal partner rather than an accompanying instrument; from Haydn the piquant surprises that could arise through experimenting with the formal structure; and from Clementi the conception of the rhetorical drama and conflict inherent in the form, which Beethoven further intensified by transferring the dramatic elements of French "rescue opera" to instrumental music.

In the first movement, the center of gravity of the sonata of the time, the highly organized structure consisted of an exposition of thematic material heightened by a conflict of tonal centers as well as themes; a development, generally of previously presented material, whose conflicts arose through thematic fragmentation and motivic development, often contrapuntally treated, underlaid by fluctuating and unstable tonalities; and a recapitulation restating the exposition with certain changes to insure that the second and closing theme-groups would appear in the tonic, thus resolving the conflicts of the exposition. Haydn, more than Mozart, contributed a slow introduction to the first movement, which Beethoven either spun out at great length (Second and Seventh symphonies) or reduced to a mere gesture (Op. 31, No. 2, Op. 78 sonatas). Although there were a few grand codas in the Classic period, like the finale of Vanhal's Symphony in A minor, the outer movements of Haydn's Symphony No. 44, and the first or last movements of Mozart's large instrumental works in C major or C minor, Beethoven raised the coda to the status of a second development section.

The formal structure and time-scale of the first movement of Beethoven's Piano Sonata, Op. 53, called "Waldstein" after one of the composer's first patrons, lies midway between the highly concentrated sonata-form movements of the Fifth Symphony or the Op. 95 string quartet and the immensely expanded first movements of the "Eroica" and the Ninth symphonies. The first theme-group is based on motives rather than themes, and the transition is long in order to prepare the rather remote tonality of E major for the hymn-like second theme. A second transition leads to A minor for the closing group, which returns smoothly to the tonic for the repeat of the exposition but then, during the second playing of this section, modulates to F major, the tonality of the opening of the development. The latter is based on motives from the first theme-group and a figuration pattern from the second theme-group (measure 49 of the exposition), treated in sequence. The retransition to the tonic begins imperceptibly, sinks to a low point (measure 142) and then rises to a peak of climactic fury, all on the dominant of C major, then subsides through scales in contrary motion to the recapitulation, in which a "bonus" of seven measures (167–173) intensifies the feeling of the home tonic through deviations from it in delaying the inevitable.

Beethoven effectively reconciles the demands that the second and closing theme-groups be recapitulated in the tonic by beginning the former group in A major but (through A minor) closing in C major and, after a slightly compressed transition, beginning his closing group in subdominant minor. His emphasis on the subdominant leads to the coda, which starts in the remote key of D-flat major and, on motives from the first theme-group that had previously been worked over in the first development, rises to a climax; but the intensity decreases with a final statement of the second theme, a slowing down in the speed, and fermatas on the leading tone. A final rush, based on the first theme in the tonic, concludes the movement. One should note throughout the movement the transitional open spaces, the "lungs" which permit the music to breathe. Many similarities in principles of formal structure, emotional intensities, and scope are found between the "Waldstein" Sonata and the comparable work in minor, the popular "Appassionata" Sonata, Op. 57, in F minor like the storm movement of the "Pastoral" Symphony.

Fidelio, Beethoven's only opera, is a middle-period work although it underwent later revisions. The libretto was based on *Léonore, or Conjugal Love* by the French playwright Jean-Nicolas Bouilly (1763–1842), which had previously been set to music by two minor composers, Pierre Gaveaux (1761–1825) and Ferdinando Paër (1771–1839). *Fidelio* is virtually the last of the rescue operas and the only one which has survived in the repertoire. Though the lesser conventions of opera, especially those deriving from the *Singspiel*, were beneath Beethoven, as the opening and Rocco's "Gold" aria in Act I will testify, the composer's freedom-loving spirit and moral integrity rises to its height in Act II during the scene of Florestan in his dungeon cell, the climactic quartet of Act II when Leonore saves Florestan from his mortal enemy Pizarro, and the finale, in C major like the finale of the Fifth Symphony, with its triumphant echoes of the spirit of French revolutionary music. Of the four overtures which Beethoven wrote for the opera (contrast this with Rossini's using the same overture for at least three different operas!), the "Fidelio" overture written in 1814 is generally used to open the opera whereas "Leonore No. 3," a virtual symphonic poem recapitulating the high points of the drama, is performed during the change of scene for the finale of the second act.

The most experimental works of this period are the three string quartets of Op. 59 which Beethoven wrote for Count Rasumovsky, the Russian ambassador to Vienna who maintained a private string quartet. In homage to his patron, Beethoven incorporated Russian themes in each quartet; the theme of the trio of the third movement of the E minor quartet was also used by Musorgsky in the Coronation Scene in *Boris Godunov* (see Examples 10-3a and 10-5c). The F major Quartet has a first movement on a grandly expansive scale; its second movement is one of Beethoven's most unusual compositions because of the irregular resolutions of what seem to be dominant harmonies and the highly unusual and irregular sonata form. The E minor Quartet has a moving slow movement and a Hungarian-type finale which oscillates between C major and E minor, whereas the C major Quartet closes with a fugue which too many performers play at breakneck speed.

Beethoven's overtures, written chiefly for dramas but transcending their original function as curtain-raisers, are among the principal forerunners of the symphonic poem. Among the best are the previously cited "Leonore No. 3"; the overture to *Coriolan* (by Collin, not Shakespeare), a characteristic C minor work; and the overture to *Egmont,* for which Beethoven also wrote the incidental music frequently called for in Goethe's drama. Beethoven's songs, a good many of which date from his middle period, are the most neglected of his compositions. Their air of nobility is most successful in the settings of devotional texts (Op. 48) by the German poet C. F. Gellert (1715–1769). The songs stem from and are the culmination of the heritage of J. F. Reichardt and other north German composers, rather than being precursors of the Lieder of Schubert.

Beethoven's second transitional period, which William S. Newman has called the "period of invasion" because of the French conquest of Austria and entry into Vienna during these years, is an experimental period and also the time when the composer's popularity was at its zenith. Among the major works of this period are the Seventh and Eighth Symphonies, the "Archduke" piano trio, the piano sonatas from Op. 78 to Op. 90, and the string quartets Op. 74 and Op. 95, as well as some lesser-known works like the Choral Fantasia, the Mass in C, and *Wellington's Victory,* or "Battle Symphony," Op. 91.

During this period Beethoven wrote genuinely neoclassic works, the F-sharp and G major Piano Sonatas, Opp. 78 and 79, and the Eighth Symphony—homages to the past with an eye to the future. His other major works of this time are more experimental: the Seventh Symphony with its monothematic first movement and its preoccupation with rhythm; the virtually athematic first movement of the Op. 74, or "Harp," quartet; and the Op. 95 quartet with its astronomically high specific gravity unequaled until Sibelius' Fourth Symphony, unusual excursions into remote keys through enharmonic modulations, intensely concentrated first movement, and almost Rossinian conclusion. Whereas the first movement of the Op. 90 piano sonata is nearly as terse as that of the Op. 95 quartet, the second and final movement, almost Schubertian in its lyricism, is as spacious and expansive as the "Archduke" Trio, Op. 97.

Beethoven's sketches for the finale of his Eighth Symphony give insight into his creative process. Composition was not easy for Beethoven; thematic ideas, of which only the germ of the final form is evident in their initial stages, had to be laboriously revised and polished. His jottings and revisions were set down in sketchbooks, many of which have been preserved though scattered among many libraries. As a reviser of his sketches, he may be compared with the mother bear of mediaeval legend whose cubs were born formless and then literally licked into shape. Example 4-7 shows this process.

In the initial sketch for the finale (a), the basic ideas of the opening are evident: the major third in triplet rhythm at the opening, the

EXAMPLE 4-7. Beethoven's sketches for finale of Symphony No. 8, Op. 93: (a) first sketch; (b) second sketch; (c) third sketch; (d) final version.[9]

(a)

(b)

(c) Meilleur

Final form
(d) Allegro vivace

[9] After Gustav Nottebohm, *Zweite Beethoveniana* (Leipzig, 1887), pp. 116–117.

consequent idea with a descending melodic contour (measure 5), and the flat submediant as a harmonic interval (measure 9). Sketch (b) seems to be a regression, although the descending melodic line is improved and continued, the meter receives its final designations as ¢, and the contrast of triplets with duplets is not entirely abandoned. Sketch (c) Beethoven designated as "better": he restored the contrast of triplets and duplets but stopped the propulsive effect of the consequent idea. In the final form, the second measure of the earlier sketches is expanded through clever repetition, the opening has more rhythmic variety, the chromatic alteration in measure 9 gives more harmonic interest, the change of pitch location in measure 6 continues the effect of a descending melodic line, and the phrase is extended. The D-flat of the first sketch is saved until measure 17 and changed to a C-sharp, the reason for which is apparent only in the coda where it becomes the dominant of F-sharp minor.

BEETHOVEN'S FINAL PERIOD

During this period, which began in 1815 and 1816 with the Op. 102 cello sonatas and Op. 101 piano sonata, Beethoven became almost totally deaf, led an eremitic and eccentric existence, and tried to gain custody of his nephew Karl, resulting in strife with the boy's mother and constant struggles between uncle and ward that culminated with Karl's running away and subsequently attempting suicide. Beethoven had increasing difficulty in conceiving, organizing, and shaping his musical ideas, which resulted in a lessened output of work, but among the compositions of this period are some of the most abstract and sublime ever written. Yet these works estranged Beethoven from his audience and alienated most of his colleagues, who could or would not follow him into the empyrean. From this period come his last five piano sonatas, his best bagatelles, his last five string quartets, the "Diabelli" Variations, the *Missa Solemnis,* and the Ninth Symphony.

This period can be called Beethoven's "contrapuntal" period. Fugues occur in the finales of the Op. 101, Op. 106 ("Hammerklavier"), and Op. 110 sonatas, and contrapuntal devices characterize the variations of Op. 109 and the first movements of Op. 106 and Op. 111. The first movement of the C-sharp minor Quartet (Op. 131) is a fugue, and portions of this fugue and the third of the variations from the slow movement of this quartet resemble the "paired imitation" of Josquin des Prez and his successors. The *Grosse Fuge,* Op. 133, originally intended to be the finale of the Op. 130 quartet, is the apogee of Beethoven's abstract counterpoint. That Handel was his principal mentor is especially apparent in the "Consecration of the House" Overture, Op. 124, and the fugal portions of the *Missa Solemnis.*

Beethoven overwhelmed the limits of Classical form in his sonata movements by blurring the demarcations between sections and theme-groups and in creating such gigantic structures as the first movements of the "Hammerklavier" Sonata and Ninth Symphony. Frequent changes of key and tempo characterize many of these movements; in the first movement of the Op. 130 quartet, of average length for this period, there are sixteen tempo changes and six changes of key signature, ranging from six flats to two sharps. These two signatures, representing the flat submediant and major mediant relationships of the tonic key of B-flat major, give further evidence of the composer's predilection, already apparent in his second period, for modulations by thirds in his sonata-form expositions.

The slow movements of Beethoven's instrumental cycles in this period often become the musical centers of gravity, and sometimes (Opp. 109, 111) are final movements. Occasionally these slow movements have programmatic titles, like "Cavatina" in the Op. 130 quartet or "Song of a Convalescent's Thanksgiving to God, in the Lydian mode" from the Op. 132 quartet. Theme and variation form, often with a final variation containing chains of trills which add to the mood of sublimity, is common in these movements. As early as 1806 Beethoven had become interested in variations on a ground bass (the C minor variations, WoO 80), and the variations of his last period emphasize as constants the structure and basic harmonic scheme of the theme, with melody, meter, rhythm, pitch-locations, and other musical elements all as variables.

The composer-publisher Anton Diabelli (1781–1858) circulated one of his waltzes among a large number of composers with the request that each write a variation on it. Beethoven complied, and in fact wrote 33 variations on the theme; these not only explore all its harmonic, motivic, and musical possibilities but also, as Geiringer has shown, fit into an architectonic scheme in which the number of variations conforms to the structure of the theme: eight groups of four variations each following the theme's eight four-measure phrases, with Variation 33 as an epilogue.[10] In contrast to the grand scope of the "Diabelli" Variations are the *Bagatelles* of Op. 126 and the last four of the *Bagatelles,* Op. 119 (the others of this set having been composed earlier); they are enigmatically terse works which had a strong influence on Schumann and Brahms.

[10] Karl Geiringer, "The Structure of Beethoven's Diabelli Variations," *Musical Quarterly,* L (1964), 496–503. A five-part structure is postulated in David H. Porter, "The Structure of Beethoven's Diabelli Variations, Op. 120," *Music Review,* XXXI (1970), 295–301.

Just as the giant "Hammerklavier" Sonata stretches the capacities of performer and listener to the utmost, so does the Ninth Symphony. All its movements are immense specimens of their type—the first of sonata form, the second of the scherzo, and the third of the "double variation." The finale is a setting of Schiller's "Ode to Joy" for soloists, chorus, and orchestra, a project which had been in the back of the composer's mind for over 30 years. Its structure is essentially that of theme and variations, a form unusual in choral music, and a few of its notable moments may be cited: the recapitulation of snatches of themes from earlier movements, each rejected by an instrumental recitative in the cellos and basses; the simplicity of the theme, which led Spohr to reject it as a "Gassenhauer" (alley) tune; the sudden modulation at the end of the fifth variation from A major (dominant of the tonic) to F major (dominant of the new key of B-flat), one of the best illustrations of Beethoven's sudden shifting of tonal planes; the military march variation for tenor soloist and male chorus, with the ensuing triple fugue followed by the statement of the theme in its entirety for the last time; the introduction of new material (G major, 3/2) after which this new material is combined with the theme in a simultaneous double fugue; the sublime and almost impossible vocal cadenzas for the soloists; and the breathtaking coda.

On the other hand, the *Missa Solemnis*, which caused Beethoven the greatest difficulty in its creation of all his compositions, is his most problematical work. The Austrian symphonic Mass had already been expanded to its limits, both musical and liturgical, by Haydn, and this medium was not as amenable to enlargement as were the sonata form and the variation cycle. Despite Beethoven's intense personal sincerity in this work and the sublimity of its outer movements (Kyrie and Agnus Dei), it is difficult to avoid considering the *Missa Solemnis* as one of the greatest failures in the history of music. For the work is uneven, even patchy in places, and the overlong conclusions of the Gloria and Credo, influenced by the choral writing of Handel, tend to stupefy rather than edify. The influences not only of Handel (whom Beethoven had come to consider the greatest of his predecessors) and Haydn, but also of Cherubini, Albrechtsberger, and the entire tradition of the heroic orchestral Mass from the early Baroque onward (Benevoli's *Mass for 53 Voices*, 1628) are brought together in this work, for which Beethoven had even studied Gregorian chant and sixteenth-century counterpoint. Beethoven's own deep feeling is most clearly evident in the personal prayers which he attached to the Kyrie and Agnus Dei, his setting of the words "et homo factus est" of the Credo in bold relief, and his transformation, in the Agnus Dei, of the fanfares and drumbeats which Haydn had earlier used in his *Mass in Time of War* (1796).

What perplexed Beethoven's contemporaries most and led them to believe that he had either taken leave of his senses or, because of his deafness, had no idea of the sounds he was writing, was actually a typical device of the period, "Romantic irony." Romantic irony in literature has been equated variously with parody, overstatement, exaggeration, misplaced emphasis, or destruction and recreation of the object or mood to indicate mastery of the material. Often in his late work Beethoven creates a sublime mood only to destroy it, as in the fourth variation of the slow movement in the C-sharp minor Quartet (Example 4-8a), or in this same quartet to contrive a musical practical joke (Example 4-8b); note

EXAMPLE 4-8. Romantic irony in Beethoven's Quartet in C-sharp minor, Op. 131: (a) variation 4 in "fourth" movement; (b) coda of scherzo, "fifth" movement.

the portrayal of musicians who seem to have lost their place in the music, their attempts to restore order, and their finally fiddling away *sul ponticello* (on the strings near the bridge) like an orchestra of infuriated dwarfs. Beethoven's supreme example of Romantic irony is the enigmatic pizzicato conclusion of his F major Quartet (Op. 135).[11]

BEETHOVEN'S LEGACY

No composer of the nineteenth century could wholly escape Beethoven's influence, for his musical activity was so universal that he must be regarded as the trunk of the tree of nineteenth-century music from which so many branches sprang.

Beethoven gave the strongest impetus, at least for music, to the idea that art was a substitute for, or at least as noble as, religion. A cluster of attitudes arose from this idea. The world, meaning publishers, music lovers, the middle-class audience, and the nobility (later the state), owed the composer a living. He, in his turn, deliberately aimed at creating the musical masterpiece, chiefly an instrumental cycle with at least one movement in sonata form, since such a work was the noblest, most serious, and most intellectually respectable sort of musical composition. The gestation period for such works was longer, as befits such higher-grade organisms; such works were individual entities to be published as separate opus numbers rather than in sets; and the greatest of these compositions were intended for posterity rather than for the demands of the musical market. Performers, instrumental or vocal, should raise their technical skill or vocal ranges to the composer's demands, and the producer should meet the composer's stipulation for an increased number of performers; this widened the resources on which the future composer could call, but began to open a gulf between the composer, who became a specialist rather than a performer who wrote his own repertoire, and the journeyman musician or singer. The sociological features of nineteenth-century music, to be further discussed in Chapter 12, became

[11] For additional illustrations, see my article "Beethoven and Romantic Irony," *Musical Quarterly*, LVI (1970), 647–664.

apparent in Beethoven's time, and he gave these trends a powerful push, partly through his own forceful personality, which encouraged later composers along the same lines.

In his large instrumental cycles Beethoven displayed two contradictory attitudes: the first, implying tight condensation, fairly strict construction, and even some degree of connection between movements or their constituent sections, best shown in his Fifth Symphony, Op. 95 Quartet, and Op. 101 Piano Sonata, continued through Schumann and Brahms, and culminated in the later symphonies of Sibelius; whereas the second, characterized by an expanded and loose construction, a flexible order and number of movements, some programmatic elements, and even the implication that the symphony or sonata was what one chose to make it (most evident in the Sixth and Ninth Symphonies, "Hammerklavier" Sonata, and Op. 131 Quartet), can be found in Schubert, Berlioz, Chopin, Bruckner, and Mahler. Beethoven widened the resources of tonality (macro-harmony), though micro-harmonic innovations (coloristic chords) were the property of his lesser contemporaries; he also strove to elevate counterpoint to the peak of nobility reached by J. S. Bach and Handel.

Beethoven's influence on instrumental music or the large choral work was stifling, stultifying, or at least terrifying to subsequent generations of composers. Many of his younger contemporaries and successors focused their attention on forms which Beethoven had somewhat neglected, such as the song, song cycle, or small character piece, yet Beethoven had anticipated even these efforts in such works as his song cycle *An die ferne Geliebte,* Op. 98, and the *Bagatelles* of Op. 119 and Op. 126.

BIBLIOGRAPHICAL NOTES

The literature on Beethoven is so extensive that only a brief selection of the best studies can be given here. Additional listings, with emphasis on recent studies, are contained in Basil Deane, "The Present State of Beethoven Research," *Studies in Music,* I (1967), 11–22, and Erich Schenk and others, "Zur Beethovenforschung der letzten zehn Jahre," *Acta Musicologica,* XLII (1970), 83–108, from 1960 through April 1970. Georg Kinsky and Hans Helm, *Das Werk Beethovens* (Munich, 1955), is a thematic catalog with copious annotations of Beethoven's works comparable to Köchel's catalog of Mozart's.

Alexander Wheelock Thayer's *Life of Beethoven,* with excellent and extensive annotations by Elliot Forbes (Princeton, 1964, 2 vols.) is the standard account of Beethoven's life, but without discussion of his music; this approach has also been followed by George Marek in his *Beethoven*

(New York, 1969), a very readable popular biography which incorporates new research. Emily Anderson's translation of the *Letters of Beethoven*, O. G. Sonneck's *Beethoven: Impressions of Contemporaries* (1926; reprint, New York, 1967), and Anton Schindler's *Beethoven as I Knew Him*, translated and extensively annotated by Donald MacArdle (Chapel Hill, 1966), give excellent portraits of Beethoven the man. H. C. Robbins Landon's *Beethoven* (New York, 1970) is an excellent documentary biography with numerous splendid pictorial illustrations. A good one-volume critical biography of Beethoven's life and works is still needed; the best is Marion Scott's *Beethoven* (London, 1934), with Donald Tovey's incomplete *Beethoven* (London, 1944) containing many valuable insights into his music. Martin Cooper's *Beethoven: The Last Decade* (London, 1970) is an excellent study of Beethoven's life and music from 1817 until his death. Essays on various aspects of Beethoven's music are contained in Nigel Fortune and Denis Arnold, *The Beethoven Companion* (London, 1970) and Joseph Schmidt-Görg and Hans Schmidt, *Ludwig van Beethoven* (English trans., New York, 1970).

Among the full-length studies of Beethoven's works in individual genres are George Grove's *Beethoven and His Nine Symphonies* (1896; reprint, New York, 1962); Donald Tovey's *A Companion to Beethoven's Pianoforte Sonatas* (London, 1951); William S. Newman's *The Sonata in the Classic Era* (Chapel Hill, 1963), with Clementi's sonatas discussed pp. 738–759 and Beethoven's pp. 501–542; and the studies of Beethoven's quartets by Daniel Gregory Mason (New York, 1947), Philip Radcliffe (London, 1965), Ivan Mahaim (Paris, 1964, 2 vols., limited to the last quartets), and Joseph Kerman (New York, 1967). The continuing publication of Beethoven's sketchbooks in facsimile, with transcriptions and commentaries, is rendering Gustav Nottebohm's *Beethoveniana* (Leipzig, 1927, 2 vols.) obsolete. Special issues of musicological journals for 1970, Beethoven's bicentennial year, contain detailed studies of individual aspects of Beethoven's life, works, and creative processes.

A new and more complete edition of Beethoven's works, replacing the old *Gesamtausgabe* (Leipzig, 1862–1865), is being published by Henle-Verlag in Munich.

FIVE

BEETHOVEN'S CONTEMPORARIES

The first three decades of the nineteenth century have frequently been called the "Age of Beethoven." This term is somewhat erroneous, for although Beethoven was the greatest composer of this period and virtually all his contemporaries came at some time into his orbit, it must be recalled that a large number of significant composers were active between 1800 and 1830. All of them had their roots deeply sunk into the eighteenth century, and some considered themselves Mozart's legitimate heirs; most of them accepted Beethoven's earlier compositions while rejecting the works of his final period. Yet in a sense the composers to be discussed in this chapter were more progressive than Beethoven and, perhaps because they refused to compete with him and sought different means of musical expression, had a more immediate influence on most of the younger composers who reached musical maturity between 1830 and 1850.

JAN LADISLAS DUSSEK (1760–1812)

The change from Classic to Romantic is most strikingly seen in the works of Jan Ladislas Dussek (Dušek, Duschek, Dusík), ten years older than Beethoven and only four years younger than Mozart. An extremely peripatetic composer even by nineteenth-century standards, Dussek's career took him from his native Bohemia to Belgium, Russia, Germany, London, and Paris. He is said to have been a pupil of C. P. E. Bach; whether so or not, one can discern Bach's influence on Dussek's style.

Even in his early sonatas of the late 1780's and early 1790's, Dussek's works show a disintegration of the equilibrium characteristic of the High Classic period. Key-relationships between first and second theme-groups are sometimes quite remote (A♭-E in the Op. 5, No. 3 sonata); sudden shifts of tonal planes to unexpected areas anticipate Beethoven (the abrupt shifts between exposition and development in the first movements of Dussek's Op. 35, No. 2 and Beethoven's Op. 10, No. 3 sonatas); phrase-dominated writing is the rule; and Dussek's harmonic Romanticism is evident in his frequent borrowings from minor to major, especially chords of the diminished seventh or minor subdominant, often reinforced with non-harmonic tones or chromatically moving inner parts. Within an individual sonata movement, Classic and Romantic melodic and harmonic patterns are often juxtaposed. Heavy and full sonorities, influenced by the English pianos, are quite frequent in Dussek's sonatas before 1800. Quite uncanny resemblances can be seen between Dussek's themes, devices, patternings, and tonal freedoms and Beethoven's slightly later sonatas.

After his Op. 44 sonata of 1800, Dussek's style became increasingly more Romantic. His sonorous piano writing remains full but is less chordal; it relies heavily on elaborate figurations and a more technically complex kind of writing, yet it retains a "singing" style for the piano. Many of these sonatas have programmatic titles.

Most surprising of all are Dussek's anticipations of a large number of subsequent Romantic composers, some of whom were not even born when Dussek composed these harbingers of their musical style. One can easily single out, for example, the anticipation of Mendelssohn in the second movement of the Op. 10, No. 3 sonata (ca. 1789); of Weber, Hummel, and many others in the "perpetual motion" kind of finales, some of which dangerously skirt the trivial; or even of such far-removed composers as Schumann and Brahms in, respectively, the "maggiore" section of the rondo and the trio of the minuet in the "L'Invocation" sonata of 1812. Rossini, Chopin, Smetana, and Dvořák are other composers whose styles seem to have been anticipated by Dussek. Yet little direct influence by Dussek on these composers can be definitely proven, since his works went out of fashion shortly after his death.

The most famous of Dussek's sonatas is his "Elégie harmonique," Op. 61, in the "Romantic" key of F-sharp minor, written as an elegy for his talented pupil Prince Louis Ferdinand of Prussia (1772–1806), an original if undisciplined composer, praised by Beethoven and Spohr, who was killed at the battle of Saalfeld. The dramatic rhetoric of the sonata, the frequent key-changes within movements, and the disintegration of the second theme-group amid harmonic complexities anticipate Chopin and especially Liszt, as shown in Example 5-1.[1]

EXAMPLE 5-1. Dussek, Sonata in F-sharp minor, Op. 61, first movement, opening of second theme-group.

[1] Published in *Musica Antiqua Bohemica,* LXIII, 1–20.

JOHANN NEPOMUK HUMMEL (1778–1837)

Possibly of Czech ancestry, Hummel at an early age studied with Mozart and even lived in his home, and later he considered himself to be the chief heir of Mozart's tradition. A brilliant piano virtuoso and prolific composer of piano, church, and chamber music, he succeeded Haydn as Prince Esterházy's music director and later held important posts in Stuttgart and Weimar.

Hummel's early works show harmonic crudities and even direct quotations from Mozart, particularly in the outer movements of his Op. 20 sonata, but his style later became more individual. Most noteworthy are the slow movements of his piano sonatas, with luxuriant fioritura figuration (even with 128th and 256th notes) well suited to the light action of the Viennese piano, as well as explorations of atmospheric devices and interesting sonorities and harmonic colors. Hummel's piano concertos, along with Spohr's violin concertos, were the chief models for the soloist-dominated nineteenth-century concerto, with their soulfully lyrical themes, frequent use of the minor mode, and brilliant pianistic fireworks, especially in the codas.

Hummel's chamber music is represented at its peak by his septets for piano, strings, and winds. The Op. 103 septet is called the "Military" because of its trumpet part. The suavity and elegance of the Op. 74 septet for piano, low strings, and winds, especially in the elfin scherzo and genial variations, is comparable only to Schubert's "Trout" Quintet. The variations of Hummel's Notturno, Op. 99 (originally for piano duet and subsequently scored for wind ensemble), show that Schubert did not have an exclusive monopoly on Viennese charm and grace.

Hummel's Masses, along with Schubert's, are the last major essays in the Viennese classical style of church music; the E-flat and D major Masses are his best despite their stiff counterpoint, whereas the Mass in B-flat major is waltzlike in the Osanna and full of the tunefully sentimental effects which were to characterize much subsequent church music.

His most significant work, the F-sharp minor Sonata, Op. 81 (1819), shows the new problems of the Romantic piano sonata. The opening theme contains the germ cells of the entire first movement; the slow movement is replete with the figuration which so strongly influenced Chopin; and the finale is dualistic, with much transitional material needed to reconcile the "Hungarian" gypsy opening with the "severe" fugal second theme—which shows that J. S. Bach's *Well-Tempered Clavier* was more widely disseminated than well-digested at this time. (Example 5-2).

EXAMPLE 5-2. Hummel, Sonata in F-sharp minor, Op. 81, third movement, opening of (a) first and (b) second theme-groups.

Hummel's music at its best is suave, elegant, and gracious rather than profound and laden with a message to the world. If the term "Classic Romanticist" is again permitted in musical discourse, it would fit Hummel far better than Schubert, the composer to whom this expression has most frequently been applied.

LOUIS (LUDWIG) SPOHR (1784–1859)

Haydn was still composing when Spohr published his first work, and Wagner finished *Tristan und Isolde* in the year of Spohr's death. Though Spohr rejected most of Beethoven's music from the Fifth Symphony onward, he welcomed the early operas of Wagner. Though as a violin virtuoso he wrote most of his compositions for this instrument, wind players are his staunchest champions today, and he is best known now not for his music but for his autobiography, which gives a vivid picture of European musical life during the first three decades of the nineteenth century. Spohr was a universal composer, for he wrote even harp music (for his first wife) and works for piano as well as much chamber music, ten symphonies, choral music (including a Mass), operas, and concertos.

Spohr's chamber music ranges from duos for two violins to elaborately scored works like the Nonet, Op. 31, for strings and winds. Quite typical are the solo quartets, which the composer described as being "for violin, with second violin, viola, and cello"; the first violin parts have twice as many pages as any other part and are really violin concertos with string trio accompaniments. His most interesting chamber works are his double string quartets, Opp. 65, 77, 87, 136, not for string octet but two opposed string quartets, and his chamber music with wind instruments like the Nonet (its slow movement is probably Spohr's finest composition), the Octet, Op. 32, and the Quintet for piano and winds, Op. 52.

Spohr's brilliant violin concertos have passed into virtual oblivion except for the Eighth Concerto in A minor, called "Gesangscene" because it was modeled after the Italian *scena ed aria*. His clarinet concertos, though not particularly grateful for the instrument, are sometimes played.

Spohr's ten symphonies range from 1811 to 1857; some have programmatic titles. The best is the Fourth, *Die Weihe der Töne* (Op. 86, 1832), which includes a romanza-type slow movement in which a lullaby, dance, and serenade are stated by themselves and then combined (with conflicting 3/8, 2/8, and 9/16 meters) in the manner of the three dance orchestras in the finale to Act I of Mozart's *Don Giovanni;* a dotted march in the style of Spontini; an "Ambrosian Song of Praise" in counterpoint to a fugato; and an extended chorale prelude in Bach's style. The curious "Historical Symphony" (No. 6, Op. 120) is "in the style and taste of four different periods": that of Bach and Handel (1720), Haydn and Mozart (1780), Beethoven (1810), and the "modern" period of 1840. The first movement is like a Baroque-era French overture; the second utilizes the chromaticism of Mozart's slow movements; the third is more like a fast minuet by Schubert than a "cosmic" Beethoven scherzo; and the finale, opening with a crashing diminished-seventh chord, is less "modern" than the later works of Beethoven or Schubert. The Seventh Symphony, titled "Earthly and Divine in Human Life" (Op. 121, 1841) and scored for two orchestras, anticipates the Liszt of *Les Préludes* in the second movement and the pseudo-religious Wagner of *Lohengrin* in the "Divine" finale. The program of the symphony would have appealed to both Liszt and Wagner, and Spohr's symphonies must be considered important antecedents of the symphonic poem.

Spohr's most important operas are *Faust* (1816), the first major opera based on Goethe's drama, and his masterpiece, *Jessonda* (1823). Spohr was intentionally trying to create the great German opera and selected as his models not only those by his idol Mozart but also the French rescue opera. The grand arias and finales are the most interesting portions, but his operas are not as attractive as Weber's because Spohr lacked dramatic instinct and musical economy; he envied Weber's ability to write popular operas.

Among Spohr's once-popular oratorios, the most representative are *The Last Judgment* (1826), *Calvary* (1835), and (his best work in this genre) *The Fall of Babylon* (1840). He also wrote a Mass for Ten Voices (1820) in which he tried to combine sixteenth-century contrapuntal techniques with the harmonies of Mozart's *Requiem*. Spohr's oratorios are out of fashion because they contain almost unbearably cloying movements characterized by such effects as over-use of 9/8 meter and slow tempos, a lavish use of chords of the diminished seventh and augmented sixth, and a melodic chromaticism often intensified by doubling the dissonant tones at the third or sixth below. Spohr's chromaticism stems from Mozart's, especially from such of his slow movements as those of the E-flat Quartet, K. 428, and the "Prague" Symphony, K. 504. Such passages as that shown in Example 5-3, with its wandering tonality finally settling into a cadence, influenced Spohr's successors.

EXAMPLE 5-3. Louis Spohr, *The Fall of Babylon.*

deem - er liv - eth   He that died is

ri - sen, and He shall live to all e - ter - ni - ty, and

He shall reign, and shall con - quer all His e - ne -

mies

Chorus

Praise His aw - ful name

Spohr's concertos had a strong influence on those of Mendelssohn and Chopin, and his chromaticism not only affected Wagner (Example 8–5b) but in its more sentimental vein the course of English Protestant church music. Although his music is of great historical importance, it lacks the sincerity and effusiveness of Weber's, the elegance of Field's, or the singing style and harmonic inventiveness of Schubert's.

CARL MARIA VON WEBER (1786–1826)

Weber has been hailed as the first genuinely "Romantic" composer, the first "modern" composer, and the first orchestrator. Although he was chiefly a composer of piano music and operas, he also wrote two symphonies, a few Masses and other choral works, songs, chamber music, and display pieces for clarinet and other wind instruments; he even began an autobiographical novel.

Weber's piano music is written in an extremely personal and individual style. With his large hands and long thumbs he could easily play the full chords spanning a tenth and the wide leaps in a rapid tempo which make his music so difficult for most pianists. A striking characteristic of his style is his transfer of orchestral idioms to the keyboard; not just a virtually orchestral range of sonority, as in Clementi and Beethoven, but an actual imitation of orchestral sounds, like the timpani strokes in the second movement of the Op. 24 piano sonata, the timpani rolls and horn-like arpeggios opening the Op. 39 sonata, or the string tremolos in the solo piano part of the Op. 32 concerto. Weber is the first composer whose piano works have been successfully transcribed for orchestra, as witness Berlioz's and Weingartner's transcriptions of *Invitation to the Dance* or Hindemith's *Symphonic Metamorphoses*, three movements of which are based on Weber's four-hand piano pieces. Other Weberian traits are a facile homophonic writing and a brilliance deriving from Mozart's sonata-rondo finales.

Weber's sonatas clearly show the weaknesses of early Romantic extended instrumental forms. The first movements have magnificent openings, but the lyrical themes are not suitable for development, the transitions sag, the second themes are not so strong as the first themes, and the developments are filled with sequences and passage-work, often over diminished-seventh chords. The slow movements and scherzos are fine, but the finales, although containing breath-taking virtuoso passages, lack the quality of "summing up" the instrumental cycle. As a composer of four-hand duets for one piano, Weber deserves to rank with Mozart and Schubert, especially in the pieces of Op. 60. His variations are chiefly ornamental; the most interesting individual ones are those in "national" styles—mazurkas, Spanish dances, and especially polaccas, which are among his favorite vehicles for virtuosity.

The concertos, chiefly for piano or clarinet, have strong links with the eighteenth century through their quasi-martial openings. Noteworthy are the abbreviated concertos, especially the Konzertstück in F minor for piano, with its exuberantly joyous finale, and the Concertino for clarinet and orchestra. The two symphonies, both in C major and both dating from 1807, are remarkably surprising and fresh works, apparently modeled on Mozart's "Paris" Symphony, K. 297, and Beethoven's First Symphony; Weber's First, with its cyclic use of the raised fourth degree of the major scale, anticipates the "Turkish" elements of *Abu Hassan* and *Oberon.*

Weber's four best operas are his masterpieces. *Abu Hassan* (1812), with only three characters and one act, is a delightful Turkish *Singspiel,* a worthy successor to works on similar topics by Gluck, Grétry, and Mozart. The other three operas share certain characteristics: the super-natural "marvelous" element is important, and all incorporate "grand arias" for the protagonists with contrasting romances for the lesser characters, a legacy of the rescue opera. *Der Freischütz* (1821) and *Oberon* (1826) contain much nature-painting, with the real hero of the former the German forest in its benign (the huntsmen's chorus in Act III) or malignant aspects (the "Wolf's Glen" in the finale of Act II). *Euryanthe* (1823), a chivalric drama with an impossibly absurd libretto, is less successful than Weber's other operas, probably because in it he was striving to write the "great German opera." *Euryanthe* is considered "connected" and "through-composed" because the numbers are linked by accompanied recitatives and ariosos rather than by *secco* recitative or spoken dialogue, but set-numbers are easily distinguishable. Weber made some use of recurrent "reminiscence motives" associated with characters (especially the villainess Eglantine) or states of mind, a technique to be developed more fully by Wagner in his leitmotives.

Weber's operatic overtures are sonata-form movements skillfully constructed from the opera's main themes. The overture to *Oberon* is a good illustration: the introduction contains Oberon's horn call, the ritornello from the fairies' chorus in Act I, and the march for Charlemagne's court in Act III; the first theme-group is the conclusion of the Act II quartet; the second theme-group contains the middle section of Hüon's aria in Act I; and the closing theme, also developed in the coda, is the conclusion of Rezia's grand aria "Ocean, Thou Mighty Monster." Weber's technique of creating operatic overtures later degenerated into the thematic potpourris that were to become commonplace as preludes to operettas and musical comedies.

Weber's musical style contains elements common to both his vocal and instrumental music. His melody is highly individual, with much of its sweetness coming from an assimilation, rather than direct quotation, of the style of German folk and popular music. His themes are conceived in terms of regular phrases, but the bravura vocal themes seem pianistic. His use of non-harmonic tones on the beat produces a romantically yearning quality and in rapid tempos gives an effect of brilliance, yet the harmonic background is diatonic in contrast to Spohr's modulatory-chromatic atmosphere. Weber's rhythm is very elastic, with much reliance on the ambiguity of hemiola, as when in 6/8 meter he produces the effect of 3/4. His love for dotted rhythms gives a martial tone to the first movements of his concertos and to his cantata *Kampf und Sieg*, written to celebrate Napoleon's overthrow, and provides a chivalric tone to his characterization of his knightly heroes (Example 5-4). Weber tends to over-use diminished-seventh chords in creating a daemonic atmosphere, as in *Der Freischütz* or the storm in *Oberon*. The chord of the major ninth as a dominant harmony is a hallmark of his style.

EXAMPLE 5-4. Weber, Adolar's aria, Act I of *Euryanthe*.

It was as an orchestrator that Weber's influence was most pronounced. His orchestra is that of Beethoven, with the trombones as
permanent members rather than occasional visitors, but he differs from
his contemporaries by making imaginative and atmospheric use of the
winds as solo instruments or choirs, especially the clarinet and French
horn. The celebrated finale of Act II of *Der Freischütz* has been called
an "arsenal of Romanticism" with its string tremolos, mysterious and
spectral harmonies in the trombones or low woodwind instruments, and
the special effects that accompany the casting of the magic bullets.
Weber's unique keyboard style had some influence on Chopin and Mendelssohn, and his last three operas, especially their orchestral colors, had
a strong effect on Berlioz and Wagner; the popularity of his music in
France influenced the *opéra lyrique* of Gounod and Thomas. Weber's
best works are his finest operas, the inner movements of his sonatas, and
the four-hand pieces of Op. 60; and the clarinetist is grateful to Weber
for having written some of the finest staples of his repertoire.

FRANZ SCHUBERT (1797–1828)

Schubert was the youngest, most prolific, and musically most important of the composers discussed in this chapter, although he was initially the least appreciated, chiefly because most of his works published
during his lifetime were songs or four-hand piano pieces and he was
unable to appear in public as a performer. His musical fecundity can be
shown by one striking illustration: during the year 1816 he wrote 179
compositions, ranging from dances for piano and songs to two sym-

phonies, an opera, and the Mass in C major. Within each of the genres of his works, e.g., song, sonata, etc., one finds compositions ranging from triviality to inspired genius. Though he wrote for every available medium, he was least successful in composing operas or duos for solo instrument with piano.

Schubert's *oeuvre* may be divided into three chronological periods. The first extends from 1811 to 1819, the year of the "Trout" Quintet for piano and strings and the A major Piano Sonata, D. 664.[2] The second period ranges from 1820 to 1827 and includes such tantalizingly incomplete works as the Quartetsatz in C minor (D. 703), the "Unfinished" Symphony, and the C major Piano Sonata (D. 840), as well as his three great string quartets. The two piano trios and the song-cycle *Die Winterreise* are transitions to his third and final period, which embraced scarcely more than a year but contained his greatest compositions. It is most convenient to consider Schubert's works by genres rather than by periods, since his songs developed along a path different from his instrumental music and his dance music resists attempts at chronological ordering.

Piano music. Schubert composed at least 23 piano sonatas, some incomplete. Isolated early piano pieces may be sonata movements. The Sonata, D. 617, for piano duet and the Grand Duo in C, D. 812, which has been orchestrated in the mistaken belief that it was the sketch of a "lost" symphony, complete the list.

The sonatas display a considerable variety. Those from the A minor (D. 845, Op. 42) onward generally have four movements. They vary in total length from the exquisitely concise A major (D. 664, Op. 120) to the expansive last Sonata in B-flat (D. 960). Although a few begin with attention-getting boldness, most open with the quiet statement of a lyrical theme, often in question-and-answer form. The titles of the third movements oscillate between "menuetto" and "scherzo"; their trios contain some of Schubert's loveliest music. The slow movements are song-like, sometimes a theme and variations; characteristic of those in three-part, rondo, or modified sonata form is a more active and interesting accompaniment at the reprise of the opening theme. The finales, the weakest movements, tend to sprawl and are generally inferior to the closing movements of the composer's best symphonies or chamber music. The sonatas lack the technical difficulties of those by Beethoven, Weber, or Hummel yet are scorned by many pianists, probably because of their general lack of brilliance and some passages which sound even more

---

[2] Schubert's works are known by their numbering in O. E. Deutsch's *Schubert: Thematic Catalogue* (New York, 1951), rather than by their opus numbers, which are chronologically inaccurate owing to the amount of music published with opus numbers after the composer's death.

orchestral than Weber's piano music, e.g., the second theme-group of the A minor Sonata, D. 784, especially in the recapitulation.

Schubert's short character pieces derive not from the epigrammatic bagatelles of Beethoven, but from the eclogues, dithyrambs, rhapsodies, and impromptus by two Czech composers residing in Vienna, Jan Vaclav Tomašek (Tomaschek, 1774–1850) and Jan Hugo Voříšek (Worzischek, 1791–1825). The forms of these pieces are generally ternary or rondo with coda. The best known of Schubert's essays in the smaller forms are the *Moments musicaux*, D. 780 (ca. 1823), and two groups of Impromptus; the finest are the *Drei Klavierstücke*, D. 946, of 1828.

Schubert also wrote copious quantities of dance music—waltzes, Ländler, ecossaises, and "German dances," chiefly in waltz tempo. The waltzes are not individual compositions but chains of dances like those of his contemporary Josef Lanner (1801–1843) or the later waltzes of the Johann Strausses (Sr., 1804–1849; Jr., 1825–1899), with each individual waltz containing six or more separate dances. The most interesting of the dance pieces are the polonaises and marches for piano duet. The spirit of Viennese popular music permeates not only the marches and dances but many of Schubert's larger works, for example the zither effect of the scherzo of the D major Sonata (D. 850, Op. 53) or the trio of the scherzo of the A major Sonata (D. 959).

Among Schubert's miscellaneous piano works are several sets of variations, for which he preferred a theme opening with a dactylic rhythm; short pieces which may be sonata movements; a magnificent Allegro in A minor for piano duet (D. 968); some rondos for piano duet which are allegretto, lyrical, and contemplative as opposed to the fast, flashy, and brilliant virtuoso rondos of his contemporaries; and a few divertimentos, all of considerable length, of which the most enjoyable is the *Divertissement à l'hongroise*, D. 818, one of the many souvenirs of Schubert's visits to Zselis as music master to the Esterházy family. The greatest of these miscellaneous compositions is the four-hand Fantaisie in F minor, D. 940, in which Schubert seemed to be aiming toward a one-movement instrumental cycle midway between Mozart's fantasies for mechanical organ (K. 594, 608) and a one-movement sonata. The work contains delightful and effective illustrations of the composer's love for contrasting minor and major forms of his themes (Example 5-5).

Orchestral music. Of Schubert's nine symphonies, the first six are early works, the Seventh is but a sketch (although attempts have been made to complete it), the Eighth is unfinished, and the Ninth (erroneously called the Seventh by some) was rejected by most orchestras during the nineteenth century. The early symphonies were written for the ensemble of the Imperial and Royal Stadt-Konvikt, where Schubert

EXAMPLE 5-5. Schubert, Fantaisie in F minor, D. 940: (a) opening theme; (b) opening theme stated in major mode; (c) closing theme of first section; (d) fugal treatment (see bass line) of (c) in minor.

(a)   Allegro molto moderato

(b)

(c)

pp legato

was a student; they call for an orchestra like that of late Haydn or early Beethoven but with solo flute and solo oboe assigned a more prominent role. It would seem that Schubert did not dare to compete with any of Beethoven's orchestral works written after *Prometheus.* Schubert's C minor Symphony (No. 4, D. 417) emulates the Beethoven of the C minor Quartet (Op. 18, No. 4) rather than the C minor sonatas or symphony; it has an unusually bumptious scherzo and some wonderful major-minor contrasts in the finale. The Second Symphony (B-flat, D. 125) is only superficially Classic, for the extensive use of winds with high tessituras in their parts, the frequent borrowed harmonies from minor, the minuet-type movement in minor (like that of the Fifth Symphony, D. 485, also in B-flat major), and the unusual yet logical tonal relationships in the sonata-form movements are all Romantic traits. The Fifth Symphony has the light instrumentation of early Haydn or Mozart and in many ways is closely modelled on Mozart's G minor Symphony, K. 550; it is the most popular of these early symphonies. The Sixth Symphony, D. 589, seems strongly influenced by Rossini's overtures.

With the Eighth Symphony, Schubert began a new style of symphonic composition. The formal structures of the two completed movements show Schubert at his most adventurous, for in the first movement the introductory material dominates both the recapitulation and the coda (the recapitulation begins directly with the oboe-clarinet theme) and the idea of the second theme appears in the closing group. The unusual development section in the second movement has confused more than one analyst, and its second theme contains one of Schubert's most magical contrasts between minor and major (C-sharp minor–D-flat major). Schubert did begin to sketch a scherzo, and even orchestrated the first two pages, but abandoned the movement in the middle of the trio. Various hypotheses have been advanced for Schubert's failure to complete the symphony; it is most logical to assume that compositional problems, rather than any incident in Schubert's life, compelled him to cease work on this symphony and proceed to compositions for other media.[3] Not until the last year of his life did Schubert resume symphonic composition by writing his Ninth Symphony; in some respects it is a regression to earlier works, especially the Third Symphony and the Grand Duo for piano duet; yet on the other hand its "heavenly length" (Schumann's term), its imaginative writing for brass instruments, its insistent dotted rhythms, and its driving finale influenced Schubert's logical successor, Anton Bruckner.

Almost all the overtures, especially those "in the Italian style," show the influence of Rossini's domination of Viennese musical life during the 1820's. The so-called *Rosamunde* Overture was actually written for a drama called *Die Zauberharfe;* in this overture Schubert seems intoxicated by his first chance to write for an orchestra of professionals and in the tutti passages tends to overwhelm the listener with sheer volume of sound.

Chamber music. From his early youth Schubert was an avid violist in the family string quartet.[4] Thirty-six chamber works (excluding duet sonatas), some only fragmentary, can be counted; of these, the last three string quartets, the String Quintet with two cellos, the "Trout" Quintet, the piano trios, and the Octet are outstanding.

The chamber music with piano is represented chiefly by the two trios (D. 929 and 989) and the "Trout" Quintet, D. 667, so called because the fourth of its five movements is a set of variations on Schubert's own song "Die Forelle." Noteworthy is Schubert's use of the singing tone of the piano, often in the high register, to the accompaniment of the strings. The Octet (D. 803) for clarinet, bassoon, horn, and strings, with its six movements a late example of the Classic-era divertimento, is among Schubert's most delightfully expansive works. Both the first and last movements have slow introductions, that of the finale quite ominous in contrast to the light-hearted main body of the movement; the slow movements include variations as well as one of Schubert's finest and most lyrical song-like forms.

Of the string quartets, the ones in A minor (D. 804, Op. 29) and D minor (D. 810) are the most popular; the G major (D. 887) is seldom performed because of its length and its fatiguing effect on performers.

[3] For the various hypotheses as well as the sketches of the incomplete third movement, see Martin Chusid's edition of Schubert's B minor Symphony in the *Norton Critical Scores* (New York, 1968). The idea that the B minor entr'acte from the incidental music for *Rosamunde* may be the missing finale and suggestions for completing the scherzo are discussed by Gerald Abraham in his "Finishing the Unfinished," *Musical Times* (June 1971), 547–548.

[4] The number of composers of magnificent chamber music who were also violists is amazing; besides Schubert, one need only mention Mozart, Beethoven, Dvořák, Hindemith, and Quincy Porter.

The A minor Quartet is noteworthy because of its major-minor contrasts in the first movement and its somber third movement with a contrasting trio in major; the D minor for its daemonic energy, unusual for Schubert, in the outer movements and its slow movement, variations on his song "Death and the Maiden." The most sublime of the instrumental works is the Quintet in C major (D. 956) for string quartet with an additional cello, which provides a warmer sonority than does the second viola of the customary string quintet. In the first movement the opening theme contains some of Schubert's finest harmonic coloring (see Example 2-7a), and the second theme-group is one of his loveliest ideas; the closing theme is a quietly mysterious Hungarian march, ending with a reminiscence of the second theme. Unusual features in this quintet include the somber trio of the light-hearted scherzo and the strange cadence, including the lowered second degree, in the Hungarian-style finale.

Vocal music. During his lifetime Schubert was principally known as a composer of vocal music. He was unsuccessful in opera but wrote much fine choral music, and he can be regarded as the establisher of one of the few new musical forms of the nineteenth century, the Lied or art-song.

Most of Schubert's larger choral works stem from his attempts to secure a position as a church composer that would provide him with both support and time for composing. His first four Latin Masses are early works and strongly influenced by Michael Haydn (1737–1806), but his A-flat (D. 678, 1822) and E-flat (D. 950, 1828) Masses are the last significant examples of the Viennese Classic Mass. The garbled texts of Schubert's Credo movements have been erroneously explained as stemming from either his carelessness or unorthodox beliefs, but he would not have been likely to jeopardize his chances for a secure position, and it is most likely that these Credos (along with his church works in the vernacular, like the "German Mass," D. 872) indicate the lingering effects of Joseph II's ill-considered attempts at "reforming" Austrian Catholicism, some of which had yet to be purged from the Viennese liturgy. Schubert also wrote two major oratorios (*Miriam's Song of Triumph* and the incomplete *Lazarus*) and delightful secular part-songs, many for male voices; their warm sonority encouraged some of Schubert's boldest harmonic experiments.

Schubert's Lieder must be understood in terms of the limitations of their predecessors. During the eighteenth century the atmosphere for solo song was restrictive: despite the efflorescence of German lyric poetry, the poets desired their works to be independent artistic productions, not merely librettos for song, and the composer was subject to the attitude "Sing your songs while composing them without using an instrument or adding a bass," which deprived the composer of the two areas in which he could operate most freely and independently: interesting accompaniment and refined harmonic expression. Poets preferred a simple strophic song that would support their verses; Schiller denounced the "constant strumming on the piano" as song accompaniment; and many songs were printed on only two staves, with the upper one being the voice part, an indication that the pianist was to sing the melody while playing.

Music assumed a more important role in the songs of the later eighteenth century. Reichardt's songs are generally strophic, often hymnlike, with sometimes elaborate melodies with wide ranges and accompaniments generally limited to doubling the voice part or to broken arpeggiated chords in the right hand. Zelter's songs were more esteemed by poets than musicians and their influence on Schubert's songs was minimal. More important influences were the songs and ballads of Johann Rudolf Zumsteeg (1760–1802), Schiller's classmate; several of his ballads resemble the operatic scena with its ritornelli, accompanied recitatives, independent piano preludes and postludes, arias in differing tempos, and even passages in the style of melodrama with the text declaimed over the music. Less well known influences on Schubert's songs are the works of the Viennese song composers, especially Nikolaus Freiherr von Krufft (1779–1818), whose songs contain quasi-folk song melodies, independent piano accompaniments, and ventures toward the through-composed song.

Schubert's songs span his entire creative career, from 1811 to 1828, and number more than 600, some of them different settings of the same poem. His choice of poets was quite catholic, including not only Goethe and Schiller but also lesser eighteenth-century figures like Klopstock, Hölty, and Matthisson; Romantic poets like the Schlegel brothers and the early Heine and Rückert; his versifying friends like Schober and Mayrhofer; and German translators of Shakespeare and Sir Walter Scott. Hölderlin and Eichendorff are the only significant German poets of the time whose words Schubert did not set to music.

Schubert's songs display a great variety but can be fitted into certain broad classifications. The strophic songs, with the same melody for each verse, include many of the fine songs in the cycle *Die schöne Müllerin;* they often have delightful piano preludes or postludes. More common are modified strophic songs, in which Schubert works changes in melody, accompaniment, or harmony (such as shifting from major to minor or the reverse). Songs in the character of the operatic scena are usually early works and influenced by Zumsteeg; they tend to be lengthy and sectional, with extraneous material (like the 60-measure piano interlude in "Der Taucher," D. 111) and, as in Zumsteeg's comparable works, sometimes an "interlocking" tonality with an ending in a key other than the original tonic. Condensations of the scena type led to Schubert's through-composed songs, sometimes in ballad style like "Der Erlkönig"

(D. 328) and generally unified through recurring themes, tonal schemas, or accompaniment patterns.[5]

In many of the strophic songs a frequent device is the placing of the melody exclusively in the vocal part with the accompaniment merely sustaining the harmony and creating rhythmic motion, as in Reichardt's or Krufft's songs; but Schubert's melody demands an accompaniment that will bring out its latent harmony. More frequent are songs in which the accompaniment holds the song together; who can forget the repeated triplets of "Der Erlkönig" or the varied patterns of "Ganymed" (D. 544)? The piano preludes and postludes, as well as many accompaniments, contain much descriptive tone-painting. The songs containing an alternation of declamation and arioso, with recurring themes or tonalities unifying the work, are less frequent but include some of his greatest compositions, ranging chronologically from "Gruppe aus dem Tartarus" (D. 583, 1817) to the Heine songs in the mis-named *Schwanengesang* (D. 957).[6] In "Memnon" (D. 541) the melodic line contains wide leaps, and in "Der Doppelgänger" (D. 957, No. 13) the declamation, reinforced by a dramatic accompaniment, borders on expressionism; such songs are among the ancestors of the vocal styles of Wagner, Hugo Wolf, and even Schoenberg and Webern.

Among Schubert's favorite song types are the hymn-like, often on a topic dealing with Greek antiquity ("Lied eines Schiffers an die Dioskuren," D. 360) or the elegiac (the settings from Goethe's *Wilhelm Meister*). Some of the most popular are those dealing with nature, especially water or night, and those which approach (and have virtually become) folk songs, like "Der Lindenbaum" from *Die Winterreise*, D. 911. Space does not permit even a list of the great Schubert songs, for over a hundred can be considered such.

Schubert did not add expression marks to the voice parts of his songs, since he felt that the text was direction enough. Leopold von Sonnleithner, one of his contemporaries, described how Schubert wanted his songs performed:

[More than a hundred times] I heard him accompany and rehearse his songs. Above all, he always kept the most strict and even time, except in

---

[5] One need only compare Schubert's "Erlkönig" with the setting by Carl Loewe (1818) to see the difference between genius and talent in early Romantic music. Only in the setting of a humorous text (e.g., Goethe's "Hochzeitslied") does Loewe surpass Schubert.

[6] After Schubert's death the publisher Haslinger arbitrarily grouped these last songs together and affixed the title "Swan Song" to create a sentimental interest; *Schwanengesang* is not in fact a song cycle, for the texts were written by three different poets.

the few cases where he had expressly indicated in writing a ritardando, morendo, accelerando, etc. Furthermore he never allowed violent expression in performance. The Lieder singer, as a rule, only relates experiences and feelings of others; he does not himself impersonate the characters whose feelings he describes. . . . With Schubert especially, the true expression, the deepest feeling is already inherent in the melody as such, and is admirably enhanced by the accompaniment. Everything that hinders the flow of the melody and disturbs the evenly flowing accompaniment is, therefore, exactly contrary to the composer's intention and destroys the musical effect.[7]

Musical style. Schubert's most beloved melodies are generally found in his strophic or folklike songs, the second themes of his sonata-form movements, his slow movements, and the trios of his scherzos. His rhythmic innovations are few but interesting; noteworthy among them are the displaced accents in the scherzo of his C minor Symphony; the hemiolas in the scherzo of his D major Sonata (Op. 53, D. 850) in which the macrorhythm consists of four measures of 3/2 followed by six measures of 3/4; or the cross-rhythms in the Allegro in A minor (D. 947). Two striking aspects of Schubert's harmony may be considered: color harmony and modulation. By the former is implied the non-functional use of such sonorities as diminished-seventh and augmented-sixth chords, for atmospheric and coloristic reasons rather than for modulation. Such color harmony may be a rhetorically amplifying device, as in the opening of the C major String Quintet, or one for establishing a mood in the piano prelude of a song, as in "Am Meer" (D. 957, No. 12). Schubert's most notable modulations are generally abrupt, often sudden shifts to a mediant or submediant. Example 5-6 is one of his most magical modulations; although it seems like an extreme shift (C-sharp minor to C major), it can be best explained enharmonically as a shift from the dominant to its mediant (G-sharp major to B-sharp major). Another surprising effect

EXAMPLE 5-6. Schubert, Sonata in B-flat major, D. 960, second movement.

[7] Cited in O. E. Deutsch (ed.), *Schubert: Memoirs by His Friends* (London, 1958), p. 116.

is an abrupt change to a different tonality in the course of a leisurely transition to what one would expect to be the dominant, as in the *Grand Rondeau* in A major, D. 951. In the course of a minor theme Schubert often ventures into the flat supertonic (Neapolitan), as in Example 5-5a.

The oft-told story of Schubert's starting to take lessons in counterpoint from Simon Sechter (1788–1867), the theorist later to be Bruckner's teacher, has created the legend that Schubert was not skilled in counterpoint, but his fugal writing is not easy to find fault with, and few composers could find more appropriate countermelodies for songlike themes. Schubert's formal weaknesses can be traced chiefly to his luxuriant melodic inventiveness and his leisurely attitude toward unfolding his musical ideas, but even his lengthiest transitions are far above the level of padding, and when he wanted to be concise, as in "Gruppe aus dem Tartarus" or the A major Sonata, D. 664, he was admirably successful. The legend that Schubert was a spontaneous composer who neither sketched nor revised is false, for his drafts for the B minor Symphony and Fantaisie in F minor show that he was as rigorous a self-critic as Beethoven or Brahms. Like all prolific composers, Schubert's work was uneven, but his best works are great and his weakest compositions possess touches of charm.

LESSER COMPOSERS, MOSTLY PIANISTS

Space permits discussion of only a few of the numerous other composers active during the first three decades of the nineteenth century.

John Field (1782–1837), Irish by birth and a pupil of Clementi, lived in Russia during most of his career, and strongly influenced not only Chopin but the entire course of Russian piano music from Glinka to Kabalevsky. Although he also wrote sonatas, concertos, and chamber music for piano and strings, he is best known for his nocturnes and was the first to use the term for piano music, since the notturnos of Hummel and Spohr are divertimentos for winds. Typical of Field's nocturnes are arpeggiated left-hand accompaniments given sonority through the sustaining pedal, over which the right hand plays, often in the high register, a dreamily singing melody elaborated with fioritura and occasional harmonic clashes with the left hand (Example 5-7); these devices had a

EXAMPLE 5-7. Field, Nocturne in C minor.

strong influence on Chopin. A less frequently encountered kind of nocturne consists of a suavely elegant melody with a simple accompaniment. One might say of Field's urbane and lyrical piano concertos (as of many of his time) that the orchestral tuttis in the first movements are quite Classic whereas the piano solo portions are Romantic. The slow and final movements of these concertos often correspond, respectively, with the two kinds of nocturnes just described. Field's polished piano concertos, despite the lack of bravura fireworks, deserve to be ranked at least with those by Hummel.

Paris was the locale of a number of transplanted virtuosos who developed techniques of performance and composition to astound the new middle-class audience whose musical background and taste were limited. The most noteworthy were Friedrich Kalkbrenner (1785–1849), Henri Herz (1803–1888), Franz Hünten (1793–1878), and the best of this group, Sigismond Thalberg (1812–1871). The salon pieces of the American Louis Moreau Gottschalk (1829–1869) stem from this tradition. The most respected of these virtuosos was the violinist Niccolò Paganini (1782–1840), whose satanic appearance and brilliant concertos and caprices captured the imaginations of Berlioz, Schumann, and Liszt, although Spohr detested his rival. Virtuosity, display, and showmanship are the primary constituents of this music, with the typical vehicles sets of variations on popular operatic airs which decorate the melody with arabesques. The musical value of most of these works is virtually nil, although Thalberg's larger works are respectable and Paganini's caprices often show piquant and imaginative touches, especially the A minor Caprice which inspired variations by such later composers as Brahms and Rakhmaninov. At least a cursory examination of the virtuoso litera- ture of this time is necessary in order to understand the reaction against it by Schumann, Mendelssohn, and Chopin, or the desire of Alkan and Liszt to surpass it.

Another group of pianists, who operated within the virtuoso tradi- tion but wrote more substantial music, was of Germanic origin; they were associates of Beethoven and transmitted his musical ideas and works, especially to England. These pianist-composers are best known today for their piano etudes, which incorporated the techniques needed to perform Beethoven's music into the fingers of subsequent generations of pianists; their other piano music is a little-explored link between Beethoven's pianistic style and that of Mendelssohn and Schumann. The most im- portant of these composers were Ferdinand Ries (1784–1838); Carl Czerny (1791–1857), one of Beethoven's few pupils who in turn gave piano lessons to Beethoven's nephew Karl and also to Liszt; and Johann Baptist Cramer (1771–1858), whose piano etudes, with Beethoven's anno- tations, Czerny used in teaching Karl.

The most imaginative and musically influential composer of this group was Ignaz Moscheles (1794–1870), whose autobiography is second only to Spohr's and Berlioz' *Memoirs* as a vivid first-hand account of musical life in the first half of the nineteenth century. Moscheles' in- fluence ranged far into the century, affecting nearly every pianist-com- poser who came to maturity between 1830 and 1860. His G minor Piano Concerto, Op. 58 (published 1820) is the most significant link between Beethoven's piano concertos and those by Liszt, Brahms, and especially Saint-Saëns. Moscheles' etudes, especially those of Op. 70 (1825–1826) and Op. 95 (1836), are surpassed only by Chopin's. One need only hear the fifth and twelfth of the Op. 70 etudes or the fourth ("Juno") of the Op. 95 set to see Moscheles' strong influence on Brahms' piano writing (Example 5-8).

EXAMPLE 5-8. Moscheles, Etude, Op. 70, No. 5.

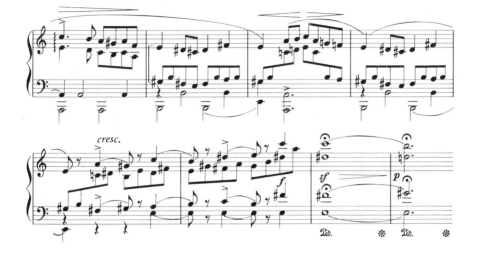

BIBLIOGRAPHICAL NOTES

A good biography of Spohr is lacking. His autobiography (1860–1861) has been issued in a corrected and copiously annotated version by Folker Göthel as *Louis Spohr: Lebenserinnerungen* (Tutzing, 1968). The English translations of the original version include a bungled piece of anonymous hack work (1865; reprint, *Louis Spohr's Autobiography,* New York, 1969) and an abridged translation by Henry Pleasants, *The Travels of Louis Spohr* (Norman, 1962). Richard Hove's "Glemte Noder II: Spohrs Kammermusik," *Dansk Musiktidskrift,* XXXI (1946) is a good survey of Spohr's chamber music. Good biographies of Weber in English are those by William Saunders (London, 1940), L. P. and R. P. Stebbins (*Enchanted Wanderer,* London and New York, 1940), and John Warrack (London, 1968). William S. Newman's magisterial *The Sonata Since Beethoven* (Chapel Hill, 1969) contains an excellent discussion of the sonatas of the pianist-composers in this chapter, especially Dussek and Hummel.

The best studies in English of Schubert's music are those by Maurice J. E. Brown, including his *Schubert: A Critical Biography* (London, 1958), *Schubert's Variations* (London, 1954), and *Essays on Schubert* (London and New York, 1966). Alfred Einstein's *Schubert: A Musical Portrait* (New York, 1951) is a fine appreciation rather than a detailed investigation, and Walter Vetter's *Der klassiker Schubert* (Leipzig, 1953, 2 vols.), a study of Schubert's life and major works from a Marxist viewpoint, is rather hazy in its distinctions between Classic and Romantic. Richard Capell's *Schubert's Songs* (2nd ed., London, 1957) is the standard study of these works. Otto Erich Deutsch's *Schubert: Memoirs by His Friends* (London, 1958) has been enlarged in a German edition (1964), forming the first volume of a new series of Schubert's complete works.

Arthur Loesser's *Men, Women and Pianos* (New York, 1954) brilliantly captures the milieu of the Paris-based piano virtuosos. The most recent study of Paganini is G. I. C. de Courcy's *Paganini the Genoese* (Norman, 1957).

Schubert, Loewe, and Prince Louis Ferdinand are the only composers in this chapter whose music is available in a set of complete works. The old series of Schubert's works (1884–1897), with many lacunae, has been reprinted and is gradually being replaced by a new edition begun by Bärenreiter in 1968. Dussek's piano sonatas comprise six volumes of the series *Musica Antiqua Bohemica*, and three of Field's piano concertos are contained in volume XVII of *Musica Britannica*. The pre-history of the Lied and ballad is easier to trace now, thanks to facsimile reprints of song collections by Reichardt and Zumsteeg, examples of the pre-Schubert Viennese song in *Denkmäler der Tonkunst in Oesterreich*, LXXIX, and several settings of Gottfried August Bürger's ballads published in *Das Erbe deutscher Musik*, XLV–XLVI (1970). Voříšek's Impromptus and his fine D major Symphony are published in volumes 1 and 34, respectively, of *Musica Antiqua Bohemica*. Almost all of Weber's music, but only a scattered sampling of the works of Hummel, Spohr, and Moscheles, is available in modern editions.

SIX

THE GERMAN
ROMANTIC EFFLORESCENCE

A large group of composers born between 1803 and 1813 dominated the music of most of the nineteenth century. The vacuum created by the deaths of Weber, Beethoven, and Schubert between 1826 and 1828 permitted the rise to prominence of younger composers, some of whom either died at an early age or changed their musical styles around 1850; it is with these men that this and the following chapter are principally concerned. Liszt and Wagner, on the other hand, took longer to mature as composers but compensated through long lives and continuing musical influence; their impact on the music of the century will be discussed in Chapter 8.

The years between 1830 and 1850 were particularly yeasty for music. The young composers, fictionally represented by Schumann's "League of David," were joined against the "Philistines," with Paris and the German cities the principal arenas of the combat and with their battles fought in the press as well as in the concert hall or opera house.

The young composers revered Beethoven, though his influence tended to paralyze their imaginations in writing in the larger forms; they highly esteemed Weber; and a few of them came to appreciate Schubert. They were more closely associated with the other arts, especially literature, than any preceding group of composers.

FELIX MENDELSSOHN-BARTHOLDY (1809–1847)

Of all these composers, Mendelssohn was closest in spirit to the eighteenth century, chiefly through his impeccable craftsmanship and sense of proportion. A highly facile and prolific composer, he left a large amount of music that still remains unpublished, and his *oeuvre* still awaits the critical scholarship and cataloging that, for example, Maurice J. E. Brown and Otto Erich Deutsch have given to Schubert's music.

Mendelssohn was second only to Mozart as a prodigy in composition. When we reflect that Mozart's first genuinely individual and independently meritorious works, like the G minor Symphony, K. 183, and the motet *Exsultate, Jubilate,* are the products of his sixteenth year, Mendelssohn's comparable precocity is apparent in such works from his sixteenth and seventeenth years as the Op. 20 Octet, the Concerto for two pianos, and the Overture to *A Midsummer Night's Dream.* Though it is fashionable to regard Mendelssohn's later works as representing a decline in his creative powers, such a verdict is as unjust as that which has been passed on Schumann's later compositions.

Mendelssohn's music must be evaluated by genres, not chronologically, and also in terms of the various facets of his creative personality: elfin and fey, soulfully expressive and sentimental, fussy-tempered, or elegiac. In various compositions Mendelssohn is the landscape painter, the Bach enthusiast, or the representative of Victorian and Biedermeier Protestantism. Many of these personalities exist isolated in individual pieces, single movements of an instrumental cycle, or even in theme-groups of a sonata-form movement constructed with impeccable craftsmanship.

Instrumental works. Mendelssohn revived the organ as a medium of composition. Although Beethoven, Moscheles, and other pianists played the organ, they regarded it as a medium for improvisation rather than composition, and the near-century between J. S. Bach's last works and Mendelssohn's organ compositions are virtually a desert for the organist. Mendelssohn's organ sonatas are more like Baroque than nineteenth-century sonatas, for sonata-form movements are few, with the first movements preludes or even variations in the style of a choralepartita. The Sixth Sonata (D minor), with its chorale variations, fugue, and concluding andante, is considered the best of these works.

Mendelssohn's piano music is underrated, partly owing to the popularity of the *Songs Without Words* as teaching pieces or the tendency to regard his two concertos for piano as "student" concertos. An occasional performance of the *Variations sérieuses*, Op. 54, brings to light the finest set of piano variations between Beethoven and Brahms; it is Mendelssohn's greatest piano work. Such smaller works as the three fantasies of Op. 16 (especially the exquisitely elfin second one), the *Album Leaf*, Op. 117, and the *Capriccio*, Op. 18, are equal in musical value to the Schubert impromptus. The Beethoven of the sonatas between Op. 78 and Op. 90, Weber, Moscheles, and to a lesser extent Field were the chief influences on Mendelssohn's keyboard style.

Mendelssohn's chamber music is little known. One must admire the freshness of the Octet, Op. 20, especially the exuberant first movement and fey scherzo, and the craftsmanship of its sixteen-year-old composer. As in some of his other early works, Mendelssohn experimented with cyclic recapitulation in its finale. His once popular string quartets have virtually vanished from the repertoire, although Mendelssohnians plead specially for the F minor Quartet, Op. 80, one of his last compositions. Perhaps the best of his chamber works is the D minor Trio, Op. 49, with its elegiac first movement and fine scherzo; highly appreciated also are his two cello sonatas, especially the D major, Op. 58, with its exuberant first movement in typically Mendelssohnian 6/8 meter, flowing but not driving (Example 6-1); its second movement is wryly wistful, with an ironic ending comparable to that of many of Heine's poems.

Mendelssohn's orchestral music is the best known part of his *oeuvre*. A large number of the symphonies written during his early years

EXAMPLE 6-1. Mendelssohn, Sonata in D major, Op. 58, first movement.

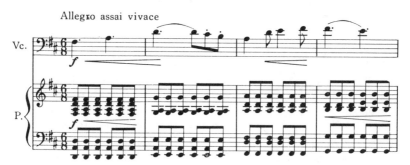

have been published only recently. The *Hymn of Praise*, often called his Second Symphony, is really a choral cantata. The "Reformation" Symphony in D minor, written to commemorate the 300th anniversary of this religious movement, and containing the "Dresden Amen" in the introduction and Luther's hymn "A Mighty Fortress Is Our God" in the finale, has a deft scherzo, a rather fussy first movement, and a finale with many skillful contrapuntal touches in its treatment of Luther's hymn but also some bombastic moments; it is interesting to compare this movement with the prelude to Meyerbeer's *Les Huguenots*, which also utilizes Luther's hymn. Mendelssohn's most popular symphony, the "Italian," is beloved because of the deftness of its outer movements and the tenderness of its contemplative inner movements; this symphony was not published during Mendelssohn's lifetime because he hoped eventually to revise the finale, with which he was dissatisfied. Mendelssohn's finest symphony is his last, the "Scotch" in A minor, with its magnificently elegiac first movement, exquisite scherzo, wistful slow movement, and driving finale which is marred, however, by a bombastic coda; all four movements are skillfully linked through a "motto" theme that appears in various guises too numerous to cite. Although Mendelssohn's piano concertos have fallen out of favor, probably because of their over-use as student concertos in the past, his Violin Concerto in E minor is one of the few works in the history of music that has an equally great appeal to performer, listener, scholar, and audience because of its pervasive melodiousness, skillful solution of the problems of balance between soloist and orchestra, exquisite scoring, and deft finale in Mendelssohn's best elfin vein.

Mendelssohn's programmatic overtures contain the best illustrations of his skillful orchestral writing. The overture to *A Midsummer Night's Dream* was followed seventeen years later by additional incidental music to the drama, but the tendency to perform this music apart from the play has resulted in the unfortunate elimination of many fine individual pieces. The best overtures are seascapes, like *Hebrides* and *Melusine;* the dramatic portrayals (*Ruy Blas*) are weaker. Excellent examples of sonata form, these overtures stand midway between those of Beethoven and the symphonic poems of Liszt and had an important influence on succeeding generations.

Vocal works. During the nineteenth century Mendelssohn's choral works were ranked above his instrumental compositions. Among his large oratorios, *St. Paul* (1836) derives from Handelian dramatic oratorio, with some movements drawing on Bach's four-part chorale style; *Elijah* (1846) is a more felicitous fusion of these elements with the oratorio style of Spohr and the English anthem, its influence evident in the motet-like choruses like "Be not Afraid" and "He Watching Over Israel." The contemplative choruses and arias are the best moments in *Elijah,* and the confrontation of Elijah with the priests of Baal is a fine dramatic moment with effective touches of satire, but the dramatic choruses (e.g., "The Fire Descends" are inferior to their Handelian models, and in the conclusion of the first part too much reliance is placed on a jog-trot rhythm. Despite its shortcomings, *Elijah* is one of the finest large choral works of the nineteenth century and for a long time was considered inferior only to Handel's *Messiah.* Among the other large choral works, the Anglican *Te Deum* (1832) is fine and the setting of Psalm 114 (1839) has a grandeur and nobility unsurpassed in Mendelssohn's works. The secular cantata *The First Walpurgis Night* (1833, revised 1843), a setting of Goethe, is a masterpiece containing Mendelssohn's best dramatic writing and loveliest landscape painting. The models for this work are the dramatic cantatas by Andreas Romberg (1767–1821). Despite attempts at imitation by Schumann, Gade, Brahms, and Dvořák, Mendelssohn's composition never had a true successor and remains unique in the musical literature.

Mendelssohn's songs are the most neglected of all his works, perhaps because they follow the tradition of the strophic songs of the Berlin school, especially those of his teacher C. F. Zelter, rather than the ideas of Schubert. As examples, "Neue Liebe" is in Mendelssohn's best elfin vein and "Die Liebende schreibt" has the intimacy that one associates with Schumann. A plea should also be made for the composer's charming duets for solo women's voices.

It is difficult to make a capsule description of Mendelssohn's general style in a limited space because of the many facets of his creative personality. The elfin and landscape-painting Mendelssohn is most familiar and popular today; such indications as "presto agitato" over a composition in the minor mode will show the fussy-tempered Mendelssohn; and Example 6-1 shows the opening of one of his best exuberant works in 6/8 meter, with a prevailing diatonic style, impeccable craftsmanship, and singing melodies. Example 6-2 shows Mendelssohn in a

EXAMPLE 6-2. Mendelssohn, Variations, Op. 83, theme.

soulfully elegiac mood: note the regularity of the phrases, the expressive but restrained harmony, the frequent internal cadences within a measure (the so-called "feminine endings"), and the wistful touches imparted by minor triads, mostly well prepared with secondary dominants, in an essentially major key. The four-part writing is in an almost vocal style, and one could imagine words, especially with religious import, set to the melody. Mendelssohn is least successful in writing music with a message or in portraying emotions of conflict or stress.

Mendelssohn frequently returned to completed compositions (*Hebrides* Overture, D minor Trio, *The First Walpurgis Night*) to make thorough revisions which are superior to the original models. He was not only a composer but a leading pianist, organist, and conductor of his day, and the administrative chores resulting from his efforts to make Germany the musical center of Europe hastened his early death. The Leipzig Conservatory which he founded set the model for professional music education in Germany as well as the Anglo-Saxon countries, and his endeavors to reform church music, though the most visible results were the anthems of the English Victorians, markedly contributed to the revived interest in the Protestant musical heritage of J. S. Bach and his predecessors, and also encouraged the infant discipline of musicology.

ROBERT SCHUMANN (1810–1856)

German Romanticism, literary as well as musical, culminates in the works of Robert Schumann. His highly individual style, which derived from many sources, chiefly Beethoven, Schubert, and Dussek, had a strong influence on the absolute music of the later nineteenth century; he was a musical journalist who battled for new music; and his life and works are a neglected field for competent psychological study, since no other composer's music is so autobiographical.

Schumann's music may be divided into four chronological periods, each demarcated by a major crisis in his life. The first period, ending in

1833 with his attempted suicide, was the epoch of the Abegg Variations, Op. 1, and the Papillons, Op. 2, and terminated with the Intermezzi, Op. 5, on a theme by his future bride, Clara Wieck. The second period began in 1834 with his recovery of mental equilibrium and ended with his marriage to Clara in 1840 despite the continued opposition of her father. During these six years Schumann assumed the editorship of the *Neue Zeitschrift für Musik* and wrote his greatest piano compositions, beginning with *Carnaval,* Op. 9, and ending with *Faschingsschwank aus Wien,* Op. 26.

Schumann's marriage to his beloved Clara in 1840 inspired a "year of song" in which 127 songs, many of them his finest works in this genre, were written (some, published several years later, carry opus numbers as high as 142); 1841 was the year of orchestral music, 1842 the year of chamber music. Opinions vary as to the termination of this creative period: Einstein (in *Greatness in Music*), seeking more for a round number than an accurate date, cites Op. 50, the secular oratorio *Paradise and the Peri;* Knepler (*Musikgeschichte des XIX. Jahrhunderts*) the year 1844; E. A. Lippman (article "Schumann" in *MGG*) 1847, the year of the D minor Piano Trio. The middle years of the 1840's were fallow for Schumann and saw his abandonment of musical journalism in 1844 and a breakdown in 1845, followed by a "cure by counterpoint" which resulted in the canonic studies and sketches for pedal-clavier (a piano with a pedal keyboard like that of the organ) and the fugues on B–A–C–H (B-flat–A–C–B-natural), replete with intricate contrapuntal devices.

It is fashionable today to deprecate the music of Schumann's last period, but the years between 1849 and 1851 were among his most productive and include his best neglected music. Yet his increasing mental deterioration resulted in his forced resignation as conductor in Düsseldorf in 1853, his attempted suicide in 1854, and his subsequent confinement in a mental institution until his death.

Piano music. Not only did the piano dominate Schumann's creative activity between 1828 and 1839, but most of his successful later works, particularly songs and chamber music, relied heavily on this instrument, and most of his essential musical characteristics are revealed in his piano music.

His split personality was incorporated in his early years in the imaginary characters Florestan and Eusebius, whom Schumann depicted in *Carnaval* and had "sign" individual articles in his journal and in the Davidsbündler Dances; a few of these dances and the F-sharp minor Piano Sonata, Op. 11, were written under "joint authorship." Florestan is the capricious, tempestuous, impulsive figure who, in the dance beginning as in Example 6-3, "stopped, and his lips trembled sorrowfully";

EXAMPLE 6-3. Schumann, Davidsbündler Dances, Op. 6, No. 9, "Florestan."

Eusebius, on the other hand, is the contemplative, introspective dreamer (Example 6-4). In many of the compositions with epilogues (Davids-

EXAMPLE 6-4. Schumann, *Carnaval*, Op. 9, "Eusebius."

bündler Dances, *Arabeske, Dichterliebe*) Eusebius has the last word. Schumann's third personality, the judicious and arbitrating Master Raro, is first evident in Schumann's articles and becomes prominent in his music after 1844, especially in sonata-form movements and contrapuntal studies.[1]

In Schumann's earlier piano works the dominant idea is that of the masked ball, wherein various characters, portrayed in short epigrammatic character pieces, flit back and forth; the earliest example is *Papillons,* based on the masked ball toward the end of Jean Paul Richter's novel *Flegeljahre,* which also contains the characters Walt and Vult, models for Florestan and Eusebius. *Carnaval* is another masked ball in which Clara Wieck (Chiarina), Schumann's temporary fiancée Ernestine von Fricken (Estrella), Chopin, Paganini, and the figures of the Italian *commedia dell'arte* appear in waltzes (influenced by Schubert's) and promenades; at the end Schumann's "League of David," his musical colleagues and their ancestors like J. S. ·Bach, Beethoven, and Weber, sally forth against the "Philistines," the purveyors of empty virtuoso piano music and the Classic epigonoi who, in Schumann's words, "wrote music by the yard." The Davidsbündler Dances, later works despite an earlier opus number than *Carnaval,* are the culmination of the masked ball idea.

This gave way to series of character pieces, either indefinite atmospheric portraits (*Fantasiestücke,* Op. 12) or the delightful pictures in the *Scenes from Childhood,* Op. 15; in later years Schumann returned to works of this type in the *Waldscenen,* Op. 82, *Bunte Blätter,* Op. 99 (incorporating movements withdrawn from *Carnaval*), and his tragic farewell to music, the *Songs of the Dawn,* Op. 133. His greatest piano works are the sets of large pieces, especially the *Symphonic Etudes, Kreisleriana,* the *Novelletten,* the *Faschingsschwank aus Wien,* and the *Fantasie* in C major.

Except for the later piano collections, the sets of piano pieces are not helter-skelter assemblages of individual pieces gathered into an arbitrary collection; they are often, if not always, unified by subtle means. Schumann's delight in musical acrostics is evident as early as his Abegg Variations (in German notation, the name is spelled out as A–Bb–E–G–G); *Carnaval* is based on permutations of the letters in the name of the Sudeten town of Asch near which Ernestine von Fricken lived; "Asch" (Ab–C–B-natural) is even permutated to S C H – u – m – A – n – n by using the notes Eb–C–B–A. Other unifying devices include

---

[1] Schumann's mental illness was not schizophrenia but a manic-depressive psychosis; Florestan and Eusebius may be viewed, therefore, not as split person-. alities but as the manic and depressive facets of Schumann's psyche, with Raro as a superego attempting to control the deviant facets through contrapuntal and formal structures.

the bass line of the theme of the Impromptus, a technique derived from Beethoven's "Eroica" Variations; harmonic structures in most of the *Symphonic Etudes;* and motivic connections between movements in his larger instrumental cycles, most evident in the G minor Piano Sonata, the Piano Quintet, and the Fourth Symphony. Schumann was not consistent in his use of cyclic forms, however, and the analyst must not expect to find cyclic relationships in all of this composer's works.[2]

Schumann's organization of his cycles of larger piano pieces may best be seen in his *Kreisleriana,* Op. 16, one of his finest sets of piano pieces (Figure 6-1). Although there is no motivic connection between the

NUMBER	KEY-CENTER	STRUCTURE	REMARKS
1 (most agitated)	d	ABA	Syncopated harmonic rhythm; influence of Bach's arpeggio preludes
2 (very expressive and not too fast)	B♭	ABACA + coda	"Eusebius in highest apotheosis"; two intermezzi in faster tempos; coda one of Schumann's most dissonant passages
3 (very excited)	g	ABA + coda	Insistent rhythms; coda the dynamic climax of the set
4 (very slow)	B♭	ABA	"Melodic improvisation"; prevailing avoidance of tonic in root position; ends with a surprise cadence to V of g
5 (very lively)	g	ABACDCBA	Scherzo; motive- and rhythm-dominated
6 (very slow)	B♭	ABA	Slow movement; songlike; delayed tonic
7 (very fast)	c	ABACBA + coda	Technique of first number; foreshadowing of scherzo of second symphony; coda with a surprise cadence in E-flat
8 (fast and playful)	g	ABACA	Persistent 6/8 "riding" figure; syncopated bass relates to number 1; avoids any resemblance to conventional finale

FIGURE 6-1. Organization of Schumann's *Kreisleriana,* Op. 16. Based, with my additions and revisions, on Karl H. Wörner, "Schumanns 'Kreisleriana,'" *Sammelbände der Robert-Schumann-Gesellschaft,* II (1966), 58–65.

[2] One writer has gone so far as to conjecture that Schumann's themes were based on a numerological code. See Eric Sams, "Did Schumann Use Ciphers?" *Musical Times,* August 1965 (and the editorial comments); "The Schumann Ciphers," May 1966.

individual numbers as in *Carnaval* or *Scenes from Childhood,* the unity of the cycle is established through subtle means, like the use of the key of B-flat for the slow numbers which serve as points of rest, the surprise cadence of Number 4 which leads directly to the following number, and the balanced contrasts in moods, even within individual numbers wherein the sections are marked by tempo as well as key changes. That Schumann did *not* intend this work to have a conventional finale is shown by his treatment of the last two numbers: the coda of the seventh piece, quiet and chordal in contrast to the agitation of the main number, leads to a cadence in E-flat major, after which the final number, in G minor, is dominated by a ghostly riding rhythm with bizarre syncopations in the bass (relating to the syncopated harmonic rhythm of the opening number) and a mysterious ending. Writers have sought to find a direct connection between individual numbers of this work and episodes in the career of E. T. A. Hoffmann's fictional character Kreisler, the eccentric, wild *Kapellmeister,* but any relationships are at best metaphorical, and none of the numbers is a programmatic painting of any of Kreisler's adventures.

Schumann's middle-sized piano works, including single compositions like the *Arabeske* or *Blumenstück* as well as individual *Novelletten* or *Nachtstücke,* are modified rondo forms, often with codas. In the *Fantasie,* Op. 17, Schumann was aiming for a new kind of form, a modified sonata in three main sections with the first a very free sonata movement. In his sonatas the treatment of form is less skillful, for Schumann was empirically trying to revitalize this structure, but in his best symphonies and chamber music the force of his imagination triumphs over the weaknesses of his larger former concepts.

Rhythm is Schumann's chief driving force. Following Beethoven's example in the first movements of the Fifth and Seventh Symphonies or the last movement of the C-sharp minor Quartet, he wrote many pieces dominated by insistent rhythms, either monorhythmic like the eighth of the *Kreisleriana* pieces or sectional, with each portion dominated by a pronounced rhythm, as in the first number of the *Faschingsschwank.* Unfortunately, Schumann overworked the idea of insistent rhythm to the point of obsession; one can count the same pattern repeated 32 times in the finale of the Fourth Symphony, for example. Yet Schumann's masterly use of syncopation, hemiola, rhythmic displacement, polyrhythms, and syncopated harmonic rhythm makes him a master of rhythm comparable only to Beethoven, Berlioz, Brahms, and Stravinsky.

Schumann's harmony is seldom strikingly dissonant. More characteristic of his style is a lingering on non-harmonic tones in the melody with a gentle accompaniment aided by the sustaining pedal, especially in "Eusebius"-like numbers such as the coda of the *Arabeske.* Another typical device consists of powerful march-like passages with full chords in both hands and a fast harmonic rhythm. Schumann's bass lines are superb, and his harmonic imagination is best shown through a lavish use of inversions and secondary dominants. Schumann, as well as Chopin, was an innovator in writing around but avoiding the tonic, as in Example 6-3, and thus directly contributed to the "psychological tonality" of Liszt and Wagner.

That Schumann was a magnificent melodist is shown not only in his songs but also in his piano music; one can easily imagine words set to the seventeenth of the Davidsbündler Dances or the sixth of the *Kreisleriana*. Often Schumann will pluck, as it were, a melody from the notes of his accompaniment. Less frequent are compositions based on motives rather than melodies, as in the fifth of the *Kreisleriana*, in which the interplay of motives, rhythms, and harmonies provides the musical interest. In some of the later works, like the fourth of the Marches, Op. 76, written under the stimulus of the revolutionary events of 1848, or the third of the *Bilder aus Osten*, Op. 66, Schumann concentrates on insistent reiteration of square-cut melodies.

Songs. Schumann wrote 127 songs in 1840, the "year of song" during which he married Clara Wieck. These songs, furthermore, are the ones most frequently performed, whether individual songs like "Mit Myrthen und Rosen" and "The Two Grenadiers" or the song cycles *Myrthen, Liederkreis,* and *Frauenliebe und Leben.*

The most striking characteristic of Schumann's best songs is the close relationship between voice and piano. What Schumann had previously confided to the singing tone of the piano was now given to the voice but without relegating the piano to the background as a mere accompanying instrument. Preludes, postludes, and interludes play a major role; the preludes are generally short, even to the point of merely getting the singer started, whereas the interludes often unify the song (as in "Der Nussbaum"), and the postludes continue and intensify the mood of the song after the singer finishes. The finest postlude is the conclusion of *Dichterliebe*, for it leads from the ironic mood of the last song back to the contemplative "Eusebius" mood of the first song of the cycle. Another trait of Schumann's songs is a close relationship between poetry and music; not since the troubadours, trouvères, and Minnesänger had words and notes been so beautifully united. Heinrich Heine's gently ironic verses inspired Schumann's best songs, as did the full-blown romanticism of Rückert and the nature poetry of Eichendorff; Robert Burns' poems inspired the best folklike settings. In Schumann's later years, when his creative imagination sometimes flagged, such good poems as those by Lenau, set as Op. 90, or by Mary Queen of Scots, used in his last fine songs (Op. 135, 1852), roused his latent talents.

Schumann's strophic songs are generally simple and folklike; those of Op. 79 are vocal companions to his *Album for the Young*. The declamatory songs, like "Ich grolle nicht" from *Dichterliebe,* are more melodious than Schubert's; the chordal, hymnlike songs are generally late works. The song-cycles are unified in various ways: cyclic interrelationships in *Dichterliebe,* similarities between the outer songs in *Frauenliebe und Leben,* or tonal relationships between songs in *Myrthen, Liederkreis,* or the Mary Stuart songs.

Orchestral music. Schumann's orchestral works include four symphonies and a quasi-symphony without a slow movement (the Overture, *Scherzo,* and *Finale,* Op. 52); concertos for piano (Op. 54) and cello (Op. 129), as well as some miscellaneous concert pieces, the best of which is the Konzertstück for four horns, Op. 86; and four overtures, the earliest written in 1851. In recent years the symphonies have seldom been performed, and the Cello Concerto is neglected because its contrasts are too subtle, its poetic atmosphere too unrelieved, and its virtuosity too unevident, though cellists know how difficult it is.

The First Symphony is partially cyclic; more so are the Second and Fourth. In the Second Symphony the main theme of the slow movement (in minor) becomes the second theme (in major) in the finale. All the movements are related in the Fourth Symphony, a highly concise work based on germ-motives like Beethoven's Fifth Symphony which set a pattern for symphonic writing that continued well into the twentieth century with Sibelius' Seventh Symphony. In some of these orchestral works Schumann attempted to dissolve the boundaries between movements, most successfully in the Cello Concerto.

In his book *Style and Idea* Arnold Schoenberg effectively contradicted the frequently encountered nonsense about Schumann's "poor" orchestration by stating that if the orchestration were changed, much of the typically Schumannesque quality of these works would be lost. Schumann wanted certain tone colors and especially wanted blends of tone, subject to the natural limitations of the brass instruments (it is interesting to note the virtual liberation of his horn parts in the later orchestral works), and we should not blame the composer for not wanting his orchestral works to sound like those of Mendelssohn or Berlioz.

Chamber Music. Most of Schumann's best chamber music was written in 1842, the year of the three string quartets, the Piano Quintet, and the Piano Quartet. After he recovered from his breakdown of the mid-1840's Schumann's renewed interest in this medium resulted in three piano trios, three violin sonatas, miscellaneous chamber music including winds, and even piano accompaniments for Bach's solo violin and solo cello works and for Paganini's caprices.

That Beethoven's later works were Schumann's models is most evident in the Piano Quartet; it is not mere coincidence that E-flat is the common key of this work and Beethoven's Op. 127 string quartet. Schumann's string quartets are the finest between Schubert's and Brahms', but the most exciting of his chamber works is the Piano Quintet. Cyclic relationships abound in his work, one of the most striking being the combination of the opening themes of the outer movements as a double fugue in the coda of the finale. All of the chamber works show some kind of formal experimentation in attempting to create new paths for the sonata form and scherzo (A-major Quartet) or finale, especially the Piano Quintet, the structure of which is shown in Figure 6-2. Note in this finale Schumann's combination of sonata-rondo principles with the expanded recapitulation and "second development" of Beethoven's larger works. The themes of this movement are all related: all but one begins on the second half of the *alla breve* measure, and that exception is a countermelody to theme (d) which is first stated in the development and recurs in the recapitulation, a section which boasts in turn a new theme which recurs after the double fugue.

Of the chamber music of Schumann's last period, the D minor Trio, Op. 63 (1847), is the best example. A complex work that demands many hearings for its message to be revealed, it shows that late Schumann can be almost as difficult as late Beethoven for the listener. Although the lyricism in this trio is sometimes hectic, and portions of the second movement and finale give the listener the impression that Schumann is merely going through the motions, there are nevertheless many adventurous harmonies, and few passages in chamber music are as striking as the *sul ponticello* section of the first movement.

Choral music. Schumann came late to this genre. His first published choral work, *Paradise and the Peri*, a secular oratorio, contains fine movements but is hindered by Thomas Moore's saccharine text. The *Mass*, Op. 147, and *Requiem*, Op. 148, both written in 1852 for Düsseldorf, are not difficult works but are quite effective. *Manfred*, Op. 115 (1848–1849), based on Byron's poem and scored for narrator, chorus, and orchestra, is a splendid work; its overture is the most frequently performed of Schumann's later compositions, and though the choral parts are subsidiary there is much fine music to accompany the narration, especially in nature-painting scenes like the invocation of the witch of the Alps; the appearances of the shade of Astarte contain some of Schumann's most expressive music. His one opera, *Genoveva* (1850), was beset with numerous problems, not the least of these the libretto. A continuation of the mediaeval-chivalric legend with virtually continuous set-numbers like *Euryanthe*, *Genoveva's* greatest misfortune was its having been composed after *Tannhäuser* and *Lohengrin*.

Schumann's greatest late work, which may well be the finest neglected composition of the entire nineteenth century, is his *Scenes from Faust*, composed between 1844 and 1853. Rather than select numbers which would make a continuous narrative, he selected individual scenes,

SECTION	THEME	MEASURES	TONAL CENTERS	CORRESPONDENCE TO RONDO-SONATA FORM
A	a	1–21	c–g	Exposition: theme
	b	21–29	E♭	
	a	29–37	g–d	
	b	37–43	B♭–V of g	Transition
B	c	43–51	G (III)	First episode, corresponding
	d	51–77	G with sequences	to second theme-group in sonata form
A	a	77–85	e–b	Theme, but in remote key
Transition		85–94	B (enharmonic) ♭VI	
Development		95–164	Tonal flux	Developmental second episode
	d	95–114		
	e/d	114–136		e as counter-melody to d
	a	136–164	c♯–g♯–d♯ (enharmonic equivalent of tonic minor)	Retransition
A	a	164–172	e♭–b♭	Recapitulation: theme
	b	172–178	G♭–V of B♭	
B	c	178–186	B♭ (V)	First episode, dominant
	d	186–212	B♭–E♭	Tonic major established
A	a	212–223	c–g (vi-iii)	Theme in related key
D	f	224–248	E♭ (I)	Closing theme of sonata-form; also re-establishes tonic major
Fugato	a	248–274	c (vi)	"Second development"
E	e/d	274–299	E♭ (I)	Unifies development with recapitulation
Transition		300–318	E♭ (I)	
Double fugue		319–378	E♭ (I)	Combines major form of (a) with opening theme of first movement
D	f	378–401	E♭ (I)	Reprise of closing theme
Coda	a	401–427	E♭ (I)	Conclusion based on major form of (a)

FIGURE 6-2. Structural analysis of the finale of Schumann's Piano Quintet, Op. 44.

mostly from the second part of the drama. Considerable cyclic unity joins the scenes; the solos are among the few instances where Schumann could transfer his mastery of song composition to the brief aria with orchestra; the declamation, especially that of Faust, must have been studied by Wagner; and the third part contains the most sublime music between

Beethoven's death and Brahms' full maturity. A comparison of Schumann's original conclusion with his later version of the ending provides an excellent illustration of how his first thoughts were superior to his revisions.

THE GERMAN ROMANTIC LEGACY

Mendelssohn's music became the model for the "academic" composer in Protestant lands, especially in Germany, Scandinavia, and the Anglo-Saxon countries, in choral music as well as for the instrumental cycle. His portrayals of nature served as a model for future generations. During the second half of the nineteenth century Mendelssohn's music was revered in England to the point of adulation, and one may speculate whether the violent reaction against his music that took place during the early years of the twentieth century was part of the general reaction against the Victorian ethic and aesthetic.

Schumann's legacy, on the other hand, was more enduring and more widely disseminated. As a music critic, he played a major role in publicizing the music of Beethoven and Chopin and in building the posthumous reputations of J. S. Bach and especially Schubert; his essays on music are equalled as literary works only by those of Berlioz, Hanslick, and George Bernard Shaw.

Schumann's influence on subsequent generations worked in several different directions. His ideas of instrumental music and especially the instrumental cycle were a happy mean between those of Mendelssohn and Berlioz and thus strongly influenced the general revival of instrumental music after 1860, and not only in Germany. Brahms was his most obvious disciple, but one must include Lalo, Saint-Saëns, Fauré, Chaikovsky, Grieg, and even Sibelius and Rakhmaninov. Schumann's example undoubtedly liberated his close friend Liszt from being merely a purveyor of virtuosic galops and opera transcriptions, and Schumann's harmony led to the "psychological tonality" of Liszt and Wagner.

Schumann's influence moved downward as well as outward. His contemporary Robert Franz (1815–1892) published about 350 songs between 1843 and the onset of his deafness in 1868; most of these are simplifications of the Schumannesque Lied, from the standpoints of the technical demands on pianists and singers as well as of the musical content itself, as can be discerned by comparing the setting of a given poem by Franz with that by Schumann. Schumann's enthusiastic and effusive emotional expressiveness and fine harmonic coloring were soon to be debased into a "hearts and flowers" sentimentality, so well exemplified by the songs and piano music of Adolf Jensen (1837–1879) or the drawing room ballads and wedding songs of the American, Oley Speaks (1874–1948). One need but compare two ballads, Schumann's "The Two Grenadiers" and Speaks' "On the Road to Mandalay" to see the downward direction that resulted from the popularization of Schumann's style.

BIBLIOGRAPHICAL NOTES

The standard biography of Mendelssohn in English is Eric Werner's *Felix Mendelssohn, A New Image of the Composer and His Age* (New York, 1963); unfortunately, the author overstates Mendelssohn's "modernism," and the book suffers from an awkward translation. Many of the letters have been translated into English (*Mendelssohn's Letters,* transl. Gisella Selden-Goth, New York, 1945). Percy M. Young's *Introduction to the Music of Mendelssohn* (London, 1949) is quite serviceable.

No biography of Schumann has the immediacy of J. W. von Wasiliewski's (Dresden, 1858; English translation, *Life and Letters of Robert Schumann,* Boston, 1871); this study by one of the composer's closest associates deserves a new and annotated translation. Joan Chissell's *Schumann* (London, 1948) is the most adequate biography in English, for André Boucourechliev's *Schumann* (New York, 1959) is filled with Romantic overstatements (if also beautiful illustrations). Eric Sams' *The Songs of Robert Schumann* (New York, 1969) contains fine analyses and paraphrased translations of the text of each individual song. Leon Plantinga's *Schumann as Critic* (New Haven, 1967) is a superb assessment of Schumann as a writer on music, reinforced by examination of the music that Schumann discussed, and it supersedes all other studies of Schumann's aesthetics. Plantinga's translations of Schumann's sometimes complicated German prose are more felicitous than those of Fanny Ritter (*Music and Musicians,* London, n.d.) or Henry Pleasants (*The Musical World of Robert Schumann,* New York, 1965).

The complete works of Mendelssohn and Schumann have recently been reprinted. Several of Mendelssohn's compositions, mostly youthful works, that were not published in the older complete edition are appearing in the *Neue Leipzig Ausgabe.*

SEVEN

ITALIAN AND
FRENCH ROMANTICISM

Musical Romanticism developed later in Italy and France than in Germany and Austria. The reasons are easy to explain: in Italy opera was the dominant medium and its audiences were conservative until the 1840's, the period of the drive for unification of Italy (the *Risorgimento*), whereas in France the rescue and revolutionary operas of the 1780's and 1790's gradually disappeared with the advent of the Directory and the subsequent rise to power of Napoleon.

ITALIAN OPERA, 1813–1853

The Italian operas of Gioacchino Rossini (1792–1868) are the culmination of the Neapolitan opera of the eighteenth century and thus represent the close of an old era rather than the beginning of a new one.

Though only a few of his comic operas and some of his overtures are performed today, he was the most popular composer in Europe during the 1820's.

Rossini's first success was *Tancredi* (1813), and so many serious and comic operas streamed from his prolific pen that he enjoyed an international reputation by the time he was 30. In 1824 he settled in Paris, where he produced French versions of his Italian works and wrote two of his masterpieces, the *opéra comique Le Comte Ory* (1828) and *William Tell* (1829). With the latter, his career as a composer of operas ended, although he continued to compose short piano pieces, songs, and church music. Among the reasons advanced for his refusal to continue operatic composition, the most probable are his difficulties with the régime of Louis Philippe, which assumed power after the July Revolution of 1830, and his distaste for competing against Meyerbeer.

Rossini's opera overtures are among the most exciting and thrilling works in this genre. They generally consist of a slow introduction, a main section in abridged sonata form with the development section replaced by a transition back to the tonic, and a coda in a faster tempo. Characteristic of them are piquant woodwind solos, driving rhythms, and crescendos consisting of a repeated motive to which instruments are added in succession.

Rossini's arias often follow a stereotyped form which includes a slow introduction featuring a florid and highly ornamented vocal writing, an allegro with virtuoso fireworks for the singer and sometimes solo instrumentalists as well, and a *cabaletta* in an even faster tempo, designed to elicit a shower of applause. Rossini was assailed for writing out his vocal ornaments, but it is necessary to remember (as Spohr testifies about his travels in Italy during this time) that both singers and instrumentalists inserted ornaments into anything they were performing, and Rossini merely codified an established tradition. The assertion has been made that Isabella Colbran, his principal singer, mistress, and, later, wife, was losing her voice and that Rossini ornamented her parts in order to conceal her vocal deficiencies, yet similar "coloratura" writing occurs in the principal male roles.

Rossini's ensembles are pseudo-canonic, with each singer entering in turn, but they bear only a surface relationship to the contrapuntal writing in Cherubini's operas or Beethoven's *Fidelio* and are really strophic with only very rudimentary counterpoint. His choral writing, like that of his successors, is extremely simple because almost all chorus singers of that time could not read music.

Touches of Romanticism are most evident in Rossini's serious operas, with their plots derived from literature or history (in contrast to the involved plots, which derived from the popular theatre, of the comic operas), and in the faint tinctures of chromaticism in his slower melodies (see Example 7-1) in contrast to the diatonic rapid vocal melodies which often sound as if designed for the clarinets in a military band.

EXAMPLE 7-1. Rossini, Cavatina, "Bel raggio lusinghier," *Semiramide,* Act I.

Rossini was the true composer of the counter-revolution which spread over Europe after 1815. In his novel *Le Rouge et le Noir* Stendhal describes an ultra-Royalist salon where the only fit topics of conversation were Rossini and the weather. The Paris of the Bourbon restoration, the London of George IV, and the Vienna of Metternich were most hospitable to Rossini's music; this hampered the careers of Beethoven and Schubert during the 1820's, and in France younger composers like Auber and Herold were driven to strong efforts to emancipate themselves from Rossini's influence. Although the anti-Rossini strictures of Boieldieu, Spohr, Wagner, and others were partially motivated by chauvinism and professional jealousy, it is nevertheless true that his influence in most European countries was stifling; perhaps this explains why Italy and France lagged behind Germany in developing a Romantic musical idiom.

Italian Romanticism during the 1830's is best seen in the music of the Sicilian-born Vincenzo Bellini (1801–1835), who wrote almost exclusively for the operatic stage during his short career. Bellini is most praised for his long, arched vocal melodies, which require a superb singer, almost always a soprano, for their proper performance (Example 7-2); he may have absorbed this style through his teacher Niccolò Zingarelli (1752–1837), whose generally undistinguished operas contain progressive moments like the aria "Ombra adorata aspetta" from *Giuletta e Romeo* (1796). A large number of Bellini's melodies consist of passages with a prevailing dotted rhythm that occasionally imparts a martial cast (see Example 7-3a). A trait typical of Bellini's ritornelli, later adopted by Verdi, is an interruption of the melody just before the final cadence, after which the prevailing accompaniment pattern is re-established and the singer begins.

EXAMPLE 7-2. Bellini, *La Sonnambula*, Act I.

EXAMPLE 7-3. (a) Bellini, *Norma*, Act I; (b) Verdi, *Luisa Miller*, Act I; (c) Donizetti, *Lucrezia Borgia*, Act I duet; (d) Verdi, *La Traviata,* Act III.

(c)

Di pes-ca - to - re ig - no - bi - le esser fig - luol cre - de - i,

Moderato

A - ma tua, ma-dre, e te - ne - ro Sem-pre per lei ti ser - ba,

pre - ga che l'i - ra pla-chi - si del - la sua sor - te a - cer - ba

(d) Allegro

Ah! gran Dio! mo - rir sì gio - vi - ne, io che pe - na - to ho

tan - to! mo - rir sì pres-so a ter - ge - re il mio sì lon-go pian - to!

Bellini's harmonic resources and orchestral palette are limited, often producing an effect of monotony, yet he was often able to create an effective psychological scene setting, as in the opening of Act II of *Norma.* Bellini excels as a melodist and as a musical psychologist.

Gaetano Donizetti (1797–1848) represents the lusty, vigorous side of post-Rossinian Italian opera. Although he was a very prolific composer, few of his many operas have survived in the repertoire, and these usually as vehicles for a star singer: *Lucia di Lammermoor* for a soprano, *L'Elisir d'amore* for a tenor, *Don Pasquale* for a comic baritone. Though he lacked Bellini's refinement and taste and was prone to writing musical crudities and vulgarities, Donizetti nevertheless had a gift for creating the "big scene," like the sextet and "Mad Scene" from *Lucia,* as vehicles for vocal display. His sentimental melodies (Example 7-3c) are often doubled with parallel thirds and sixths.

Giuseppe Verdi (1813–1901) was the greatest Italian composer of the nineteenth century. Although his musical development was slow and his first major work, *Nabucco* (based on the Biblical story of King Nebuchadnezzar), was not performed until 1842, his career as a composer spanned more than fifty years. His work can be divided into four major periods; for the sake of chronological organization and to account for the changes in his musical style after 1853, this chapter will include only the works of his first two periods, with the operas and other compositions after *La Traviata* to be discussed in Chapter 11.

Verdi's operas before 1851 have been disdained by some critics because of their vulgarity, earthiness, and unshamed portrayal of raw emotions, the techniques for which came largely from the operas of Saverio Mercadante (1795–1870). Yet these works nevertheless display a powerful dramatic sense, deep psychological insights (especially in *Luisa Miller,* his masterpiece of this period), and a skillful treatment of the devices which he inherited from Bellini and Donizetti. Compare Bellini's gentle tenor cantilena (Example 7-3a) with Verdi's powerful baritone aria (Example 7-3b), and the greater intensity that Verdi gives in Example 7-3d to a musical formula that sounds quite ordinary in Donizetti's style (the Moderato of Example 7-3c).

An understanding of Verdi's early work is incomplete without a knowledge of the political drive for the unification of Italy known as the *Risorgimento.* Many of Verdi's early operas (*Nabucco, I Lombardi, La Battaglia di Legnano*) are thinly disguised political tracts into which the audiences could read appeals for liberation from foreign, especially Austrian, domination. Passages that seem like vulgar, bouncy brass band music are really intonations of the mass songs of the revolutionary Carbonari or "Young Italy" movements, and Verdi's early period really closed with the suppression of and temporary setbacks to the unification movement after the Austrian victories over the Italian insurgents in 1849.

Verdi's operas of the early 1850's—*Rigoletto, Il Trovatore,* and *La Traviata*—can with equal correctness be considered the culmination of the works of his early period, as products of a self-contained period, or as harbingers of the future. The first two operas are concerned with the portrayal of such violent matters as murder, torture, kidnapping, seduction, dishonor, and hatred, with little concern for the subtleties of musical or dramatic character portrayal, whereas *La Traviata* is a psychological drama, a bourgeois tragedy in contemporaneous dress.

Many of the traits of Verdi's earlier operas survive in *Rigoletto* and *Il Trovatore* and can be seen in the soldiers' chorus from the latter opera, the bouncy chorus of courtiers in Act II of *Rigoletto,* or stereotyped set-numbers like "Di quella pira" in *Il Trovatore* or the duet at the end of Act III in *Rigoletto.* On the other hand, musical tendencies which were to flower in Verdi's later operas become apparent at this time; foremost is an impassioned musical declamation, neither recitative nor aria nor Wagnerian sung speech, but rather to be compared to the vocal parts in Monteverdi's Venetian operas of the 1640's. As a general rule, such declamation is given to the baritone (Example 7-4). The combination of subtle harmonic refinements, effective ritornelli which set the scene rather than merely announce a favorite aria for the audience, and restraint in the use of vocal fireworks or other musical stereotypes gives greater depth to the soprano arias, evident in the "Miserere" from *Il Trovatore,* Gilda's aria in Act II of *Rigoletto,* or the whole third act of *La Traviata.*

EXAMPLE 7-4. Verdi, *Rigoletto,* Act I.

FRENCH OPERATIC GENRES

French opera throughout its history presents a Hegelian picture of thesis, antithesis, and synthesis. The thesis is the serious, stately, and sometimes pretentious *grande musique* of Lully, Rameau, Gluck, Meyerbeer, or d'Indy, whereas the antithesis is the *petite musique agréable* of *opéra comique*, operetta, or parodies of serious works. The synthesis occurs when the *petite musique* approaches its serious counterpart in style and topic, as in the rescue opera or *opéra lyrique*.

Gluck's legacy persisted in France longer than in any other nation. The nobility of his style, combined with the powerful expressive devices of the *Sturm und Drang* which were brought to Paris by German instrumental composers, the melodious tunes of the eighteenth-century *comédie mêlée d'ariettes*, and the ideals of the French Revolution contributed to the rescue opera which arose in the mid-1780's but lost its vitality after 1800. Gluck's ideas were also continued by Antonio Salieri (1750–1825), who spent most of his life in Vienna; Luigi Cherubini (1760–1842); and especially Gasparo Spontini (1774–1851), whose grand historical operas, like *La Vestale* and *Fernand Cortez*, display a heroically monumental simplicity, contain rich orchestration, and were to influence both Berlioz and Wagner. At the same time, *opéra comique* was reverting to its earlier form of a sentimental play interspersed with musical interludes, chiefly syllabic and strophic ariettes, romances, and couplets, with simple ensembles and finales. In 1800 the leading composer in this genre was Nicolas Dalayrac (1753–1809), who also wrote rescue operas and string quartets.

During the first two decades of the nineteenth century the rivalry of François-Adrien Boieldieu (1775–1834) with Niccolò Isouard (1775–1818) stimulated the growth of *opéra comique*. Boieldieu was the better composer, but Isouard could write more popular tunes and had the better librettos, many of which poke fun at the pretentions of bourgeois society. The rivalry exhausted both men: Isouard died in 1818 and Boieldieu's muse was fallow between that year and 1825.

The advent of Rossini in Paris threatened to extinguish a viable French school of composition. After the failure of his *Olympie* in 1819 Spontini left for Berlin, and the younger French composers shamelessly aped Rossini's musical mannerisms. Yet *opéra comique* as a native French genre was revived in 1825 with Boieldieu's *La Dame blanche* and *Le Macon* by the prolific D. F. E. Auber (1782–1871). *Opéra comique* was to enjoy two decades of success with such works as Auber's *Fra Diavolo*, *La Part du diable*, and *La Sirène*, and *Zampa* and *Le Pré aux clercs* by L. J. F. Herold (1791–1833). Though Rossini's influence remained audible in the overtures and the vocal fireworks of the *première chanteuse de roulades*, the French style was prominent in the delightful ariettes, deft ensembles, and the prevailing dance-like rhythms (Example 7-5). Around 1845, with the later works of Auber and the early works of Ambroise Thomas (1811–1896), *opéra comique* assumed a depth of seriousness and expression which was to become the *opéra lyrique* of the 1860's.

EXAMPLE 7-5. Herold, *Le Pré aux clercs*, Act III.

Allegro moderato ma appassionato

Auber's *La Muette de Portici* (or *Masaniello*, 1828) was the first example of French Grand Opera, a genre characterized by a historical plot with elements of realism, influenced by the historical dramas of Friedrich Schiller and the historical novels of Sir Walter Scott (1771–1832), and by a mixture of various musical styles, from the symphony and the grand aria down to the trivial dance tunes of the ballet. It was designed to appeal to all the tastes of the middle-class audience which patronized the Opéra after the July Revolution brought the high bourgeois class to power. Spontini's influence was strong on Auber's work and its immediate successor, Rossini's operatic swan song *William Tell*. Of the composers of Grand Opera, Giacomo Meyerbeer (1791–1864, *recte* Jakob Beer) was the most important.

Meyerbeer, a virtuoso pianist in his boyhood, studied operatic composition in Italy before becoming a permanent resident of Paris in 1826. In 1831 his *Robert le diable* established his reputation as a composer of Grand Opera. *Les Huguenots* followed in 1836, *Le Prophète* in 1849, but his masterpiece, *L'Africaine*, though begun in 1838, was not performed until after his death. The supreme musical eclectic of all times, Meyerbeer combined virtually every known device in his operas for the sake of creating telling effects. His style ranges from the crassest vulgarity, as in the "Shadow Song" from *Le Pardon de Ploërmel* (1859) or the quickstep in *Les Huguenots* derived from the Lutheran chorale "Ein' feste Burg," through melodies which had a telling effect on the listeners of the time but today seem bombastic, as in Example 7-6, to

EXAMPLE 7-6. Meyerbeer, *Les Huguenots*, Act IV.

the expressive movements of the love duets in *Les Huguenots* and *L'Africaine* and Vasco da Gama's grand air "Ô Paradis" in Act III of the latter opera. Meyerbeer rivaled Berlioz in introducing new orchestral effects. Much of his music has a veiled sonority because of his predilection for extreme flat or sharp keys, with the result that the sympathetic vibrations of open strings are not available as they are in such "brilliant" keys as G, D, or A major; his harmonic effects, chiefly enharmonic modulations, were widely plagiarized. Meyerbeer had an extremely important influence on the opera of the second half of the century, especially on Wagner's earlier operas, the nationalist historical operas of eastern Europe, and Verdi's operas between *La Traviata* and *Otello*. The exoticism of *L'Africaine* and the orientalia of Félicien David (1810–1876) were models for such operas as Verdi's *Aïda* and Saint-Saëns' *Samson and Delilah*.

Opéra lyrique, which began around 1850, was a more intimate counterpoise to the grandiose operas of Meyerbeer, and the best works in this genre have a charm and delightfulness not present in any of the contemporaneous schools of operatic composition; Charles Gounod (1818–1893), Ambroise Thomas (1811–1896), and Jules Massenet (1842–1912) are its best composers. The plots deal almost exclusively with love and are often distortions of literary masterpieces; the classic example is Thomas' version of *A Midsummer Night's Dream* in which Queen Elizabeth, Shakespeare, and Falstaff are among the *dramatis personae*. The expressiveness of *opéra lyrique* derives chiefly from piquant chromatic seasonings, compound meters (especially 9/8 and 12/8), and long, lyrical melodies, frequently with "feminine" endings in internal cadences. Example 7-7, from the love duet in Massenet's masterpiece *Manon*, is an excellent illustration of *opéra lyrique* at its best; Gounod's *Faust* and *Romeo and Juliet* and Thomas' *Mignon* are the other major representative operas of this genre. The operas by Georges Bizet (1838–1875) also belong to the tradition of *opéra lyrique*, including his masterpiece *Carmen*, notwithstanding the realism of its libretto or its Spanish local color. Massenet's *Werther*

EXAMPLE 7-7. Massenet, *Manon*, Act I.

(1892), one of the last of the true *opéras lyriques,* exhibits a considerable tonal freedom (such as the unrelated tonal plateaux that lead to a climactic theme in the Act I love duet) and may be regarded as one of the most important precursors of the style of Debussy's *Pelléas et Mélisande.*

Operetta arose as a reaction to *opéra lyrique,* a genre scorned by Théophile Gautier as "Gluckism . . . broad, slow, slow . . . going back to plainchant." Adolphe Adam (1803–1856), a pupil of Boieldieu and a prolific composer of *opéras comiques,* began a lighter style of composition which culminated in the vivacious operettas of Jacques Offenbach (1819–1880), whose musical style is summed up in the title of one of his biographies, *Can-Can and Barcarolle.* Much of Offenbach's music faithfully depicts the vulgarity of Napoleon III's "Second Empire"; however, his posthumously performed *The Tales of Hoffmann* is free of the tawdry effects that characterize many of his operettas and should be considered one of the major *opéras lyriques.* The vogue of operetta continued in France well into the twentieth century and simultaneously spread to other nations, most significantly to Vienna where a special tradition of operetta arose, represented at its peak by *Die Fledermaus* and *The Gypsy Baron* by Johann Strauss, Jr., and *The Beggar Student* by Karl Millöcker (1842–1899), perhaps the best work of this genre.

Contemporaneous with the new French opera was the development of the dramatic ballet in France. The ballet had been an integral part of Grand Opera, and many ballets were inserted into operas adapted for the Opéra in Paris, whether *opéras lyriques* like Gounod's *Faust,* foreign operas of the past like Mozart's *The Magic Flute* or Weber's *Der Freischütz* (for which Berlioz arranged the music), or even Wagner's *Tannhäuser.* The leading composer of French ballet music was Léo Délibes (1836–1891), whose *Sylvia* and *Coppélia* are the scintillating acme of this genre; Délibes also wrote *opéras lyriques,* of which *Lakmé* is the most famous. Throughout the nineteenth century French ballet had an extremely strong influence on its Russian counterpart, whether in Glinka's operas or in Chaikovsky's ballets.

After 1870 opera lost its almost exclusive domination over French music and became only one of the forms of musical expression open to the rising generations of French composers who will be discussed in Chapters 9 and 11.

FRYDERYK (FRÉDÉRIC) CHOPIN (1810–1849)

Chopin permanently left his native Poland in November 1830 and settled in Paris in the following year. In *Lutetia* (1837), the poet Heine evaluated him as a composer and pianist of the first rank and the darling of the aristocratic public of Paris; assessing the national influences on Chopin's music, Heine remarked that Poland contributed chivalric sensitivity and historical sorrow; France, grace and easy charm; and Germany, Romantic melancholy. (One might add that Italy gave Chopin his melodic cantilena through Bellini's music and the traditions of operatic singing, including ornamentation.) Heine continued that Chopin "is therefore neither Pole, Frenchman, nor German; he betrays a much higher origin . . . from the land of Mozart, Raphael, Goethe; his true fatherland is the realm of poetry."

Chopin was essentially a composer for the piano; the songs and chamber music are peripheral in his *oeuvre,* though his Cello Sonata is the most significant duet sonata between those of Beethoven and Brahms. Though Chopin has been regarded as a composer who could work effectively only in the smaller forms, only in the preludes is he a genuine miniaturist like Schumann, Grieg, or MacDowell. The small number of his instrumental cycles has often been cited as evidence that he could not successfully write large-scale compositions. Yet in his larger free forms (polonaises, ballades, fantasias, etc.) he often displayed a considerable structural imagination, as shown in Figure 7-1.

Although the influences of Hummel, Field, and Weber are pronounced in the early works, written before his departure from Poland, many of Chopin's individual stylistic traits are also evident in these compositions. The best of them, like the Polonaise for cello and piano, the slow movements of the two concertos, several of the Etudes, Op. 10, and the Variations, Op. 2 (which elicited Schumann's remark, "Hats off, gentlemen, a genius!"), could not be mistaken for works by any other composer. Most of Chopin's popular compositions were written between 1831 and 1840, a period of composition which can be demarcated by the Nocturnes, Op. 9, and the B-flat minor Piano Sonata. A last period began with such major works as the F-sharp minor Polonaise and the A-flat major Ballade and, except for a few mazurkas and waltzes written during his last series of illnesses, concluded with the Cello Sonata, Op. 45 (1846). The best of these late works have a spaciousness of conception (which was not always successful) in the larger pieces, and interesting refinements in the smaller works, like the cross-rhythms in the so-called "Minute" Waltz.

Almost all of Chopin's smaller compositions are based on dances, especially the Polish mazurka and the international waltz. The forms, basically ternary, are sometimes expanded into rondos. Though such dances as the E-flat (Op. 18) and G-flat (Op. 70, No. 1) waltzes and the D major Mazurka (Op. 33, No. 2) are suitable for dancing, as witness their orchestral transcriptions in the ballet *Les Sylphides,* most of the dances are as highly stylized as the movements of J. S. Bach's suites; representative specimens are the A minor Waltz (Op. 34, No. 2) or any of the mazurkas in C-sharp minor. The mazurkas, spanning Chopin's entire creative career, show the greatest variety in mood and contain some of the most interesting melodic and harmonic ideas of any of his compositions.

Chopin's middle-sized works include relatively minor compositions like the variations and impromptus as well as such major works as the nocturnes, scherzos, polonaises, and ballades. The nocturnes, popular because of their relative technical ease, range in expression from salon pieces like the F-sharp major (Op. 15, No. 2) to such major works as the C-sharp minor (Op. 27, No. 1) and G major (Op. 37, No. 2); the C-sharp minor (Example 7-8a) is one of the composer's most pessimistic compositions, relieved by a stirring middle section and a consolatory coda, whereas the G major has some of the composer's most adventurous modulations. Among Chopin's four scherzos, the one in B-flat minor is most frequently performed; the middle section of the one in B minor is the Polish Christmas carol "Lulajze Jezuniu."

Chopin's six mature polonaises are considered his most important group of compositions. They display a wide variety of mood: delicacy in the C-sharp minor, funereal lament in the E-flat minor, a stirring processional quality in the A major (the so-called "Military" polonaise), lament again in the C minor with its harmonically interesting trio, Sarmatian wildness in the F-sharp minor, and powerful virtuosity in the A-flat major.

Of the fantasias, the relatively early but posthumously published *Fantaisie Impromptu* is on a small scale and is one of Chopin's most popular works, especially in its simplified versions. The *Polonaise-Fantasia* (Op. 61), a late work, contains a magical introduction whose harmonic freedom may possibly have influenced Liszt and Wagner, yet despite its beautiful sections it does not give the impression of a genuinely unified composition. The Fantaisie in F minor, Op. 49, is one of the composer's most significant works; apart from the opening march, its structure, resembling a free sonata form, was one of the most important antecedents of the "double-function" form of Liszt's B minor Sonata. The G minor, A-flat major, and F minor Ballades are among Chopin's most important compositions (though the C major Ballade is less successful) and excellently illustrate his technique of creating a large work through juxtaposing and effectively repeating short sections which by themselves would have been admirable preludes or nocturnes.

Chopin's few large instrumental cycles have been dismissed by critics from Schumann and Liszt to the present because of their supposed imperfections in form. The two piano concertos, both early works, stem from the tradition of Dussek and Field, and Spohr's influence is strong in the F minor Concerto. Apart from the juvenile C minor Sonata, Chopin's three essays in this genre consist of the B-flat minor (Op. 35) and B major (Op. 58) piano sonatas and the G minor Cello Sonata. Common to them all are recapitulations which begin directly with the second theme-group in the first movement, the first theme being either omitted because of its having been worked over so intensively in the development (B-flat minor Sonata) or presented later in a kind of "mirror" recapitulation (Cello Sonata); Brahms was somewhat influenced by these recapitulations. The finales range from the terse, enigmatic, toccata-like finale based on triplet figuration in the B-flat minor Sonata, a complete antithesis to the usual "optimistic" or "climatic" finales of the nineteenth-century instrumental cycle, to the well-developed and extensive finales of the other two sonatas.

Chopin's architectonic genius at its best is seen in the Third Ballade, Op. 47, where he skillfully creates a musical structure loosely based on sonata form yet ingeniously and freely treated, with a tonal structure akin to that of the sonata-rondo form. Figure 7-1, a structural analysis of this ballade, can only show this in outline, for space does not permit

SECTION	SUBSECTION	MEASURES	KEY-CENTER	REMARKS
Exposition (1–155)				
A (1–53)	a	1–8	A♭ (I)	
	b (with variants)	9–26	A♭ (I)	
	c	27–36	A♭–V of F	
	a	37–53	A♭ (I)	
B (54–115)	d	54–63	F (VI)	Modulates through C as common tone
	d'	64–104	f–V of C	
	d	105–115	C (III)	
C¹		116–135	A♭ (I)	
C²		136–144	A♭ (I)	Variant of d'
B	d	145–155	A♭ (I)	No modulation
Development (156–211)				
	d'	156–183	c♯–B (♭III)	
	d	184–187	E (♭VI)	B pedal
	a	188–211	E–c–E♭ (V)	Retransition 204–211
Recapitulation (211–240)				
A	a	212–229	A♭ (I)	Climax; only *ff* section in the Ballade
C¹		230–238	A♭ (I)	
Final cadence: V₇ of vi; vi; V₇; I (238–240)				

FIGURE 7-1. Chopin, Third Ballade, Op. 47.

citation of the numerous examples of the melodic variation which further serves to unify this work.

Chopin's melody ranges from figuration and passage-work whose main interest is harmonic and pianistic to a languid cantilena with its ornamentation often derived from vocal music, particularly the vocal portamento; Chopin would often exquisitely vary his melody with ornamental figuration, as in the F minor Ballade. Many of Chopin's singing melodies, whether major (the Op. 9, No. 2 Nocturne or the middle section of the *Fantaisie Impromptu*) or even minor (Op. 63, No. 3 Mazurka), were carried over into twentieth-century popular music.

Chopin's "modal" effects do not derive solely from deliberate and consistent use of the lowered second and seventh or sharpened fourth degree of the scale, but rather from the ambiguity between the diatonic and altered forms of these scalar degrees. The early polonaises of Op. 71 best show the ambiguous leading tone, whereas the mazurkas contain the best illustrations of the conflict between the raised and natural fourth degrees of the scale (Example 7-8a, b) often found in Slavic folk music (Example 7-8c). The lowered second degree of the scale is the reverse of the leading tone's drive to the tonic; this gives the melody in Example 7-9a its despairing character and in another composition results in the kind of cadence typical of Bartók's music, where the leading tone and lowered second degree are sounded simultaneously (Example 7-9b).

Liszt perceptively remarked that Chopin's main harmonic contributions were the extension of chords, chromatic and enharmonic inner parts, and embellishing notes in melodic figuration which are found in Italian vocal ornamentation. Abraham has coined the term "tonal parenthesis" to describe the extension of chords; it consists of a passage in fast

EXAMPLE 7-8. Ambiguous use of raised and natural fourth degree of scale in (a) Chopin, Mazurka, Op. 56, No. 2; (b) Chopin, Mazurka, Op. 50, No. 3; (c) Slavic folk music (from Jan Seidel [ed.]), *Národ v Písni*, Prague, 1941, p. 247).

EXAMPLE 7-9. Lowered second degree of scale in (a) Chopin, Nocturne, Op. 27, No. 1 and (b) Chopin, Mazurka, Op. 56, No. 3.

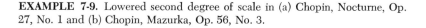

harmonic rhythm containing mostly dominant-tonic relationships which starts in the home key and returns to it and thus cannot be considered a true modulation. One of the simplest illustrations of this device is shown in Example 7-10. In larger and later works like the sonatas, ballades, and

EXAMPLE 7-10. Chopin, Nocturne, Op. 9, No. 2.

fantasias such tonal parentheses are longer and more extensive and often involve a lavish keyboard figuration. One of Chopin's favorite modulatory points of departure is an unresolved dominant-seventh chord in third inversion, fortissimo, followed by runs and scale passages. Nontonic beginnings are among Chopin's favorite devices; among them are the opening of the G minor Ballade with a cadential formula beginning with the "Neapolitan" chord (its root the flatted supertonic) which continues into the opening theme of the Ballade, and the magnificent dominant preparation of the A-flat major Polonaise. The mazurkas Op. 17, No. 4, Op. 24, No. 2, and Op. 59, No. 1 are wonderful specimens of tonal ambiguity equalled only by the A minor Prelude. Chopin sometimes relied on an "interlocking" tonality in which a composition begins in one key and ends in another; for example, the F major Ballade ends in A minor (Chopin's deliberate intention, according to Schumann).

Ignaz Moscheles' comment about Chopin's "harsh modulations which strike me disagreeably when I am playing his compositions" has been quoted out of context so often that the remainder of his statement needs to be supplied; he further said that such modulations no longer shocked him, since when Chopin played them "he glides over them in a fairylike way with his delicate fingers." Moscheles evidently could not play Chopin's music with understanding, for almost all of Chopin's dissonances are passing, not to be intensified or emphasized, and are an integral part of his (as well as Schumann's) piano coloring. Chopin's harmony had some influence on that of Liszt and Wagner (compare the ending of the Op. 48, No. 2 Nocturne with the finale of the *Faust Symphony* and the "Magic Sleep" motive of Act III of *Die Walküre*), but had its strongest impact on early twentieth-century composers like Ciurlionis and Skryabin, who extended Chopin's ideas to perhaps the ultimate reaches of tonal harmony.[1]

Chopin's rhythm, though dominated by the dance, is highly flexible; one need but think of the cross-rhythms between 3/4 in one hand and 6/8 in the other in the A-flat Waltz, Op. 42, and the E major Scherzo. He has two kinds of rubato: one kind where, in his words, "the singing hand may deviate . . . but the accompanying hand must keep time," appropriate to some of his music in which a steady left-hand accompaniment supports the right hand's silvery washes of color, often in irregular groupings of notes, characteristics of the *Berceuse* and *Barcarolle;* another kind is an alteration of tempo, either slowing or quickening, necessary for his nocturnes or stylized dances.

Chopin carefully marked the proper preparation of his trills, and the performance of his compound appoggiaturas should be generally on the beat as in the eighteenth-century style. Since the pedals of Chopin's time gave the piano less sustaining power than today's, the composer's indications for pedaling should be approached with caution.

HECTOR BERLIOZ (1803–1869)

Occasionally a composer will appear whose music is so original and so apart from the musical mainstream of his time that he is misunderstood not only by his contemporaries but also by succeeding gen-

---

[1] In her study "Zur Genesis des 'Prometheischen Akkords' bei A. N. Skrjabin," *Musik des Ostens*, II (1963), 170–183, Zofia Lissa shows that the "Chopin chord," a major thirteenth spelled C–Bb–E–A, is the ancestor of Skryabin's "mystic" chord C–F♯–Bb–E–A).

erations. Gesualdo, Wilhelm Friedemann Bach, Janáček, and Varèse are such composers, and Berlioz is the only nineteenth-century composer to be compared to them. ▌

▌In comparison with his contemporaries, Berlioz's *oeuvre* is relatively scanty, consisting of a dozen major works plus songs, concert overtures, occasional pieces for ceremonial occasions, and early works written for the Prix de Rome competition during his student days.▐Frequently several years elapsed between completion and performance of a major work; one of the most tragic passages in Berlioz' memoirs is an account of the deliberate suppression of a symphony lest its completion and performance beggar him and his family. Berlioz earned his living not through composition but through musical journalism, arrangements of Weber's and Gluck's operas for performance in Paris, and poorly paying sinecure positions. Few composers have had to persist in their creative work in the face of so much official discouragement, misunderstanding, and lack of support; comparable examples are more apparent in the annals of science or medicine.

Berlioz' works may be divided into three chronological periods. The first was one of apprenticeship, chiefly devoted to writing works in competition for the Prix de Rome, which provided a government stipend for study in Italy and Germany; these compositions served as sources of themes and ideas for later works, and Berlioz has been criticized for such borrowings—by critics who forget similar re-uses of ideas by a host of composers, including J. S. Bach and Handel. The second period, characterized by an expansion of musical resources, began with the *Symphonie Fantastique* and ended with the *Damnation of Faust* (1846, although some numbers were written in 1829). The final period, which a few writers have termed neo-classic, culminated in his greatest work, the opera *Les Troyens* (1856–1859, performed in 1863).

Berlioz was the last heir of the grand, monumental, Classic tradition of Gluck, Lesueur, and Spontini, and took Beethoven's innovations, especially those of the Ninth Symphony, as points of departure. Weber's operas and the best ideas of the lyrical aspects of French *opéra comique* were lesser influences. One cannot state with certainty whether Berlioz or Chopin was the first to employ certain new structural and harmonic devices, or whether Berlioz or Meyerbeer initiated certain orchestral effects. Certain it is, however, that Berlioz' visits to England, Germany, and especially Russia had a most invigorating effect on the younger composers of these countries. His *Treatise on Instrumentation* founded the science of orchestration; he was among the first of the modern conductors, being driven to this profession by the indifference or incompetence of the conductors in Paris; and his writings on music are equalled only by those of Schumann, Eduard Hanslick (1825–1904), and George Bernard Shaw (1856–1950).

Berlioz is one of the most misunderstood composers. His tempestuous life and love affairs were well publicized, but much of his apparent eccentricity was a kind of "role playing" on his part to help call attention to his music. The occasional massive effects which he specified for actually a small fraction of his music were inviting to caricaturists (one Parisian portrayal had him riding in a giant, horse-drawn bass drum), and even today the general impression of Berlioz' music held by those not well acquainted with his works is that of noise, tempest, daemonic dissonance, and legions of brass and percussion players.

Berlioz' religious works show the contradictions of his style. The *Requiem* (1837) and what he called his "Babylonian" and "Ninevite" *Te Deum* (1855) are the two works which have been most responsible for the legend about his music's noisiness and the immense numbers of players necessary to perform it, yet *L'Enfance du Christ* (1855) is a delicate, gentle work which derives not only from the intimate oratorios of Lesueur but also from the socially conscious aspects of the French Catholic revival during the nineteenth century. In a class by itself is the song cycle *Nuits d'été* (1841), with its long melodic lines for the voice and its subtle orchestration; this work wholly contradicts the typical misconceptions of Berlioz' music.

Berlioz' operas have been unsuccessful not on musical or dramatic grounds or even because of their vocal problems (though a few singers gave Berlioz the excuse that his music would ruin their voices) but because they are not adaptable to the limitations of the conventional operatic stage. *Benvenuto Cellini* (1838) is known today only through its overture and the "Roman Carnival" finale of Act II. His masterpiece *Les Troyens* contains a wide variety of musical and dramatic effects and moods, from the multi-orchestral statement of the "Trojan March" in Act I to the intimacy of the love duet in Act IV; the weakest parts of this opera are the bows to operatic convention in Act III. *Les Troyens* is particularly impressive in its retrospective, summarizing, and "testamentary" character as the culmination of the tradition of idealized Humanism in opera that began at the very end of the sixteenth century and continued through Baroque opera, Gluck, and Spontini. In a way, one could call *Les Troyens* a neo-classic opera. A similarly retrospective opera, *Béatrice et Bénédict* (1862), the composer's last work, is a deft *opéra comique* in the best traditions of this genre and the one opera by Berlioz which can best be accommodated to the restrictions of the stage; as a musical farewell it ranks with Verdi's *Falstaff* or the last movement of Beethoven's Op. 135 quartet as a masterpiece of gentle, enigmatic humor.

Aside from the concert and operatic overtures, Berlioz' five remaining large works are orchestral compositions, with or without voices. Four of them have been called "symphonies" although only the first, the

Symphonie Fantastique, really deserves this title. *Harold in Italy* (1834), with an obbligato solo viola, is neither symphony nor concerto but a bit of both. The "dramatic symphony" *Romeo and Juliet* (1839) contains extensive choral passages in its outer movements, but its central second movement is purely orchestral, for Berlioz felt that such scenes as Romeo's solo meditation, the ball, and the love scene between Romeo and Juliet would be best expressed without the hindrance of words. The *Funeral and Triumphal Symphony* (1840) is exclusively for winds, although strings and a chorus were subsequently added to the finale; it consists of a grand funeral march, an "oration" for solo trombone, then after a thrilling fanfare an "apotheosis" in quick-march style. The change of instrumentation in French army bands, wherein oboes and bassoons were supplanted by saxophones and saxhorns, has made this work a rarity in performance. The symphonic idea disappeared with *Lélio* (1832), an unsuccessful "sequel" to the *Symphonie Fantastique* that adds narrator and chorus to the orchestra. *The Damnation of Faust* is neither symphony, oratorio, opera, nor cantata but contains elements of all these genres; seldom performed in its entirety, it is generally known through such orchestral excerpts as the Racoczy March.

Berlioz' musical style is misunderstood because it differs so greatly from that of his contemporaries or even his immediate successors, and his antecedents like Spontini and Lesueur are unfamiliar even to musical scholars. Berlioz is the true founder of the "modern" orchestra, as his stipulation for numbers of instruments, especially in the string section, shows. Berlioz demanded his additional performers not for volume but for sonority, especially in his brass writing; he knew that it took many string players to achieve a true pianissimo, and he wanted additional winds in order to have unified tone colors on a chord. He requested additional timpani not only to have a triad or four-part chord playable on those instruments but also to provide additional sonority for orchestral chords on the mediant. Occasions when volume for volume's sake is demanded are few in his music; more characteristic are passages with extremely delicate scoring (the third movement of the *Symphonie Fantastique* or the inner movements of *Harold in Italy*) or a festive brilliance of violins and winds in their high registers (the ball scene of *Romeo and Juliet*). Berlioz was the first composer to utilize fully the improvements in instruments, particularly the French woodwind and brass instruments, that had resulted from the technological and metallurgical innovations of the Industrial Revolution. Yet in his use and disposition of even his largest vocal and instrumental resources, Berlioz at all times remained the practical musician.

Largely because of the satirical "Amen" fugue in the *Damnation of Faust* and Ferdinand Hiller's remark that Berlioz believed "neither in God nor in Bach," Berlioz has been erroneously viewed as a hater of counterpoint. His contrapuntal point of departure was the last movement of Beethoven's Ninth Symphony, and the number of fugal passages in his works, of which the finale of the *Symphonie Fantastique* or the introductions to *Harold in Italy* and *Romeo and Juliet* are representative, should lay to rest any statements that Berlioz was anti-contrapuntal; in fact, the opening chorus of the *Te Deum* is as good fugally as any of Mendelssohn's essays in this genre. Berlioz' most characteristic contrapuntal device is the combination of two themes, often for a programmatic purpose; this derived from the double-fugue variation in the last movement of Beethoven's Ninth Symphony.

Berlioz' harmony is strikingly original, chiefly because of his free use of diminished-seventh chords as modulatory pivots, his love for "weak" or so called "modal" progressions to the third or sixth degrees of the scale, his employment of orchestral timbres to reinforce harmonic change or to underline the part writing, and his use of seemingly arbitrary or even dissonant effects which on closer examination are surprisingly logical (e.g., the relationship between B natural and C natural in the second movement of *Harold in Italy*, which at first seems gratingly dissonant but highly reasonable after one hears the coda of this movement). Berlioz hated abuses of non-harmonic tones, especially appoggiaturas, and criticized even the tame use of them in Herold's *Zampa* (1831) as well as Wagner's more radical employment of them in *Tristan*. One of Berlioz' favorite dissonances consists of suspensions delayed well past the expected moment of resolution. He also delighted in the flat submediant, often in an inner part, as an expressive degree of the scale.

Berlioz' melodic gifts escape many listeners because his melodies are often long, asymmetrical, and even seemingly arbitrary: recently the melody in Example 7-11 has been claimed as a quasi-serial melody, but note how the sparse accompaniment and harmony give it a tonal direction. Berlioz often loved to reharmonize melodies on their recurrence, a technique best shown in the second movement of *Harold in Italy*. Berlioz' melody also has a wonderful rhythmic flexibility, seen not only in Example 7-11 but also in the opening allegro of the *Benvenuto Cellini* overture and the horn theme of the hunt and storm in *Les Troyens*.

Rhythm is the most exciting aspect of Berlioz' music. In his letters and memoirs he repeatedly complained about the inadequacies of many orchestral musicians in coping with his rhythmic writing. It is not so much the use of syncopation or rhythmic experiments like the 7/4 meter of the dance of the soothsayers in *L'Enfance du Christ* that makes his rhythm so original, but the subtle "sprung rhythms," the cross-rhythms, the entrances stipulated where the performers do not expect them, the differences between macrorhythm (meter) and the micro-

EXAMPLE 7-11. Berlioz, *Romeo and Juliet*, Part II (Romeo Alone).

Andante malinconico e sostenuto

rhythm of individual lines or short groupings of notes, and even what Renaissance composers would have called "proportions" (the coda of the third movement of *Harold in Italy*).

Berlioz' form is loose but logical. His use of the recurrent *idée fixe* in the *Symphonie Fantastique* and his recapitulation of previously heard themes in *Harold in Italy* (deriving directly from the finale of Beethoven's Ninth Symphony) and the *Requiem* were supplanted by less obvious and systematic procedures in his later works. According to Barzun, rhythm and tempo have structural functions for Berlioz. Tonality does not play so important an organizing role in his music as it did in the works of his Germanic contemporaries, and Berlioz must share with Chopin the responsibility for weakening the effect of tonality as a major structural device.

For the listener, the impact of the rhythm and the orchestral sonority in Berlioz' music often obscures the unconventional and original treatment of other musical materials. So much is made from the idea of contrast: compare the sheer massiveness of the *Te Deum* with his meticulous attention to detail, especially in varying the accompanimental patterns of a repeated theme, or the variety and brilliance of his allegros with his deliberate uses of monotony to create an expression either of humility (the offertory of the *Requiem*) or of inexorable, relentless power (the

"Judex crederis" of the *Te Deum*). Berlioz paints a better picture of Hell than any other composer (*Symphonie Fantastique, The Damnation of Faust*) but his contrasting heavens are rather bland. Berlioz' structural niceties are often obscured by the wealth of detail in his transitional passages.

Berlioz changed many elements of his style from work to work. With the "apotheosis" of the *Funeral and Triumphal Symphony* or the *Reverie and Caprice* for violin and orchestra he showed that he could write in a popular vein, but his heart was in the monumental works which were accepted by only a limited segment of his audience. Each of his major works differs in several essential respects from its companions, and Barzun has pointed out the disagreement among students of Berlioz' music about which of his works is the greatest or most representative. Few composers, moreover, are less amenable to pigeonholing, categorizing, or the tracing of influences; Berlioz exists in a kind of splendid isolation, though his influence is greater than is generally supposed or was generally admitted.

BIBLIOGRAPHICAL NOTES

Donald J. Grout's *A Short History of Opera* (2nd ed., New York, 1965) remains the best general survey of opera during the first half of the nineteenth century. The panorama of Italian opera is best seen through the biographies of its composers: Stendhal's *Life of Rossini* (Henri Beyle, Paris, 1824; English translation, New York, 1957) is better as a picture of attitudes of the time than as a biographical source, and the older biographies of Giuseppe Radiciotti (Tivoli, 1927–1929, 3 vols.) and Francis Toye (London, 1934) have been replaced by the standard Italian biography by Luigi Rognoni (Turin, 1968) and by the biography in English by Herbert Weinstock (New York, 1968). Recent biographies of Donizetti in English are by Herbert Weinstock (New York, 1964) and William Ashbrook (London, 1965); of Bellini by Leslie Orrey (London, 1969) and Herbert Weinstock (New York, 1971). Verdi has been well served by several biographies: in addition to Franco Abbiati's standard Italian biography (Milan, 1959, 4 vols.) and Hugo Gerigk's German biography (Potsdam, 1932), biographies in English are Francis Toye's (London, 1931) and the best, Frank Walker's *The Man Verdi* (New York, 1962). Charles Osborne's *The Complete Operas of Verdi* (New York, 1970) is a convenient one-volume study of the operas. More detailed investigations of individual operas appear in a series of monographs, *Verdi*, published by the Instituto di Studi Verdiana in Parma (1960–   ), which include English translations of each article.

W. L. Crosten's *French Grand Opera* (New York, 1948) is an unsurpassable study of the cultural milieu of this genre. Martin Cooper's essay on Meyerbeer in his *Ideas and Music* (London, 1965) is the best recent study of Meyerbeer's music. Cooper's *Opéra Comique* (New York, 1949) and my dissertation on D. F. E. Auber (University Microfilms, 1957) survey the lighter counterpart, but *opéra lyrique* has yet to receive a definitive investigation. The memoirs of Gounod (English translation, New York, 1895) and Massenet (English translation, Boston, 1919) and the biographies of Bizet by Mina Curtiss (New York, 1958) and Winton Dean (London, 1962) and James Harding's biography of Massenet (London, 1970) give at present the best picture of *opéra lyrique* in English. Offenbach's work in its cultural milieu is marvelously studied in Sacheverell Sitwell's *La Vie parisienne* (London, 1937) and Moss and Marvin's *Can-Can and Barcarolle* (New York, 1954); the portion of his diary dealing with his American voyage has been translated by Lander MacClintock as *Orpheus in America* (New York, 1957).

Chopin's life and works have produced chiefly rhapsodic, quasi-poetical appreciations, not only from critics (for example, J. G. Huneker, *Chopin: The Man and His Music,* New York, 1901) but even from scholars (Hugo Leichtentritt, *Chopin,* Berlin, 1905). Gerald Abraham's *Chopin's Musical Style* (London, 1939) is a splendid study of his music, and Arthur Hedley's *Chopin* (London, 1947) corrects many of the legends about this composer. Edward Waters' annotated translation of Liszt's *Life of Chopin* (New York, 1963) makes available a fine appreciation and memoir, even if this biography is probably Liszt's ideas as written down by the Countess Marie d'Agoult. Recent investigations include a collection of essays edited by Alan Walker (London, 1966), in which Walker's own study of Chopin's musical structure and thematic process is quite forced, and a pictorial biography by Enzo Orlandi (English translation, London, 1968).

Jacques Barzun's *Berlioz and the Romantic Century* (3rd ed., New York, 1969) is a superb "life and times," influenced in its musical portions by Tom S. Wotton's *Berlioz* (1935; reprint, London, 1969). A special number of *La Révue musicale* (1956) contains several articles on Berlioz' musical style, and I am greatly indebted to Philip Friedheim's study of Berlioz' harmony in *Music Review,* XXI (1960). Berlioz' collected literary works have been reprinted, and a new edition of these with annotations is in progress. English translations of Berlioz' literary writings include Jacques Barzun's *Evenings with the Orchestra* (New York, 1956) and the translations of his memoirs, with detailed annotations, by Ernest Newman (1932; reprint, New York, 1966) and David Cairns (London, 1969, with additional information.)

Recent investigations have shown that the available scores of Italian operas from Rossini through Verdi contain many errors with few, if any, accounts of the variant versions of individual arias, cabalettas, or other portions. Even the "standard" edition of Chopin's complete works, the Paderewski edition, has been accused of containing editorial tamperings to achieve consistency, and the formerly standard edition (1900–1907) of Berlioz' works by Charles Malherbe and Felix Weingartner has several lacunae and is filled with gratuitous changes of instrumentation and other editorial tinkering. The *New Berlioz Edition,* begun in 1968, is a model of scholarship and editorial integrity; hopefully, a comparable edition of Verdi's music will appear in the future.

EIGHT

THE MUSIC
OF THE FUTURE

The year 1848 is the dividing point in the musical as well as the narrative, social, and cultural history of the nineteenth century. The revolutions of 1848 and 1849 which convulsed continental Europe all ended in failure. During this time Berlioz and Chopin sought safety in England; Schumann and Johann Strauss paid tribute with marches, the former to commemorate the revolutionaries and the latter to celebrate the victors; Liszt wrote his heroic elegy *Funérailles* as a memorial to his friends who fell in the Hungarian uprising; and Wagner was so actively involved in revolutionary activities that he was driven into exile.

Although literary historians consider 1848 the terminal date of Romanticism, the changes in music that took place after that year gave nineteenth-century Romanticism in music a new lease on life which was to be valid for another 45 years. It is true that the deaths of Mendelssohn,

Chopin, and subsequently Schumann created a vacuum which was filled by Liszt and Wagner, though these two composers had written important works before 1848; that Berlioz and Verdi substantially changed their musical styles; and that as Meyerbeer's reputation was waning, *opéra comique* and Grand Opera coalesced into *opéra lyrique.* Yet all the new developments had important roots in the immediate past, and though 1848, like 1870, is an important "watershed date" in the general history of the nineteenth century, it is not a year marking stylistic convulsions like 1600, 1740, or 1910; 1848 is a date dividing a musical epoch like 1550, 1690, 1770, or 1933.

Terms like "music of the future" and "new German school" are often used to describe some of the musical developments that took place after 1848, but neither Liszt nor Wagner consciously used them. The phrase "music of the future" has been attributed to a hanger-on in Liszt's circle and became a pejorative term among conservative critics in Germany and France; the term "new German school" appropriately describes only the compositions by Liszt and his circle during the 1850's and 1860's. This "new music" had several important antecedents: Beethoven's late works, Berlioz' and Chopin's compositions, and less "respectable" parents like Spohr, Spontini, and Meyerbeer.

Protagonists of the "new German school" felt that Beethoven had said all that was worth saying in the media of absolute music and that the symphonies, sonatas, and string quartets produced after his death were inferior to their models. Spohr and Berlioz had shown that the program symphony was a way to a new ideal of expression, and Berlioz had also revealed the new orchestral colors available to the composer. Paganini exhibited a new concept of virtuosity which Liszt transferred to the keyboard, and Weber, Spohr, and Berlioz had been the principal founders of the discipline of conducting. Beethoven's ideas for the enrichment of the large instrumental cycle to large works intended to be played without pauses between its movements and with thematic links between them —Schubert's "Wanderer" and F Minor Fantaisies, Mendelssohn's Violin Concerto and "Scotch" Symphony, Schumann's Fourth Symphony and Cello Concerto, for example. The declamatory songs of Schubert were just becoming known. Although the Italianate "number opera" provided opportunities for the singer, it was coming to be viewed as dramatically false and musically sterile; Meyerbeer's Grand Operas were more theatrically effective but made too many concessions to the public. Harmonic and instrumental colors were to provide the main channels for musical expression in new forms, instrumental or vocal, and thus provide edification and emotional release for an audience that had to be specially trained through musical journalism.

FERENC (FRANZ) LISZT (1811–1886)

Liszt was born only 30 miles from Vienna, his mother was Austrian, and from childhood he resided chiefly in central or western Europe; though bearing a Hungarian name he could not speak the language (he was most at home in French), and despite his Hungarian rhapsodies he was not a truly nationalist composer. He was, in fact, the most international musical figure between Gluck and Stravinsky.

Liszt's works fall into five chronological periods with the years 1839, 1848, 1861, and 1869 as the approximate points of demarcation. His work, however, has not been subjected to the searching examination or chronological-bibliographical study that the works of other major composers have received. He revised most of his early works during the 1850's, and his songs span his entire career without revealing the radical changes of, for instance, his piano music.

First period. Virtually all the works of Liszt's Parisian period (1826–1839) were either unpublished or were revised several years later. The changes were chiefly in the pianistic layout and structural cohesion, and Liszt may have delayed their publication until he felt that the public was ready for his new musical ideas. The important works of this period are the first two books of the *Années de pèlerinage* (Switzerland and Italy), the *Transcendental Etudes*, and the *Grand galop chromatique* (1838), the only major work of this period that Liszt did not later revise.

Most of the *Transcendental Etudes* are works of great virtuosity, although "Paysage" with its premonitions of Brahms' style, the delicate "Feux follets" with its use of a motive which Bartók later employed in his Fourth String Quartet, and "Harmonies du soir" provide poetic contrasts. The final version of 1852 was a simplification of the virtually insuperable pianistic difficulties of the 1826 and 1839 editions. The fourth of these etudes well illustrates the varied treatment of a melody which Liszt developed into the "transformation of themes," as Example 8-1 shows,

EXAMPLE 8-1. Liszt, excerpts from "Mazeppa," *Transcendental Etudes.*

(b)

il canto marcato e vibrato assai

Animato

(c)   *leggiero*

mp

as well as Liszt's piano technique; Example 8-1b is a specimen of the so-called "thumb melody" for which Liszt was famous.

In contrast, the individual pieces of the *Années de pèlerinage* range from the quietly lyrical piece ("Eclogue," "Sposalizio") to full-fledged symphonic poems for the piano like "Vallée d'Obermann," the most remarkable work in the two sets, or the dissonant "Il Penseroso," which anticipates the strange harmonies of his late works. Such harmonic devices as altered chords or unresolved dissonances are evident even in these early compositions. The *Grand galop chromatique*, a fine specimen of bravura display, anticipates not only Offenbach's can-cans but also the circus-like music with piquant dissonances later effectively employed by Prokofiev and Shostakovich. Many critics have difficulty in reconciling the advanced style of these works with their chronology, for they are contemporaneous with the most popular piano compositions of Schumann and Chopin; Liszt was later to write polonaises, ballades, and a berceuse with a pedal point on D-flat like Chopin's. Paganini's violin playing influenced not only Liszt's keyboard technique but also his sense of "showmanship," whereas Berlioz' influence was important chiefly in guiding Liszt's steps toward program music.

Second period. Liszt spent the years from 1839 to 1847 as a touring virtuoso and had little time for composition, though he began to write songs and sketched several of the works which were later to be completed in Weimar after he had retired from his hectic performing career. The most representative compositions of this period are Liszt's piano transcriptions, though some of these date from his Paris years and he continued to arrange works in other media for the piano throughout his life. The operatic transcriptions were meant to be appreciated by those who knew their operas well and were among the most popular works on Liszt's tours. He also transcribed songs, chiefly Schubert's or his own (the Petrarch sonnets and the *Liebesträume* were originally songs); orchestral works by Beethoven and Berlioz; and even J. S. Bach's Weimar organ works. In a day when permanent symphony orchestras were rare, Liszt's transcriptions brought many unfamiliar works before the general public and undoubtedly aroused in many the desire to hear the original versions. During these virtuoso years Liszt showed himself altruistically willing to devote his talents to playing the major works of Schumann and Chopin, since they were physically incapable of doing so.

Third period. From 1848 to 1861 Liszt was musical director and conductor in Weimar, producing concerts and conducting operas. During this period he wrote his most frequently performed large compositions, devoted his energies generously to helping Berlioz and Wagner, revised almost all of his earlier compositions into their final form, and assumed responsibility for the writings on music which appeared under his name.

The piano works of this period include the intimate Consolations and the *Harmonies poétiques et religieuses*, essentially a continuation of the *Années de pèlerinage*, which include reworkings of earlier compositions, transcriptions, and the grand heroic elegy *Funérailles* (its middle section, similar to the trio of Chopin's A-flat major Polonaise, has given rise to the legend that this piece is a "tombeau de Chopin"). The two polonaises, two ballades (the second fine if repetitious), and a few shorter works seem directly inspired by Chopin. The most significant of Liszt's piano compositions of this period, and the most influential piano composition for the second half of the nineteenth century, is the B minor Piano Sonata, completed in 1853 and dedicated to Schumann.

For this one-movement, cyclically connected structure which combines the salient elements of contrast and unity of both the sonata-form first movement and the multi-movement instrumental cycle, Liszt had several precedents: the later fantasies of C. P. E. Bach, Mozart, and Schubert; the first movement of Clementi's G minor Sonata, Op. 34, No. 2, in which the pervasive thematic transformation of a single motive in all sections of the movement, including the slow section between development and recapitulation, anticipates the structure of Liszt's B minor Sonata; a one-movement *Grande sonate mélancolique* (1814) by Moscheles which surprisingly anticipates Liszt's rhetorical devices; and the ballades, *Polonaise-Fantaisie*, and especially the F minor Fantasy of Chopin. Liszt pursued this one-movement form to its logical conclusion not only in the B minor Sonata but also in his symphonic poems and A major Piano Concerto.

Figure 8-1 shows in outline form the combination of structures in the Sonata in B minor, with significant motives and some of their transformations. Note the overlapping between "development" and "slow movement," although the "finale" corresponds with the recapitulation. The apparently capricious introduction, with its tonal center of G minor, is later seen as ingeniously logical: G is a pivot note for the diminished seventh that serves as the dominant of B minor. A tonic chord of B minor in root position (which earlier composers would have considered essential to establish the tonality) does not appear until the start of the transition to the second theme-group. Notice how the "closing group" is a lyrical transformation of the originally driving and hectic motive C.

Much of the "development" corresponds to the slow movement of an instrumental cycle. New material (X), which is a contrast through its tonal stability in F-sharp major and its homophonic texture, is introduced and later returns in the coda. The use of motive A in the return of the introduction, with a tonal center of F-sharp, leads one to expect a tonal as well as thematic recapitulation, but the enharmonic reading of F-sharp as G-flat and its use as a springboard for the diminished seventh as the

"MOVEMENT"	SECTION	MOTIVE	KEY CENTER
"First Movement" (mm. 1–330)	Slow Introduction (1–7)	A	g
	Exposition (8–178)		
	First theme-group (8–24 + 25–31)	B, C	b
	Transition (32–104)	B, C, A	b to V of D
	Second theme-group (105–119)	D	D
	Second transition (119–152)	B, C	around D
	Closing group (153–178)	C′	D
	Development (179–459)		
	Continuation of allegro (179–300)	B, C′, D	Tonal flux
	Recitativo (301–310)	D	c♯, f
	Transition (311–330)	B, C, B/C	to B pedal
"Slow Movement" (331–459)	Andante sostenuto (331–346)	X	F♯
	Quasi adagio (347–396)	C, D, B	A, F♯, g, to V of F♯
	Retransition (397–459)	X, C, A	F♯
"Finale" (460–769) "Scherzando" (460–532)	Recapitulation (460–649)		
	Fugue = first theme-group (460–522)	B + C	b♭–E♭
	Correspondence to mm. 25–31 (523–532)	B, C	E♭–b
	Transition (533–565)	B, C, A	b
	Second theme-group (600–615)	D	B
	Second transition excised		
	Closing group (616–641)	C′	B
	Transitional close (642–649) (parallels 179–196)	B	to V of g♯
Coda (650–769)	Stretto quasi presto (650–682); (parallels incalzando, 255–276)	C′	g♯–V of B
	Presto (683–691)	A	to B
	Prestissimo (692–709)	B	B
	Apotheosis (710–719)	D	B
	Peroration, andante sostenuto (721–737)	X	B
	Epilogue, allegro moderato (738–769)	C, B, A	B

FIGURE 8-1. Liszt, Sonata in B Minor.

A   Lento assai

B Allegro energico

D Grandioso

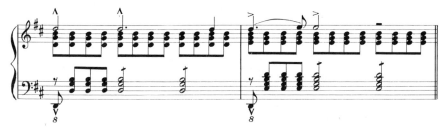

C′ Cantabile espressivo

X Andante sostenuto

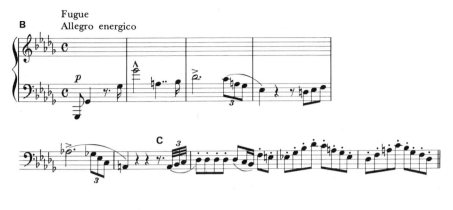

Transformation of motive A in coda:

dominant of B-flat minor, the key of the fugue, is a surprise; the proper "recapitulation" occurs only with the appearance of the "second theme" (motive D) in the tonic B major. Despite transient modulations, the coda is in B major throughout.

Unity in other respects is only apparently broken down: although there are 15 changes of key signature, 12 major tempo changes, and 17 changes of time signature, these have mostly structural functions; the "second theme" is in 3/2 meter, almost all of the key changes are in the development, and almost all of the tempo changes are in the coda. That Liszt intended this work to be one of high integrity rather than a virtuoso showpiece is shown by its ending, quiet and almost mystical rather than a shower of fireworks.

Among the other important works of the Weimar period are compositions for piano and orchestra, three of them major works. The earliest of these, the E-flat Piano Concerto, loosely adheres to a four-movement form with cyclic interrelations between movements, an omnipresent first theme, and interesting transformations, with the lyrical theme of the slow movement becoming the bumptious march of the finale. The A major Piano Concerto is a more successful work, in one movement with two contrasting themes, the first of these subject to the greatest variety of changes. The *Totentanz* is a set of free variations on the "Dies Irae" chant of the Requiem Mass and the finest example of Liszt's "satanic" compositions, which had so much influence on Stravinsky and Prokofiev.

As a result of the urgings of his friend the princess Carolyne de Sayn-Wittgenstein, Liszt directed his attention to purely orchestral compositions and while in Weimar wrote twelve of his thirteen symphonic poems and two programmatic symphonies. Though he needed help in orchestrating the *Mountain Symphony* (the weakest and most padded of his symphonic poems) and the first version of *Tasso*, with the final version of this work Liszt showed that he could handle the orchestra effectively if somewhat conventionally, his scoring being more like Spohr's than that of Berlioz or Wagner.

The symphonic poems derived on one hand from the concert overtures of Beethoven and Mendelssohn and on the other from the programmatic symphonies of Spohr and Berlioz; in scope and extent they occupy a position midway between overture and symphony. Programmatic works, their general structure corresponds to that of the B minor Sonata. *Les Préludes* is the finest structural specimen, with *Tasso*, *Mazeppa* (based on the fourth Transcendental Étude, with elaborate introduction and coda), *Orpheus* (a restrained work which many regard as Liszt's masterpiece in this genre), and the *Battle of the Huns* the other major works. These and Liszt's other symphonic poems influenced virtually every subsequent composer except such devotees of absolute music as Bruckner and Brahms: one can clearly see the influence of *Orpheus* on Franck, *Héroïde funèbre* and *Mazeppa* on Mahler, and *Tasso* and *Die Ideale* on Richard Strauss; and the achievements of the eastern European nationalists or the French composers after 1870 would have been unthinkable without Liszt's orchestral works.

Of Liszt's symphonies, the *Faust Symphony*, composed in 1854 and first performed in 1857, is regarded by many as Liszt's greatest composition. Its introduction is very "modern," with much use of the augmented triad; Example 2-8a shows how Liszt used this triad to harmonize an aspect of the "Faust" theme that contains all twelve notes of the chromatic scale without any repetition and thus can be regarded as a "proto-tone-row." The first movement, "Faust," contains almost all of the themes of the symphony, whereas the second movement, "Gretchen," is chromatically lyrical and almost sensuous. The third movement, "Mephistopheles," is Liszt at his most interesting, for although he diabolically parodies the Faust themes to show that Mephistopheles cannot create, only destroy, when Gretchen's theme recurs toward the end of the movement it is undistorted, thus showing that she has escaped Mephistopheles' baleful control. The work concludes with a setting of the final chorus from Goethe's drama. The *Dante Symphony* is less successful; although the first movement, "Inferno," depicts the empty desolation of Hell and is even more terrifying than Berlioz' lurid canvases, the second movement, "Purgatory," is wandering, vague, and goes nowhere. In the concluding "Magnificat" (Liszt made no setting of "Paradise") the composer uses many secondary triads with unexpected resolutions in a manner which almost anticipates that of Vaughan Williams.

Liszt's songs are the least known of all his works. The Petrarch sonnets and *Liebesträume* are more successful in their piano versions, but "Es muss ein Wunderbares sein" has the intimacy of Schumann; "Tristesse," a late song, anticipates the chromaticism of Hugo Wolf; and the best song, "Ihr Glocken von Marling," anticipates the lyric song of the twentieth century. Many of Liszt's songs have overwritten piano accompaniments, and "Die drei Zigeuner" even sounds like a Hungarian rhapsody with vocal accompaniment; the French songs, of which "Oh! quand je dors" is the best, belong to the tradition of the romance rather than the German Lied.

Fourth period. After several disappointments in his efforts to make Weimar a major musical center, Liszt resigned his post as musical director in Weimar in 1858 and in 1861 followed Princess Carolyne to Rome. After deciding not to marry her, Liszt went into a period of semi-retirement and focused most of his attention on religious works. Of the important piano compositions of the time, the Legends have religious topics, but in style they and the Mephisto Waltz (better in its piano than its orchestral version) hearken back to the Weimar period, during which years Liszt had become interested in choral music.

Liszt's first major Mass, the festive Mass for the dedication of the basilica in Esztergom (Gran), dates from 1855 and is orchestrally and stylistically related to the best symphonic poems, the Consolations, and the *Harmonies poétiques et religieuses;* along with the very subjective setting of Psalm 13, it exemplifies Liszt's ideas for a "humanitarian" church music which would be "devotional, strong, and drastic—uniting on a colossal scale the theatre and the Church, dramatic and sacred, superb and simple, fiery and free, stormy and calm, translucent and emotional." In this statement—and in these works—one is reminded not only of the social Catholicism of the Abbé Lamennais and his followers who remained in the Church but also of the "triumphalism" of Pius IX, Pope from 1846 to 1878 and a friend of Liszt. In contrast, the *Missa Choralis* (1865) is a very austere work for chorus with light organ accompaniment, without any of the fanfares, cymbal crashes, and rich harmonies of the Esztergom Mass or the Hungarian Coronation Mass of 1867.

Liszt's two oratorios, *St. Elizabeth* (1857–1862) and *Christus* (1862–1867), are similarly contrasting, for the former is virtually an opera, akin to the historical works of Meyerbeer and early Wagner, whereas the restrained *Christus* resembles in spirit the *Missa Choralis.* Almost all of Liszt's organ works date from this period and range from short offertory-like numbers to such extended works as the fantasia on the chorus "Weinen, klagen" from J. S. Bach's Cantata No. 12 (known better, in a modified form, as the "Crucifixus" of the B-minor Mass).

Fifth period. Liszt's "twilight," as Szabolcsi has called it, began in 1869 and was marked by a sharp change in style, as astonishing as that in the music of the late Beethoven or Stravinsky. Although in public life Liszt was constantly shuttling between Rome, Budapest, and Weimar, the recipient of many honors and the teacher of an international coterie of piano students, in his creative life he was essentially cut off from the main currents of music, his late work refused by publishers and rejected by his former disciples.

These late works, almost entirely works for the piano or for the church, show harmonic experimentation and a breaking down of tonality. *Via Crucis* (Stations of the Cross), Liszt's major work of this period, contains contrasts between austere modal harmonies and adventurously altered chords, a free use of the augmented triad (found also in his late piano piece "Unstern," Example 2-8b), and even the whole-tone scale. Many of the piano works contain clashing harmonies employed with the economy and even the brutality of Musorgsky. In contrast, the last book of *Années de pèlerinage* is a major source for a new kind of effect: to quote Szabolcsi, "anybody desirous of becoming thoroughly familiar with French impressionism has to begin with Liszt's 'Eclogue' and 'The Fountains of the Villa d'Este' so as to be able to continue with Debussy's gardens and Ravel's fireworks."

Liszt's influence was felt throughout the entire second half of the nineteenth century and well into the twentieth. One of the greatest altruists in the history of music, Liszt aided nearly every composer who came into his orbit, from Chopin to Rimsky-Korsakov, and trained an entire school of pianists. Echoes of Liszt's harmony and musical rhetoric can be found in the work of nearly every composer of the late nineteenth century; Example 8-2 shows Liszt's "anticipation" of the harmonic practices of two composers who are not generally considered among Liszt's disciples, Grieg (Example 8-2a) and MacDowell (Example 8-2b).

EXAMPLE 8-2. (a) Liszt, "Le Mal du Pays," *Années de pèlerinage,* Book I; (b) Conclusion of Second Ballade.

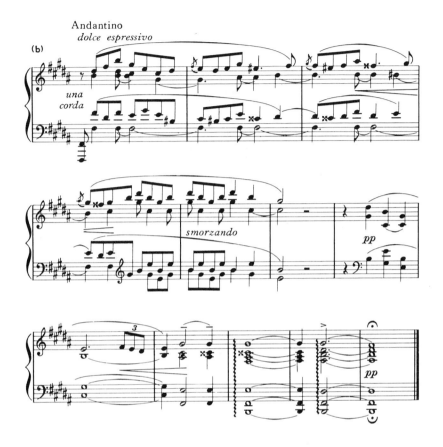

In fact, Liszt, rather than Berlioz or Wagner, is the truly seminal figure for most twentieth-century music. The variegated facets of his musical personality were to find many echoes—the heroic in Mahler, the satanic diabolism in late Mahler, Stravinsky, and Prokofiev, the landscape painting (how different from Mendelssohn's) in Debussy and Ravel, the economy of means and use of striking dissonances in Schoenberg's Op. 11 piano pieces and in the works of Bartók, who considered Liszt more important than either Wagner or Richard Strauss in the development of music. Liszt was the dominant figure of the "progressive" trends in music, even though many today reject his aesthetic, his melodrama, his rhetoric, his optimism—which shows most clearly in the apotheoses of his symphonic poems—as well as his lapses of taste into bombast, roaring chromatic octaves, delicate chromatic filigrees at cadences, or overly rich harmony; those who dislike Liszt's music on these grounds should examine his more astringent late works.

RICHARD WAGNER (1813–1883)

Wagner is still the most controversial composer of the nineteenth century. Though his influence on the subsequent history of music was not as overwhelming as was once believed, no one can deny his important position in the second half of the century, the magnitude of his achievement, or the problems he posed for virtually every operatic composer who came after him. We should therefore look at the musical milieu from which his operatic ideas came (his other works are relatively unimportant in comparison), his chronological development as seen in his operas, and the salient aspects of his musical style.

After Weber's death in 1826 German opera became provincial again, for Germany, still a geographical abstraction, lacked the musical centralization and splendor of Paris or the many urban agglomerations of Italy which supported opera. Musical conditions outside Berlin and Vienna were rather primitive, and German opera had to compete with the French and Italian repertoire, which was better sung and easier to conduct or perform. The "great German opera," for these and other reasons, seemed an unattainable dream, though models existed in Beethoven's *Fidelio* and Weber's *Euryanthe;* Spohr labored in vain, Mendelssohn and Liszt evaded the challenge, and Schumann made the last unsuccessful attempt with *Genoveva* in 1850. Some of the younger German composers saw in *Der Freischütz,* Weber's most popular opera, a model: Albert Lortzing (1801–1851) found his inspiration in the folklike *Gemütlichkeit* of Max's aria in Act I and the Huntsmen's chorus in Act III, while the horror story elements like the Act II finale inspired Heinrich Marschner (1795–1861) in *Der Vampyr* (1828) and *Hans Heiling* (1833). French and Italian influences dominated the most successful German works like *Martha* (1847) by Friedrich von Flotow (1812–1883) and *The Merry Wives of Windsor* (1849), its third act a minor masterpiece, by Otto Nicolai (1810–1849).

Wagner's ideal was a German opera that would occupy an artistic position and status equal to that of the greatest symphonic music, with the theatre a locus for edification and ennoblement rather than mere entertainment (an idea that Schiller had pursued since the mid-1780's) and through his ambition, his will, and his egomania he succeeded, after numerous setbacks that would have broken ordinary spirits. The help he received from Spontini, Liszt, King Ludwig of Bavaria, and the members of the cult that grew up around his music were valuable, but his single-minded and egocentric determination was the principal factor in his eventual triumph; even some of his obstacles were of his own making.

Wagner's early works extend to 1848; his juvenilia need not detain us here, and we should concentrate on his four major operas of this period: *Rienzi* (1840, performed 1842), *The Flying Dutchman* (1841, performed 1843), *Tannhäuser* (1845), and *Lohengrin* (1848; performed 1850, though the composer, then in exile, was not to hear it until much later). *Rienzi* is a grand historical opera written, it was thought, to outdo Meyerbeer, but its real parents are the grand operas of Spontini; only its overture is now generally known, but this work established Wagner as an operatic composer and obtained for him a post as conductor in Dresden. *The Flying Dutchman,* a work of greater significance, is the first of the "psychological dramas" in which Wagner was to excel, and the first practical demonstration of his theory of myth as the best source of plot for the music drama. *Tannhäuser* and *Lohengrin* are syntheses of Grand Opera devices, psychological music drama, and the mediaeval legends that excited many Romantics.

One who studies these works is struck by the various points at which Wagner either adheres to or departs from the operatic conventions established by Weber or Meyerbeer. Despite the continuous texture, arias and "set-numbers" are evident. *The Flying Dutchman's* arias are overwritten, especially Senta's ballad in Act II; Elisabeth's "Dich, teure Halle" in *Tannhäuser* is a magnificent specimen of the traditional grand aria; and Wolfram's song to the evening star in this opera shows that Wagner could write a "hit tune" as well as any composer. Not until *Lohengrin* did Wagner display a thorough mastery of the duet. Wagner's large-scale ensembles are the most spectacular parts of these early operas and are most successful when they follow traditional conventions, like the march in Act II or the pilgrims' choruses in Acts I and III of *Tannhäuser.* Almost all of the finales follow the Spontini-Meyerbeer tradition, with the whole company on the stage; the weakest finale is that of Act II of *Tannhäuser* with its prolix tournament of song and its hero's praising the charms of Venus in the chivalric accents of Weber's knightly heroes like Adolar or Hüon. *Lohengrin* contains the most interesting departure from the conventional spectacles, for they become muted, restrained, and subdued, and what seems to be a massive buildup to a climax in Elsa's procession in Act II is thwarted by Ortrud's denunciation. In all these operas Wagner shows a great love of contrast: Act III of *The Flying Dutchman,* in which Wagner effectively contrasts the merrymaking of the Norwegian sailors with the spectral atmosphere of the Dutchman's ship, is an excellent illustration.

In retrospect, Wagner did not make as much of a break with traditional operatic and musical conventions as either his enemies or his admirers claimed. Wagner's treatment of the voice in his early operas is quite noteworthy: though the voice dominates the orchestral accompaniment, much of what is to be sung is in a measured, quasi-melodious recitative akin to arioso (Wagner insisted that his singers perform from the standpoint of dramatic realism rather than for vocal effect), with the orchestra interjecting comments or even serving as a giant continuo. At times this results in dull music, as in the duet in Act I of *The Flying Dutchman* between Daland and the protagonist, but it can also rise to the heights of dramatic declamation, as in the hero's narrative in Act III of *Tannhäuser*. Wagner's orchestra in these operas is not unusually large, and the additional resources he demands are chiefly for on-stage fanfares, but in *Lohengrin* he discovered the expressive effects of the English horn and bass clarinet. Wagner's use of the brass ranges from the "heavy artillery" noise of *Rienzi* to the great restraint of *Lohengrin*. Harmonically, Wagner was no more adventurous than Spohr, Liszt, or Chopin at this time; it is Spohr's chromaticism that pervades the Pilgrims' chorus and Elisabeth's prayer in *Tannhäuser*. Beginning with *Lohengrin*, Wagner associated keys with certain characters or incidents: A major (also the key of the prelude) for Lohengrin, F-sharp minor for the conspiracy of Telramund and Ortrud, A-flat minor for accusations. In his recitatives Wagner is most tonally adventurous: in "Die Frist ist um" of Act I in *The Flying Dutchman* he uses one of his finest recitatives to get from B minor to C minor, although the ensuing aria has a conventional tonal scheme. The third act of *Tannhäuser* shows how Wagner was groping to achieve the dramatically and tonally unified structures characteristic of his later operas: the heightened declamation, accompanied by reminiscence motives, of the hero's pilgrimage (in A minor) is a harbinger of his later style, but set-pieces like the Pilgrims' chorus and Elizabeth's prayer are reminiscent of the Grand Opera tradition, and the tonality of E-flat major begins and closes the act.

With *Lohengrin* Wagner stopped composing, not only because his time was occupied with disputes with his superiors in Dresden, participation in the abortive revolution of 1849, proscription and exile to Switzerland, but because he felt that this opera marked a terminal point in his musical style. He had found it necessary not only to write his operas but also to train his performers and educate his audience; now he would need to begin all over again, first by setting forth in a series of essays (especially *The Art-Work of the Future* and *Opera and Drama*) his theories of what opera should be. In 1850 he began his sketches for his tetralogy *Das Ring der Nibelungen*, which he was not to complete until 1874. *Das Rheingold* was finished in 1854 and *Die Walküre* in 1856, but he abandoned *Siegfried* in the middle of the second act in 1857, not to resume work on this opera until 1869. The twelve-year hiatus was filled by *Tristan und Isolde* (1859), originally intended as a "practical" opera which would not require elaborate staging or scenery, and *Die Meistersinger* (1861), Wagner's most beloved opera, hailed even by those who dislike his other works. *Die Götterdämmerung*, the last and greatest of the *Ring* cycle, was completed in 1874 and *Parsifal*, his last opera, in 1882.

Although Wagner often went counter to his theories in the actual composing of his operas, we should nevertheless examine the basic philosophy of his operatic ideals as stated in his essays.

Wagner first of all sought to restore the idea of drama as a thoroughly integrated art, in which plot, poetry, music, scenery, costume, and action would be combined (the *Gesamtkunstwerk*); in Wagner's own words, "The highest collective art work is the drama; it is present in its ultimate completeness only when each kind of art, in its own ultimate completeness, is present in it." Hence Wagner wrote not only the music but also the words and the stage directions for his music dramas.

From his survey of the history of dramatic music, Wagner felt that this art had grown corrupt and separated from its original purpose. The drama was no longer the ultimate object but merely a vehicle for music; music, which should be the means for the fullest realization of the drama, had become in itself the ultimate goal. In addition, music had become separated from poetry and dance and had developed its own autonomous laws, thereby becoming artificial. Song had degenerated into the operatic aria; the sacred dance had declined into the French ballet with its quadrille tunes; and music itself had become a concern not of the heart but of the mind through the use of musical artifices, particularly counterpoint. The orchestra, which Beethoven had raised to a peak as an expressive medium, was relegated by the Italians to service as a mere accompaniment for the singers or was utilized by the French (especially by Meyerbeer) as a means for producing stunning but superficial effects.

Wagner's two basic problems in creating music dramas were the unification of speech and song and the reconciliation of drama and music. In unifying speech with song, Wagner sought a middle ground between bald prose on one hand and rhymed poetry on the other. His solution, seen most clearly in *The Ring of the Nibelungs* (its poetry composed before its music), was a reversion to the technique of ancient north European poetry in which common consonants in alliteration (the *Stabreim*) would not only provide coherence but would also permit contrast and antithesis which could be underlined by the music, especially through harmonic modulation. Speech, thereby, could be intensified into tone language, with equal parity given to words and music. This tone language would be the principal vehicle for dramatic action, for soliloquy, and for dialogue.

The reconciliation between music and drama was to be provided by the orchestra, which would serve, in Wagner's words, as "the soil of infinite universal feeling . . . the perfect complement of scenic environment . . . [to dissolve] the solid motionless floor of the actual scene into a fluid, pliant, yielding, impressionable, ethereal surface whose unfathomed bottom is the sea of feeling itself." Instrumental music, as

Beethoven had shown, could express everything that speech could not; it could arouse indeterminate emotions and, through the power of association, could recall past incidents, ideas, and feelings, and could actually produce more precise impressions than words alone could do. The orchestra would thereby complement the voice, bearing it along on the surface of harmony as a boat is borne on the surface of the ocean.

The form of the opera was to be a continuous unfolding of musical ideas as dictated by the plot. This was in contrast with the "number opera," in which self-contained arias, ensembles, and choruses were linked together by spoken dialogue, recitatives, or transitions. The plots were to be based on myth or legend; although Wagner wanted a "human" drama, the personages of myth or legend were larger than life and thus better able to serve as the incarnations of the basic questions of life itself: love, goodness and evil, heroism, faith, renunciation. In *The Flying Dutchman, Tannhäuser,* and *Lohengrin,* Wagner had already made use of mediaeval legend, which he was to continue in *Tristan and Isolde* and *Parsifal; The Ring of the Nibelungs,* on the other hand, was based on pagan Nordic mythology.

Wagner did not consistently apply his theories of opera to his music dramas. To begin with, he was too good a musician and too experienced a man of the theatre to be completely fettered by theories, even his own. In a way, *Die Meistersinger* is a repudiation of his operatic theories, for it is written in rhymed verse, the characters are drawn from sixteenth-century Nuremberg and seem like real persons rather than mythological beings or legendary personages, and there are numerous set-numbers of the kind encountered in traditional opera—choruses, arias (especially Walther's "Prize Song"), a ballet, even a quintet—embedded in the musical fabric. On the other hand, Wagner showed that his essential ideas of continuous musical flow, supported and re-inforced by the orchestra, could be effectively applied to the "comic opera."

Revolutionary as Wagner's theories may have seemed at the middle of the nineteenth century, his music dramas nevertheless had many antecedents: the "symphonic style" of the operas by Mozart, Cherubini, and Beethoven; the continuous texture of Weber's *Euryanthe* and Meyerbeer's mature operas, in which the boundaries between the set-numbers were blurred; and the cyclic instrumental forms, with thematic linking, from Beethoven's Fifth Symphony onward. Wagner's concept of the *Gesamtkunstwerk,* where all operatic devices are united in a whole, stemmed not only from Gluck's operas but also from the dramas of Goethe, Schiller (whose *Die Braut von Messina* of 1803 would have been the first *Gesamtkunstwerk* had there been adequate musical and theatrical resources in Weimar), and Schubert's friend Franz Grillparzer (1791–1872). Even at his most innovative, Wagner preserved links with the musical past.

Only in *Das Rheingold* (effective because of its stage effects and fast action) and *Siegfried*, the least popular of Wagner's mature operas, did the composer's theories interfere with his instinctive musical and theatrical sense. Wagner's vocal melody, often just another strand in the orchestral texture and chiefly devoted to expressing the text, is sometimes perfunctory or is doubled by the orchestra, yet one sometimes finds full-fledged arias or dry but measured recitative, with the string section serving as the continuo. Wide leaps, generally fifths or minor sevenths, are one of Wagner's favorite expressive devices; the most extreme example may be found in Kundry's part in *Parsifal*, which established a precedent for the even wider leaps in the operas of Richard Strauss, Schoenberg, and Berg. Wagner's vocal melody is seldom "tuneful," for it is designed to carry the short textual lines and quick exchange of dialogue in the dramatic poem. Wagner's declamation demanded a new type of singer,[1] but there were several precedents for those roles which demanded endurance: Meyerbeer's heroic tenors or the heroines of Cherubini's *Medea*, Beethoven's *Fidelio*, and Weber's *Euryanthe* and *Oberon*.

Except for the on-stage brass instruments, Wagner used in his early operas a more conventional and less adventurous orchestration than Berlioz. The orchestra in the *Ring* is the largest because Wagner was creating an entire dramatic world in which special effects were necessary. In Wagner's orchestra the increased number of wind instruments allows a homogeneous timbre on a chord; the English horn and bass clarinet (especially in *Tristan*) are as expressive for Wagner as the clarinet and horn were for Weber; the Wagner tubas for the *Ring* provide a solemn tone color to contrast with that of the horns or the heavy brass (best seen in the "Annunciation of Death" in Act II of *Die Walküre*); the bass trumpet, contrabass trombone, and tuba extend the compass of the brass section downward. Correspondingly, an increased number of string players is required to balance the additional wind instruments. Wagner's fortissimos are not constant, and he could orchestrate as delicately as any of his successors. His design for the sunken orchestra pit at Bayreuth, with the brass and percussion farthest under the stage, proves conclusively that he was interested more in sonority than in volume. Several features are typical of Wagner's orchestral sound: extended vertical structures with many doublings of chord-tones; upward extension of the ranges of the string instruments; frequent division of the string sections into many parts; string unisons on short turning figures accompanying a sonorous wind melody, evident as early as the overture to *Rienzi;* a great use of the cellos and even violas as melodic instruments; and a lavish employment of both fingered and bowed tremolos. Wagner often used the valved

---

[1] It is interesting to note that throughout the history of his operas their heroines have been better cast than their heroes (Heldentenors), most of whom were originally baritones.

brass instruments, especially the horns, to strengthen the middle register of his orchestra, and such dramatic brass unisons as the trombone entrance in the *Tannhäuser* overture or the "treaty" motive in the *Ring* are still vividly exciting.

The leitmotive, which may be most simply defined as a musical identification of a character, an object, or a state of mind, is Wagner's most important external means of unifying his operas. In his early operas the leitmotive is melodic, sometimes even phrase-like (Example 8-3a),

EXAMPLE 8-3. Wagner's leitmotives: (a) The Forbidden Question (*Lohengrin,* Act I); (b) Destiny (*The Ring of the Nibelungs*); (c) Hunding (*Die Walküre*).

and should really be termed a "reminiscence" motive which re-inforces the impression of a situation which occurred earlier (Verdi and Erkel were among the more conspicuous utilizers of this device). In his mature operas Wagner treats the leitmotives differently, owing much to the thematic transformations of Berlioz, Schumann, and especially Liszt; other precedents for such melodic, rhythmic, and harmonic alterations of still recognizable motives can be traced to Beethoven's development sections and even the development of subjects and countersubjects in J. S. Bach's fugues. Most of Wagner's leitmotives are melodic, but a striking chord progression (Example 8-3b) or even a rhythmic pattern (Example 8-3c) may suffice to recall earlier incidents.

The transformation of leitmotives occurs mainly through distortions of intervals or rhythmic patterns and reharmonizations. Significantly, the great majority of leitmotives in Wagner's mature operas are "open at both ends" in that they can be preceded or followed by a modulation, or the leitmotive itself can be modulatory, often enharmonically; Example 8-3b constantly fulfills this function in the last three operas of the *Ring*.

Attempts have been made to reduce the basic number of leitmotives and to find relationships between apparently dissimilar ones; like all the sweeping theories that have been applied to Wagner's unconscious creative process, there are grains of truth in such attempts, but also a tendency to read too much into the existing musical evidence. There is some association between leitmotives and keys, evident in the earliest sketches for the *Ring:* the Valkyries ride in B minor, the Norns spin in E-flat minor; and just as Brünnhilde awakens, in *Siegfried,* to a harmonic progression from E minor to C major, so Siegfried, in Act III of *Die Götterdämmerung,* regains consciousness after his assassination by Hagen to the same progression, but from E-flat minor to C-flat major. Often there is much repetition of leitmotives since Wagner did not wish to leave too much to the audience's imagination; thus in Act I, Scene 3 of *Die Walküre,* where Siegmund discovers the sword in the ash tree, the "sword" motive is repeated some twenty-one times. One of the essential functions of the leitmotive is to substitute for the dramatic "aside," wherein the audience is informed of a situation not known to the actors on the stage; a good example occurs in *Siegfried,* when the orchestra tells the audience of Mime's plot against the hero.

The *Ring* contains the most extensive use of leitmotives because of the necessity for continuity in this long tetralogy which depicts a mythological universe divorced from mundane reality. Leitmotives are fewer in the other operas; because they depend so much on atmosphere (especially *Tristan* and *Parsifal*), there is less need for recapitulatory reminiscence, and the few leitmotives used are even more striking and have more of an individual character than those of the *Ring.* Leitmotives are essential ingredients of Wagner's musical fabric, which has been called "endless melody" but is really a replacement of authentic cadences with deceptive cadences or other modulations. Although leitmotives sometimes occur in the voice part, they are usually embedded in the orchestra.

As the leitmotive is Wagner's most important external unifying device, harmony and tonality are his principal internal architectonic means. Although an extensive discussion of Wagner's harmony is not possible here, we should at least examine the principles of his harmonic practices and some of their applications.

Wagner has been called a "chromatic composer," but even in *Tristan*—his most notoriously chromatic work—he writes lengthy diatonic passages, as in the parts associated with Kurvenal. In the more chromatic sections Wagner achieves tonal stability by using "tonal cells" which often consist of a major or minor triad (the tonic), usually inverted, and containing a leitmotive; a diminished or half-diminished seventh chord; a dominant seventh, also containing a leitmotive; then a deceptive cadence, after which another character often sings or there occurs an orchestral interlude. The "open-ended" leitmotives permit several possible resolutions—sometimes to the tonic, more often to the dominant or a new tonic through a deceptive cadence, or to a diminished-seventh chord, which even in traditional practice has four possible resolutions. The longer leitmotives, like those signifying Valhalla or Siegfried's destiny, can be treated sequentially to give the effect of rising tonal plateaux. When Wagner concludes a musical section within a scene, the cadence is often to the dominant of the tonic. When he interrupts the effect of tonal stability, he uses deceptive cadences or coloristic harmony, chiefly the famous "Tristan chord" (Example 8-5c) or another chord of the half-diminished seventh or the augmented triad, yet in the passage shown in Example 8-4 he uses the diatonic "Grail" leitmotive to create a contrast with the tonal ambiguity of augmented triads in sequence.

Parsifal, Wagner's last opera, has the sharpest contrasts in its harmonic vocabulary. In the second act Wagner seems to be reverting to the earlier style of *Lohengrin* in the scenes with the Flower Maidens, and the Parsifal-Kundry duet in this act utilizes the altered harmonies characteristic, not of *Tristan,* but of the erotic piano pieces of Adolf Jensen, e.g., the *Chants d'Ionie,* Op. 44. The motive of the "Dresden Amen," symbolizing the Grail, and the "Faith" motive are sternly diatonic yet "open-ended," as shown by the ending of the Grail motive on an augmented triad in the fifth measure of Example 8-4; both motives are treated sequentially as a series of tonal plateaux. The anguish and tor-

EXAMPLE 8-4. Wagner, *Parsifal,* Act II.

ment of *Tristan* are raised exponentially in the prelude to the third act of *Parsifal* in what is most probably the most tonally free and unstable passage in nineteenth-century music; one can interestingly trace Wagner's harmonic and tonal development in capsule form by comparing the preludes to the third acts of *Tannhäuser*, *Die Meistersinger*, and *Parsifal*. In sharp contrast, the "Good Friday Magic" scene of the third act, which has been pointed out by Chappell White as "the height of what Alfred Einstein so aptly called a composer's 'second naïveté,' is very clear-cut in its tonalities (mostly D major), with only a slightly widened diatonic harmonic vocabulary similar to that of Brahms. Every harmonic tendency of the second half of the nineteenth century, except the devices of the Russian composers, can be clearly seen in *Parsifal*.

Certain operas get their "tone" from individual chords. The "Tristan chord" in Example 8-5 and other uses of the half-diminished-seventh chord in a non-functional role, especially in the love duet in Act II, are the basic atmospheric ingredients of *Tristan*. The major-minor sonority of *Die Meistersinger* is given variety by the use of the half-diminished seventh in its functional role as a chord of the dominant ninth with missing root. The augmented triad supports the chromatic portions of *Parsifal* in portraying pain and anguish (Wagner may have copied this idea from Liszt) but has no independent significance in Wagner's other operas; in

Die Meistersinger it accompanies Walther's rejection by the Master-singers and especially Beckmesser; in *Die Walküre* it is the harmoniza-tion of the "Ho-jo-to-ho" motive of the Valkyries; and in *Die Götterdam-merung* it distorts diatonic leitmotives.

In discussing Wagner's "microharmony" (individual chords and their immediate contexts) one must remember that many of the most typical "Wagnerian" progressions were very much in the air during the first half of the nineteenth century; Example 8-5 shows a few specimens thereof. Wagner neither invented these harmonic ideas nor was he the last to use them, but by employing them in striking dramatic and musical configurations he made them seem exclusively his own. His followers mis-interpreted his harmonic thought by trying to write harmony for its own sake and by seeking, often in vain, completely new and novel sonorities and effects. Examples 8-5d and 9-2a show how difficult it could be for Wagner's successors to escape his influence, and how the use of this chord (perhaps inadvertent on Chausson's part) could so easily lead to a charge of plagiarism, since Wagner had made this particular harmonic sonority so indisputably his own personal property.

EXAMPLE 8-5. (a) Beethoven, Sonata, Op. 31, No. 3, first movement (1801–1804); (b) Spohr, *Der Alchymist*, Act II (1830); (c) Wagner, *Tristan und Isolde*, Prelude (1859); (d) Chausson, *Le Roi Arthus* (posthumously performed, 1903).

(d)

Ta   voix   chan - te dansmon â - me.

Wagner's elaborate and extensive tonal structures serve to unify scenes, acts, and even entire operas. His macrotonality (the tonal plan of an act or even a long scene) extends over lengthy stretches of time-space through his use of a "psychological" tonality more evident to the ear than to the eye. This derived from the tonal plateaux in Beethoven's longer development sections; the "writing around the tonic," by emphasizing its dominant, so characteristic of Schumann, Chopin, and Liszt; and Chopin's "tonal parentheses" and lengthy dominant preparations. We should also remember that after 1850 it was no longer necessary to define the tonic of a key by stating it in root position on a strong beat; when this occurs it is usually a signal that a modulation is about to take place.

A study of scenes in Wagner's opera shows a frequent, though not invariable, use of melodic, dramatic, and tonal inner patterns organized either in a three-part structure (A–B–A) or a so-called "Bar" form (A–A–B); this latter pattern is chiefly associated with *Die Meistersinger* but occurs elsewhere: the opening 67 measures of Act III, Scene 3, of *Die Walküre* is a bar-form with introduction. Sectional divisions within scenes are often marked by orchestral interludes. Massive dominant preparations occur in individual acts: the "Ride of the Valkyries" of Scene 1 of Act III is in B minor, and the scene and motive recur in the same key at the end of Scene 2; this is preparation for the E minor-major tonality of Scene 3, with E major the basic key of Wotan's farewell, the "coda" of the third act. Figure 8-2 shows both the dramatic and the tonal structure of this act.[2]

Wagner's counterpoint is not traditional but is empirically derived from part-writing. Following Berlioz' example, he combined leit-

---

[2] For additional tonal and dramatic analyses of Wagner's *Die Meistersinger* and *Tristan*, see Graham George, *Tonality and Musical Structure* (New York, 1970), pp. 53–71.

SCENE	DRAMATIC ACTION	TONAL CENTER
1	Ride of the Valkyries	B minor-major-minor
	Brünnhilde enters and begs her sisters for help	Modulatory, but basically D minor
	Sieglinde pleads for help	Modulatory to G major (climax)
	Wotan's approach	Modulatory, tonal weight on F (third of D minor, tonic of F minor)
2	Wotan enters, seeking Brünnhilde	D minor
	Brünnhilde re-enters; Wotan reproaches her and decrees her punishment	F minor
	The Valkyries express shock and dismay	D minor
	Wotan more emphatically sentences Brünnhilde	F minor
	Exeunt Valkyries	B minor, to B major as dominant of E minor
3	Brünnhilde pleads for mitigation of her sentence	E minor, climax in E major
	Wotan reproaches her for disobedience	Modulatory, main center F minor, subsidiary A-flat major
	Brünnhilde announces that Sieglinde bears Siegfried	Modulatory, but toward E minor; climax on dominant of E minor
	Wotan repeats his sentence. Brünnhilde requests that she be protected from being taken by a coward	Sleep motive starts modulation to long stretch in C minor
	Brünnhilde begs for a fire to surround her rock	D major
	Wotan assents; puts her to sleep	E major-minor-major
	Wotan summons Loge	Dominant preparation for E; "Loge" motive
	The fire; Wotan's last statement (to "Siegfried as Hero" motive)	E major

dominant ... *tonic*

FIGURE 8-2. Wagner, *Die Walküre*, Act III.

motives for programmatic purposes, but such passages as the combination of three motives in the prelude to *Die Meistersinger* (Example 2-11) are *tours de force* rather than normal practice. Wagner's bass lines, especially in the *Tristan* prelude, repay study, and the active inner parts in his chromatic passages inspired Richard Strauss and the young Schoenberg.

Wagner's music, especially his mature operas, did not become internationally known until the last quarter of the nineteenth century, after the construction in 1876 of the *Festspielhaus* in Bayreuth, which became a place of pilgrimage for aspiring musicians. The international Wagner cult was more literary than musical, and Debussy's remark that Wagner had been "a beautiful sunset mistaken for a dawn" was lost not only on composers but also on musical historians. Those who tried to follow directly in Wagner's footsteps were generally unsuccessful: Engelbert Humperdinck (1854–1921) had the best luck with his *Hansel and Gretel* (1893), in which German folk songs and children's songs were blended with a fairy-tale libretto in a musical fabric similar to that of *Die Meistersinger*. Though Wagner's chromaticism and empirical polyphony inspired Hugo Wolf, Richard Strauss, and Schoenberg, the reaction against his heavy sonorities and mythologizing led to the lightened textures and sonorities of much French music, culminating in Debussy and Fauré. *Tristan* (particularly such passages as the prelude, opening scene, and love duet in Act II) and *Parsifal* had a stronger influence than the *Ring* on late-Romantic French music. This is evident not only in Example 8-5d but also in the opening of Chabrier's *Gwendoline* (whose librettist, Catulle Mendès, was a leading French Wagnerite) or the ascending tonal plateaux in the love duet of the first act of Massenet's *Werther*. Only deliberate acts of anti-Romantic "sacrilege," such as Chabrier's "Souvenirs de Munich," a set of quadrilles in dance tempo based on motives from *Tristan,* could fully expunge Wagner's influence from the minds of many French composers.

Wagner created more problems for the future of opera than he solved. Despite Nietzsche's claim that Bizet's *Carmen* had "Mediterraneanized" music, the "number opera" was equally a dead end for the composer, and its future was that of entertainment music like Franco-Viennese operetta and American musical comedy or of deliberate archaism, as in Stravinsky's *The Rake's Progress* (1951). The composers who chose to follow Wagner's operatic path had to choose between two pitfalls: was the music to be subordinate to the text and accompany a vocally declaimed libretto, as in the *Ring*, or was opera to be a "symphonic poem with words" like *Tristan?* These questions still remain unanswered.

OTHER COMPOSERS

A few other composers were allied with the trends of the "music of the future" and thus deserve at least brief mention. Charles-Valentin Alkan (*recte* Morhange, 1813–1888), an eccentric, eremitic composer of Jewish origin, wrote piano works of nearly impossible length and difficulty, of which his Symphony for Piano and his "Aesop's Banquet," the variations which conclude his *Etudes in all the Minor Keys,* are his best. Alkan paralleled rather than influenced Liszt, and Franck is the most important composer who came within his orbit. Many pianists concede the effectiveness of Alkan's music in performance but question whether it is worth the time that must be spent to master its intricate technical difficulties.

Of all the composers in Liszt's circle, Peter Cornelius (1824-1874) was the best. Because so much of his time was spent in being Liszt's secretary and translator, his output was limited. *The Barber of Bagdad* (1858) is a masterpiece which is excelled only by *Die Meistersinger* and *Falstaff* among nineteenth-century comic operas; it contains exquisite Lisztian harmony without sentimental effusions, one of the finest love duets in the literature, and magnificent choral writing. Cornelius' expressive art-songs, of which the *Christmas Songs* of Op. 8 are good illustrations, undoubtedly influenced the sensitive religiosity of many of Wolf's songs. Those acquainted with Cornelius' works deplore the altruism which drove him to furthering the careers of Liszt and Wagner instead of writing more music.

Though associated with Liszt, the highly prolific Joachim Raff (1822–1882) was an eclectic whose early works were influenced by Mendelssohn and whose late works presage the revival of Baroque instrumental forms (see Example 11-9a). He wrote in all the genres, but chiefly instrumental music; the Third (*Im Walde*) and Fifth (*Lenore*) are regarded as the best of his eleven symphonies, and his "geographical suites"—musical travelogues—provided models for Richard Strauss' *Aus Italien* and the *Caucasian Sketches* of M. M. Ippolitov-Ivanov (1859–1935). The music of Felix Draeseke (1835–1913), who considered Liszt's late works too radical, is very eclectic but is better constructed than Raff's.

BIBLIOGRAPHICAL NOTES

Humphrey Searle's *The Music of Liszt* (1954; 2nd ed., New York, 1966) is the best survey of this composer's music in English. Good recent biographies in English include those by Sacheverell Sitwell (revised edition, New York, 1967) and Ernest Newman (1934; reprint, 1969). Bence Szabolcsi's *The Twilight of F. Liszt* (Budapest, 1959) is an excellent, if slightly chauvinistic, account of his late years and contains a musical supplement. Zsigmond László and Béla Mátéka have collaborated on a pictorial biography of Liszt (English translation, London, 1968). *Franz Liszt: The Man and His Music,* edited by Alan Walker (London, 1970), is a collection of uneven essays, the best of them Walker's own study of Liszt's musical background and his subsequent influence on twentieth-century music. Walker's thematic catalog of Liszt's works replaces the earlier ones by Raabe and Searle. A sizable sampling of Liszt's letters, assembled by Marie Lipsius and published under her pen name of La Mara, has been reprinted in English translation (1894; reprint, New York, 1968). The standard biography of Liszt, however, is in German, Peter Raabe's *Liszt* (2nd ed., Tutzing, 1968), the first volume devoted to his life and the second to his works. The numerous writings that appeared under Liszt's name are of uncertain authorship; they are generally, however, assumed to be Liszt's ideas as expressed orally, organized and written down in French by members of his circle, and translated into German by Cornelius.

Perhaps more has been written about Wagner than about any other composer in the history of music. Chappell White's *An Introduction to the Life and Works of Richard Wagner* (Englewood Cliffs, N.J., 1967) is an excellent and readable introduction with a fine annotated bibliography. The standard biography in English is Ernest Newman's monumental *The Life of Richard Wagner* (New York, 1949, 4 vols.); his studies of the operas, *The Wagner Operas* (New York, 1949) and *Wagner Nights* (reprint, London, 1968), are devoted to the operas in the standard repertoire and intended for general readers but are excellent also for the student. Robert Donington's *Wagner's 'Ring' and Its Symbols* (2nd ed., London, 1969) is an interpretation according to Jungian psychology and contains searches for thematic relationships among leitmotives; its bibliography is more extensively annotated than that in White's introductory volume. Elliott Zuckerman's *The First Hundred Years of Wagner's Tristan* (New York, 1964) exaggerates the posthumous influence of this opera but corrects some erroneous ideas about Wagner's influence. The musical discussions in Robert W. Gutman's gossipy *Richard Wagner: The Man, His Mind, and His Music* (New York, 1968) are brief and superficial.

Special studies of Wagner's music are innumerable and only a few can be mentioned here. Detta and Michael Petzet's *Die Richard Wagner-Bühne König Ludwigs II* (Munich, 1970) is lavishly illustrated with pictures of costumes, sets, and performers of nineteenth-century productions of Wagner's operas. Various interpretations of Wagner's harmony in the prelude to *Tristan and Isolde* are offered by Ernst Kurth, *Romantische Harmonie und ihre Krise in Wagners Tristan* (1920; reprint, Tutzing, 1968); Horst Scharschuch, *Gesamtanalyse der Harmonik von Richard Wagners Musikdrama Tristan und Isolde* in the series *Forschungsbeiträge zur Musikwissenschaft*, XII (Regensburg, 1963, with supplementary volume), which has a complicated but interesting set of symbols for harmonic analysis; William J. Mitchell, "The Tristan Prelude: Techniques and Structure," *The Music Forum*, I (New York, 1967), 162–203, which is based on Heinrich Schenker's principles of musical analysis; and Roland Jackson, "The 'Neapolitan Progression' in the Nineteenth Century," *Music Review*, XXX (1969), 41–42.

Wagner's prose writings are not too well served by William Ashton Ellis' Victorian translations (1892–1899; reprint, London, 1966). Important primary source materials on Wagner are now being published in Germany, particularly his letters, to appear in approximately 15 volumes, and various documents about his life and career in the series *19. Jahrhundert*.

New editions of the complete works of both Liszt and Wagner are in progress. The older edition of Liszt's works has been reprinted by Gregg Press, Inc., with many of the previously unpublished late piano pieces appearing in the Liszt Society Publications. The complete works of Cornelius are to be reprinted, and selections of Alkan's piano music have been edited by Raymond Lewenthal (G. Schirmer, Inc.) and Georges Beck (in the series *Le Pupitre*, Vol. XVI, 1969).

NINE

THE REBIRTH
OF ABSOLUTE MUSIC

An observer of the musical scene in 1860 would have been forced to conclude that sonatas, symphonies, and string quartets would soon be as extinct as canzonas or trio sonatas, yet during the next four decades absolute music won a new lease on life even though it did not dominate the minds of composers as it had during the Classic period. Nor was this revival a repudiation of the aesthetic of Berlioz, Liszt, and Wagner, for the harmonic, structural, and orchestral resources of the "music of the future" were at least partially retained, and in France and the Slavic nations many composers demonstrated allegiance to both camps by writing both instrumental cycles and symphonic poems.

The principal composer to keep the ideals of absolute music alive during the heyday of Liszt and Wagner was Robert Volkmann (1815–1883), a German who spent most of his life in relative obscurity in Hungary. Volkmann is best known for his light, tuneful chamber music, of which the best examples are the B-flat minor Trio, Op. 5 (dedicated to

Liszt), and the string quartets in G minor, Op. 14, and E-flat major, Op. 43. His two symphonies are interesting; the First, in D minor, furnished Borodin with the structural model for the first movement of his Second Symphony. Of greatest import for the future were Volkmann's serenades for strings, prototypes not only for Chaikovsky's but also for the Opp. 1 of two important twentieth-century composers, Leoš Janáček and Carl Nielsen. Such serenades reflected an important, if paradoxical, strain in the predominantly Romantic music of the nineteenth century, that of neoclassicism.

NEOCLASSICISM IN NINETEENTH-CENTURY MUSIC

The term "neoclassic" has often been applied to the composers to be discussed in this chapter, especially Brahms, Franck, and Saint-Saëns. The term would seem to imply a return to the artistic canons of the period between 1750 and 1800, with its emphases on clarity, balance, and proportion, and its doctrines of simplicity, objectivity, and the elevation of form over content. These attitudes played a part in neoclassicism after 1850. After this date neoclassicism was almost as pervasive as Romanticism; yet, like Romanticism, it displayed so many individual manifestations that we should seek trends and tendencies to describe this movement rather than a universal definition.

Neoclassicism among nineteenth-century composers was a look back to the past, but not just to that period bounded by Pergolesi and Haydn. For the Romantics, the past was the entire remembered past of musical history, at least back to the sixteenth century, and in fact both Beethoven (for the *Missa Solemnis*) and d'Indy, composers at opposite ends of the nineteenth century, did research in Gregorian chant for their music.

A shift to a neoclassic orientation is evident as early as the 1840's. Schumann's turning from the characteristic piano piece and the art-song, typically Romantic media, to the symphony and chamber music is one of the first decisive indications. From the standpoints of form and structural balance, Chopin's B minor and G minor Sonatas are more "classic" than his earlier B-flat minor Sonata, and the same is true of his later nocturnes and mazurkas. Berlioz jokingly tried to pass off his *L'Enfance du Christ* as the work of a seventeenth-century composer; his operas *Les Troyens* and *Béatrice et Bénédict* are culminations of tendencies from the past, less "modern" than the contemporaneous operas of Meyerbeer, Verdi, Gounod, or Wagner. A date that is frequently cited as marking the firm establishment of neoclassicism is 1860, the year in which

Brahms signed a manifesto attacking the "New German School" of Liszt. After 1860, neoclassicism was an important counter-tendency to Romanticism. It appeared in a wide variety of individual manifestations, and with a typically Romantic air of contradiction, but two basic themes can be associated with it (if not in the same composer at the same time or with equal emphasis): (1) an emphasis on musical forms and attitudes from the past and (2) a simplification of musical style.

The forms inherited from the Classic period—sonata, symphony, string quartet, and the re-discovered serenade—were the ones that most frequently embodied the idea of neoclassicism, yet earlier forms were also revived. The Baroque suite of contrasting abstract dances (as opposed to the ballet suite or the musical travelogue) was discovered again, not just by obvious neoclassics like Saint-Saëns or Raff but also by composers usually associated with late-Romantic nationalism like Chaikovsky, Dvořák, and MacDowell, whose two "Modern Suites" (1883) epitomize the idea of reconciliation of the legacy of the past with the musical ideas of the future. Preludes and fugues were written by composers from Mendelssohn to Hindemith in frank emulation of Baroque models, and the motet for unaccompanied chorus was a medium not just for anti-quarians seeking to revive Renaissance and early Baroque church music but also for such progressive composers as Bruckner and Brahms.

Even in the works most closely fitted to Classic-era models one sees no slavish return to eighteenth-century styles; this is evident as early as the first six symphonies of Schubert. Yet in several respects the neo-classic works are "simpler" than the original models; the slow movement of Bizet's youthful Symphony in C (1855) is "simpler" than its prototypes, the slow movement of Beethoven's Op. 18, No. 1 Quartet and the fugato in the second movement of his Op. 18, No. 4 Quartet. Bruckner, Saint-Saëns, and Chaikovsky present far more clearly articulated sonata-form movements than do C. P. E. Bach or Haydn; one senses that the neo-classic composers had a self-conscious image in their minds of a standardized sonata form.

In the broader sense, one can even postulate the emergence of a neoclassic ethos in a composer's deliberately setting himself a compositional problem to solve. Brahms' love for this is well known, yet virtually every composer of the second half of the nineteenth century shared it and regarded the subsequent work not as a student exercise but as a piece of music worthy to stand alone in its own right. Verdi's one string quartet, by a composer who had previously warned young Italians against following the model of the German *quartettisti*, epitomizes this. Another illustration, from a composer not especially famous as a composer of absolute music, is Bizet's *Variations chromatiques* (1868), wherein the theme, usually stated in the bass, consists simply of the ascending and descending chromatic scale; one is reminded of the *inventio* of Byrd and Sweelinck in their fantasias on abstract note-patterns. Yet if Bizet's attitude was old, his harmonies were as novel as Franck's.

Simplicity in neoclassic music implies not only a return to clear-cut musical forms but also to the simplification of other musical elements as well, for instance, harmony. Around 1860 a "diatonic reaction" against the altered chords and chromatic modulations of Liszt and Wagner became evident: the symphony in C major by Woldemar Bargiel (1828–1897) is one of the best illustrations. However, not all composers who have been called neoclassic followed the path of harmonic simplification: Franck was one post-Wagnerian composer who developed a completely individual style of chromatic harmony (Example 9-5), and Bruckner, though his chromaticism is usually a shifting of microtonal planes (Example 9-2), became quite chromatically complex in his later works, especially the Eighth Symphony.

The return to diatonicism was genuinely a return to Beethoven's emphasis on tonality rather than harmonic color, a widened tonality in which natural or flattened mediants and submediants were significant tonal anchors or modulatory pivots. Added to this were Schubert's free interchange between major and minor harmonies, a renewed emphasis on secondary triads outside the dominant-tonic axis, and the utilization of altered or borrowed chords when desired. The result was a greatly widened harmonic vocabulary, diatonic in ethos, that permitted modulations to quite remote keys: both Brahms and Bruckner, for example, found that a modulation to the flattened submediant or mediant (a major triad) could be extended by using the minor form of this same chord as a further pivot, thus permitting modulation to even remoter keys. Even a purely diatonic harmony, as in the first theme of Saint-Saëns' Fifth Piano Concerto (Example 2-9), could be written in such a way as to avoid the dominant-tonic pull that had characterized Western music for the previous two centuries. Bruckner, Brahms, Saint-Saëns, and Fauré widened the vistas of tonality diatonically as Liszt and Wagner had expanded them chromatically. Even Wagner, in some of his later works—*Die Meistersinger,* the *Siegfried Idyl,* and the "Good Friday Magic" from the third act of *Parsifal*—returned to an essentially diatonic, triadic, and clear harmonic palette.

Other elements of music were equally simplified. The term *clarté latine* has been applied to much French music from Saint-Saëns to the present and has been defined as "a restoration of lucid musical form."[1] This embraces, however, not only structural but harmonic and melodic simplicity as well, and is not limited only to France, for it is perceivable

---

[1] Michael Mann, "Reaction and Continuity in Musical Composition," *Music Review,* XV (1954), 43.

in several works by such disparate composers as Bruckner, Chaikovsky, Dvořák, and Grieg. A further aspect is the reduction of orchestral resources, strikingly seen in numerous serenades (Volkmann, Brahms, Dvořák, Chaikovsky, Elgar, and many others), in Wagner's *Siegfried Idyl,* and in the renewed interest in chamber music, quite often for large ensembles with unusual combinations of instruments. Even among composers who specified large orchestral resources, from Berlioz to Mahler, one finds 'many passages that are scored with a simplicity and delicacy appropriate to chamber music.

If neoclassicism avoided the dangers of Romantic eccentricity (Alkan), grandiloquence (Liszt), seeming chaos (Wagner's *Tristan*), or excessive subjectivity (Chaikovsky, Mahler), its idiom had pitfalls of its own: epigonism, a sterile academicism, triviality, or a precious cuteness. One senses in much neoclassic music at its most extreme a reversion to the Classic idea that composition was a craft and music a product: the result was much music that simply filled gaps in the repertoire, such as Saint-Saëns' later sonatas, the instrumental solos that Fauré commissioned as jury pieces for the Paris Conservatoire, or the concertos for such relatively neglected instruments as flute, cello, harp, and clarinet by Reinecke—music that is well put together, sounds well, and never sinks below a certain minimum standard of quality, yet somehow lacks the vigor, spontaneity, individuality and freshness of even the worst music by such prolific early Romantics as Dussek, Auber, Weber, or Donizetti. Many neoclassic composers were extremely productive and prolific, yet one can make the same criticism of their music that has been made of that by their eighteenth-century counterparts like Dittersdorf and Pleyel: it is written according to formula, lacks individuality or is too close in spirit to that of a major composer of its time, and, frankly, it all sounds too much alike.

One aspect of neoclassicism that prevailed throughout the nineteenth century and well into the twentieth is in fact strongly Romantic: neoclassicism as nostalgia. The minuet movements in Schubert's A minor Quartet (D. 804) and Mendelssohn's D major Quartet, Op. 44, No. 1, are not Classic minuets, but yearning looks back to a faintly remembered past; Schubert's minuet was taken from his earlier setting of portions of an equally nostalgic poem, Schiller's "Die Götter Griechenlands," with the words "Schöne Welt, wo bist du?" (Lovely world, where are you?). Examples of later and equally fervent longing for the past, using neoclassic means, are the Ländler in Mahler's Second Symphony, his depictions of the child's view of heaven in his Third and Fourth Symphonies, and Strauss' yearnings for the ambience of Rococo and Classic times in *Der Rosenkavalier* and *Ariadne auf Naxos.*

In summary, nineteenth-century neoclassicism is a paradox: it is a reaction against Romanticism, but also in its historicism a continuation of it. It exemplifies a return to principles of formal construction that had never really been absent from Romantic music, but places stronger, and often self-conscious, emphases on them. Its reliance on simplicity was not shared by all who have been called neoclassics, and among composers from Schumann to Strauss, Berlioz to d'Indy, Glinka to Glazunov, there are oscillations, sometimes in the same composition, between neoclassic and Romantic elements. As clearly seen in the music of Busoni and Reger, neoclassicism was another ingredient in the turbulent pot of post-Romanticism, and the neoclassicism of Stravinsky, Milhaud, Prokofiev, and Hindemith was a descendent from, but also a reaction against, its post-Romantic antecedent. Yet with the major composers discussed in this and subsequent chapters who committed themselves to or casually flirted with neoclassicism, Romantic individualism remained paramount.

ANTON BRUCKNER (1824–1896)

A cathedral organist in Linz and later a professor of counterpoint in Vienna, Bruckner is known today chiefly through his symphonies (eleven, two of them unnumbered) and his church music. Although many of the anecdotes about his naiveté and self-effacement can be dismissed as *petite histoire,* his deep humility, piety, and personal integrity made him the most noble figure of nineteenth-century music. They also contributed to his lack of self-confidence in his musical ability, complicated by few opportunities to hear his music performed; he was thus led to consent to revisions, often disastrous, of many of his best works.

Bruckner is the direct descendant of the Beethoven of the Ninth Symphony and the Schubert of 1828. Though he esteemed Wagner highly, Bruckner was influenced by the Bayreuth master chiefly in aspects of instrumentation and certain harmonic devices, notably enharmonic modulation; the Third Symphony (see Example 9-2) most clearly shows Wagner's influence.

In his earliest orchestral works, ranging from the Overture in G minor (1863) to the First Symphony, even in its revision of 1890, Bruckner's mature symphonic style is perceivable only embryonically or in scattered places, for instance, in the second theme-group of the first movement or the ponderous scherzo of the First Symphony. After major personal crises, Bruckner's mature style materialized with his Second Symphony in 1871. From this symphony onward, Bruckner utilized certain musical devices which are virtually fingerprints of his style, yet he gave them enough variety to avoid mannerism. One can almost reconstruct a "typical" Bruckner symphony—with the reservations that the

Fourth and Sixth symphonies are "lighter" works and that the last three symphonies soar to a pinnacle of achievement. Bruckner begins his symphonies "out of nothingness," either with a string tremolo (Fourth, Seventh, Ninth Symphonies), a rhythmic pattern (Sixth Symphony), or, rarest of all, a slow introduction (Fifth Symphony, the allegro opening with a soft tremolo). With the significant exception of the chromatic opening of the Eighth Symphony, his longest, most fully scored, and most "philosophical" (in the Lisztian sense), Bruckner's first themes are usu-

EXAMPLE 9-1. Bruckner, Symphony No. 5, finale, recapitulation of second theme-group. Note the use of pseudo-imitation in the first section and double counterpoint in the second.

ally based on either the open fifth or the triad. He called his second themes "song themes"; in slow movements and finales as well as in first movements, the theme will be closely interwoven with a counterpoint which is an essential part of the theme-complex, and his love for exploring possible permutations of the themes in invertible counterpoint (Example 9-1), adds to the length of the second theme-groups. The closing themes can be forceful (Fifth Symphony, finale) or quietly stark (Seventh Symphony, first movement). Bruckner's expositions are not cluttered with padded transitions; often, after a pause, he will begin a new theme-group without preparation, which adds to the granitic effect of his symphonies.

Bruckner's developments are like Schubert's in that both composers rely on repeating themes in sequence; the great double fugue of the development in the finale of the Fifth Symphony is an exception. Bruckner's recapitulations are shorter than his expositions and his codas are modeled on Beethoven's. In these codas one often sees a favorite Brucknerian device: a crescendo consisting of an immense buildup out of nothingness, over a pedal point, frequently culminating in the glowing sonorities of the full brass section.

Except for the slow march in the Fourth Symphony, the slow movements are Bruckner's centers of symphonic gravity; they generally consist of solemn hymnlike adagios in sonata form, with the contrasting "song theme" often a letdown in the mood of exaltation. The scherzos are often deliberate and ponderous, less often (as in the Sixth Symphony) fantastic; the trios range from the dance-like one in the Fourth Symphony to the mysteriously shadowy one of the Ninth.

Like the other composers of the century, Bruckner struggled with the problem of the finale; there is none for the Ninth Symphony, though Bruckner began this composition in 1887. Sometimes themes from previous movements are recapitulated in the finale, and there are sometimes sharp contrasts between themes, often with programmatic significance; in the last movement of the Third Symphony the juxtaposition of a dance-like melody with a trombone chorale symbolized for Bruckner a funeral ceremony inside a church with street life going on outside its portals. A climactic chorale is a frequent, but not essential, ingredient of the finales; that of the Fifth Symphony is treated in counterpoint with the fugue subject that figures in the first theme-group of this movement.

Bruckner's melodies tend to be long, based either on a triad or on wide leaps, and are often treated as "double sequences" a third apart; this leads, in notation, to what seems to be a frightening enharmonic thicket, since part of the sequential treatment includes a Schubertian love for contrasts between major and minor. A sequence from A major, for example, can include F major, D-flat major, and C-sharp minor. In the passage shown in Example 9-2b, Bruckner begins his melody in the

EXAMPLE 9-2. Bruckner, Symphony No. 3, second movement.

(a)   Adagio bewegt, quasi andante   **(b)**   Andante quasi allegretto

tonic, modulates to distant areas, and returns securely to his home key; here one can see the roots of Hindemith's melodic-harmonic style. Bruckner's rhythmic fingerprint is the contrast of triplets and duplets in a given melody; when they occur in cross-rhythms (Fifth Symphony, second movement; Sixth Symphony, first movement), they create an effect of intricacy.

When Bruckner uses rich altered chords, he usually employs them as functional harmonies to go from one tonal center to a transient internal center. Often, after a pause, Bruckner shifts his tonal planes abruptly, a device derived from Beethoven's late works. His orchestration has been criticized as "organist's scoring": frequently one hears an effect comparable to changing organ manuals (from pure string color to woodwind color to another "manual" of glowing brass), in tutti passages he uses the contrabass tuba like an organ pedal playing an active bass line, and his tremendous octave passages, either against string figurations or powerful unisons with 32′, 16′, 4′, and 2′ "registrations," produce a massive organ-like effect. Yet he eschewed the reedy, flutey, or "voix céleste" sonorities of his fellow organist-composer César Franck.

Bruckner's well-meaning but hopelessly misguided pupils persuaded their mentor to agree to many disastrous cuts in his symphonies; after his death they changed his orchestration to achieve a more Wagnerian blend and committed mayhem on his music, for example, hacking out most of the recapitulation of the finale of his Fifth Symphony. In explanation, but not defense, one should mention that this was a period when musicians often "improved" the works of their predecessors: thus Grieg's second piano parts for some of Mozart's sonatas, MacDowell's reharmonizations of pieces in the "Anna Magdalena Book" once attributed to J. S. Bach, and the differing versions of Monteverdi's *Orfeo* by d'Indy and Respighi.

Much of Bruckner's church music, especially the motets, derives from the ethos of the Cecilian reformers who sought to restore Catholic church music to a pristine *a cappella* purity, but his Masses in D minor and F minor and his *Te Deum* are in the tradition of Viennese symphonic church music; despite many lovely passages, especially the Benedictus of the F minor Mass, these works sound overwritten. A magnificent synthesis of symphonic and Cecilian trends in church music is the E minor Mass (1866, revised 1882), which succeeds where Spohr failed in his attempts to unite sixteenth-century counterpoint and nineteenth-century harmony.

Bruckner failed to found a "school" of composition, and during his lifetime he seldom heard his symphonies in their entirety or without some kind of fiasco. Although his influence on Mahler was strong, it was not overwhelming, and linking the two composers together, as is often done, is as unjustified as bracketing Bach with Handel or Debussy with Ravel.

JOHANNES BRAHMS (1833–1897)

Though writers agree on the existence of a youthful period ending around 1855 and a final period beginning in 1891 with the works from Op. 114 onward, Brahms' creative life is difficult to arrange chronologically. It is difficult to speak of internal "periods" in his music (although Geiringer's citation of the *German Requiem* as a dividing point is quite convincing), since Brahms' first work for any medium has a certain tentative and experimental quality about it, even as late as the First Symphony or the Violin Sonata in G major; yet even in his very early works one finds so many salient traits of his mature style. One can best speak of periodization in each of the forms and media for which Brahms wrote.

Piano music. Brahms' first published works include three piano sonatas, evidence that he was beginning his career as a "strict" composer; a marvelous Scherzo, Op. 4, the earliest work he deemed fit for publication; the Ballades, Op. 10; and some variations, crowned by the magnificent Variations and Fugue on a Theme by Handel, Op. 24, which Wagner praised, and the virtuoso Variations on a Theme by Paganini, Op. 35. Brahms thereafter limited himself to short piano pieces: those of Op. 76 are highly concentrated; the Rhapsodies, Op. 79, are magnificent specimens of his "Sturm und Drang" Romantic piano writing; and the short piano pieces from Op. 116 through Op. 119 are the culmination of his achievement as a piano composer.

These brief pieces bear such noncommittal titles as "capriccio," "rhapsody," and especially "intermezzo." Generally ternary in form, the individual sections show highly subtle internal links and are often inter-related. The few passionate pieces (e.g., Op. 116, Nos. 1 and 3) are re-strained and concentrated in comparison with the Rhapsodies of Op. 79; others, like Op. 116, No. 5 and Op. 118, No. 4, are highly abstract plays on rhythmic motives. Such warm and contemplative pieces as Op. 118, No. 2 and Op. 116, No. 4 may be contrasted with the somber Op. 118, No. 6, the songful Op. 117, No. 1, and the reflective Op. 119, No. 1. These late pieces are the complete antithesis of the Romantic "salon piece"; comparing them with Liszt's *Consolations* shows a striking con-trast between the aesthetics of two different composers working within the same self-imposed limitations.

Brahms often sketched his larger chamber or orchestral works for two pianos; the scanty original literature for this medium counts among its cornerstones the two-piano versions of the Piano Quintet and the Haydn Variations. Among the fine works for piano duet are the Waltzes, Op. 39; the intricate and difficult Variations on a theme by Schumann, Op. 23; the Liebeslieder Waltzes, to which vocal parts were later added; and the familiar Hungarian Dances, which helped start a virtual ava-lanche of "national" dances for piano duet of which those by Dvořák, Grieg, Moszkowski, and Gilbert are the most worthy successors.

Chamber music. This medium occupied Brahms during all his creative life and contains perhaps his best work. In number of perform-ers, the range is from duet sonatas to string sextets, and there are interest-ing contrasting timbres in the Trio for horn, violin, and piano (Op. 40) and the Trio for clarinet, cello, and piano (Op. 114).

In all the media except for quintets, the first work reveals not only a certain tentativeness, as if Brahms were exploringly feeling his way, but also a certain expansiveness, for each first work tends to be longer than its successors. The B major Trio, Op. 8, the first of his chamber works, was originally so long that Brahms later condensed it drastically, but it is still his longest chamber work. These first works often have a serene contemplativeness, as in the B-flat String Sextet (Op. 18) and E minor Cello Sonata (Op. 38), but the extremely somber C minor String Quartet (Op. 51, No. 1) is a striking exception. As a rule, the second work in each medium is the best or most "Romantic" in its effusiveness, especially the A minor String Quartet (Op. 51, No. 2) or—Brahms' most "Romantic" chamber work—the A major Violin Sonata (Op. 100). The third work in each medium can either be the most "Classical," like the B-flat major String Quartet (Op. 67), or the most abstract, like the D minor Violin Sonata (Op. 108).

The growth of professional string quartets stimulated Brahms' muse; his chamber works, unlike Volkmann's, are not for amateurs play-ing *Hausmusik*. Generally his chamber music is highly restrained, disci-plined, and even somber (C minor Quartet, B minor Clarinet Quintet), but few more exuberant chamber works exist than the gypsy rondo which closes the G minor Piano Quartet (Op. 25) or the light-hearted first movement of the B-flat String Quartet. A few of his chamber works have an almost "orchestral" sound, especially the two string quintets, and Schoenberg thought that the G minor Piano Quartet should be given orchestral garb. Many performers of the duet sonatas complain that the competition with the piano is an unequal one, and that the close relationship between solo instrument and piano is uncongenial to the kind of virtuoso who considers his instrument the center of a duet sonata.

Orchestral music. Though Brahms' four symphonies are no longer considered the acme of his *oeuvre*, they are still among the major orchestral works of the nineteenth century. His four concertos—two for piano, one for violin, and the "Double Concerto" for violin and cello—revert to the Beethovenian tradition of a symphony with obbligato solo instrument. The two early Serenades (Opp. 11, 16) and the "Tragic" and "Academic Festival" overtures complete the short list.

Not only is the first work in each orchestral genre tentative, whether serenade (Op. 11), concerto (Op. 15), or even symphony (Op. 68), but when each is compared with a work written soon after it in another genre, as with the A major Serenade and the Second Symphony, the second work shares the expansiveness of the first. Brahms' orchestration, stemming from that of Beethoven and Schumann, is characterized by great restraint in using orchestral "heavy artillery" and by a rather dark brown, somber coloring thanks to the importance of the violas, the blended tone colors, and the doubling of notes, particularly the thirds of chords, in the low registers (a characteristic also of his piano and chamber music). Only in the D minor Piano Concerto does he write poorly for his instruments. The serenades are works for chamber orchestra; in the second, in A major, he even (as in the first movement of the *German Requiem*) omits violins.

Songs. Brahms wrote over 200 songs in the tradition of the German Lied. Except for the romances from *Magelone* (Op. 33), settings of a poetic cycle by Ludwig Tieck, and the *Four Serious Songs* (Op. 121) on Biblical texts, Brahms avoided the song cycle, preferring to write a group of songs to texts by a variety of poets.

From a strictly evolutionary standpoint Brahms' songs are regressive, for he limited the role of the accompaniment to short preludes and postludes, occasional interludes, and to doubling the vocal melody or playing arpeggiated chords, often in cross-rhythms, without, however, any semblance of hackneyed accompanimental patterns. The voice is the center of attention; the occasional wide leaps demanded are generally triadic, and irregular (three- or five-measure) but balanced phrases frequently occur. The most typical songs are either those in folk song style

("Sonntag" from Op. 47, or the German folk songs with piano accompaniment) or are slow and contemplative, like "Sapphic Ode," "Feldeinsamkeit," or "Wie bist du, meine Königin." When he examined a song by another composer, Brahms would cover all the parts except the vocal melody and the bass, evidence that he considered these the most important elements of a song.

Choral music. Only Handel and Mendelssohn can be said to have written as grateful music for choral voices as Brahms, a choral conductor who thoroughly understood the medium. His choral music is the culmination of the German tradition, embracing not only the large festival chorus but also the small mixed, male, or women's choruses that fulfilled important social as well as musical functions. Brahms' largest accompanied choral work, the *German Requiem,* is based on Biblical rather than liturgical texts and contains not only dramatic fugal passages and a song-like soprano solo in the fifth movement but also, in the outer movements (in F major, one of the composer's favorite keys) and the fourth, the finest choral writing of the century. Among the shorter accompanied works the *Song of Destiny* and the exquisite *Nänie* deserve particular mention. His *a cappella* choral works include not only motets based on the seventeenth-century choral tradition, which Brahms thoroughly understood by having conducted these works as well as several of J. S. Bach's cantatas, but also delightful arrangements of folk songs.

Musical style. As with any major composer, a capsule description of Brahms' musical style is difficult to make, but several stylistic traits are prominent in his music. His melodies emphasize the triad (characteristic also of German folk song, in which he was deeply interested), and triadic leaps give a virile strength and energy to even the most contemplative passages. When the melodies tend to be long, as in reflective works like the B major Trio, E minor Cello Sonata, and B-flat major String Sextet (like the opening melodies of Beethoven's "Archduke" Trio or Schubert's B-flat Piano Sonata, D. 960), they indicate that the work is to be on an extensive time-scale. Brahms' long melodic arches are evident even when interruptions must be taken for breath, as in the songs or the slower movements of the works for clarinet, or when the melody itself is seemingly broken up by rests, as in the third movement of the Op. 108 Violin Sonata. As Example 9-4 will show, his handling of simple phrases by extending them motivically is magnificent.

Rhythm is Brahms' driving force, and his treatment of this element, which he shared with Beethoven, Schumann, and Berlioz, raises his music far above that of his contemporaries like Raff and Reinecke, who were too easily satisfied with static or jog-trot rhythms inseparable from the meter. Although Brahms occasionally used irregular meters or (like Schumann) added another beat to a measure to extend a phrase or delay a cadence, he generally relied on syncopation, sometimes united with a syncopated harmonic rhythm (as in the first movement of the Third Symphony or Example 9-3c) that gives the impression to the casual observer that the conductor is a fraction of a beat behind or ahead of the orchestra. Cross-rhythms, with triplets in one hand and duplets in the other, are most obvious in his piano music and song accompaniments and are one of his favorite ways of giving added interest to a homophonic passage.

Brahms' most striking rhythmic device is his use of hemiola, which pervades most of his movements in 3/4 or 6/8 meter. Quite often this is a "sprung rhythm" wherein a prevailing pattern in 3/4 will give way to measures of 6/8 or vice versa (Example 9-3a) and there are also combinations of the two meters to provide another variety of cross-rhythm (6/4 and 3/2 in Example 9-3b).

EXAMPLE 9-3. Selected rhythmic devices in Brahms' music: (a) 3/4 and 6/8 meters within a theme (Horn Trio, Op. 40, last movement); (b) Hemiolar cross-rhythms (Violin Sonata, Op. 78, first movement); (c) Syncopated harmonic rhythm (Handel Variations, Op. 24; end of second variation leading into third variation).

Though Brahms was the most contrapuntal composer of the century, he was the least ostentatious about it and in this respect is surpassed only by Mozart, for even in Beethoven's music one often senses that the composer is deliberately calling attention to his use of a "learned" device. Especially in the large choral works Brahms' fugues are "accompanied," perhaps to keep the rhythmic propulsion from sagging (the fugues in the third and sixth movement of the *German Requiem* are excellent illustrations), but in the motets he reverts to more archaic techniques. The best instrumental fugal finales conclude the E minor Cello Sonata and F major String Quintet; Beethoven's keyboard fugues in the late sonatas are the most obvious models, but the ultimate ancestor is J. S. Bach's *Well-Tempered Clavier* rather than the organ fugues of the Weimar epoch which Liszt and his disciples were transcribing as virtuoso piano solos. In his variations Brahms took great delight in canonic problems, as Bach did in his "Goldberg" Variations, and in setting compositional limitations for himself, especially in the use of invertible counterpoint, where soprano and bass melodies may exchange places, or of such difficult tasks as occur in the tenth of the Schumann Variations, Op. 9, where the bass line is the mirror image of the soprano melody. Occasionally Brahms utilized ground bass techniques, as in the finales of the Haydn Variations and the Fourth Symphony.

Although Brahms used many of the harmonies of the "new German school," particularly the half-diminished seventh chord as dominant preparations in cadences, to him harmony was strictly functional, neither coloristic nor rhetorical. Along with his love for folk song came a desire for authentic sounding harmonizations requiring a lavish use of secondary triads, even to the point of blurring the tonal center of the melody, as in Example 9-4; the beginning sounds like F major but the middle A major or minor. Brahms' rather somber harmonic coloring derives from his fondness for subdominant harmony, the "dark" side of the circle of fifths as opposed to the "brightness" of dominant harmony. Often when Brahms goes to the dominant side of the circle of fifths he returns via the subdominant to the tonic. The minor forms of the subdominant and the tonic are his favorite pivots for modulation, and many of his diminished-seventh chords consist of the third of the minor subdominant

EXAMPLE 9-4. Brahms, Quartet, Op. 51, No. 1, third movement, trio.

(B-flat in the key of D) added to an incomplete dominant harmony (C-sharp–E–G) and are thus functional; similarly, chords of the augmented sixth are not used as color harmonies but serve as intensified dominants to reinforce the tonic (F-natural–A–B–D-sharp to an E major triad, as in the seventh and eighth measures of the finale of the Fourth

Symphony), and chords of the half-diminished seventh, usually in first inversion (G–E–B-flat–D in the key of D major) as dominant preparations in cadences.

Though writers disagree about the actual amount of thematic or psychological interrelationships there is between movements of his instrumental cycles, Brahms occasionally uses material from the opening movement in a finale, as in his skillful insertion of material from the first movement into the final variations of both the Op. 67 String Quartet and the Clarinet Quintet. The introductions to the outer movements of the First Symphony contain most of the salient thematic material. Most frequently Brahms creates cyclic links within his movements, especially by using crucial motives in transitional passages or by transforming a theme from one section and using it in another.

In his sonata-form movements Brahms follows the models of middle-period through late-period Beethoven, late Schubert (especially the sonatas), or the Chopin of the B minor and G minor sonatas. His expositions are clear-cut, with considerable contrast among the themes. When he does not indicate a repeat of the exposition (which should be observed in performance when so marked), his developments usually begin in the tonic with a restatement of the opening theme to give the effect of a repeated exposition. When this occurs, and especially if the material of the first theme dominates the development, the recapitulation is highly truncated, in the manner of Beethoven's Quartet, Op. 95, first movement, or Chopin's mature sonatas; it may be even a sort of "mirror" recapitulation, as in the first movement of the Op. 25 Piano Quartet. The slow movements, like Schubert's (and, later, some of Mahler's), are modeled on the art-song rather than the aria, hymn, or romance; this is especially evident when the "accompanying" instruments open the movement with a ritornello. The form is generally ternary on a large scale, with some reprises characterized by melodic variation.

Brahms' scherzo movements are seldom of the bumptious sort; only that of the Fourth Symphony really fits that description. Sometimes the scherzo is mysterious, deft, and fantastic, as in the Trio, Op. 87; sometimes it is a sturdy movement in 6/8 meter replete with duplets, as in the Horn Trio or the Op. 99 Cello Sonata. In the Op. 88 String Quintet and Op. 100 Violin Sonata the slow and scherzo movements are "telescoped" into one movement. But the most typical kind of third movement is a contemplative intermezzo, sometimes with varying tempos and thematic transformation as in the Second Symphony, most often highly poignant as in the Op. 67 Quartet or any of the late instrumental cycles; the comparable movements in Beethoven's Op. 130 and Op. 132 Quartets are the most evident models.

Considerable variety exists among Brahms' finales. One exciting kind, which Liszt appreciated most in Brahms' music, is the Hungarian rondo, at its most fiery in the G minor Piano Quartet and also found as a highly effective close to the Violin Concerto and the "Double" Concerto. A relaxed and expansive conclusion, often a rondo or set of variations, is characteristic of such works in B-flat major as the Op. 18 Sextet, the Op. 67 Quartet, and the Piano Concerto in B-flat. Some of the finales are contrary to the "optimistic" and "victorious" instrumental cycle by being in minor, even when the first movement is in tonic major. Most of the finales are in sonata form, but the conclusion of the Fourth Symphony freely utilizes ground-bass techniques with numerous variations, refinements, motivic play, and harmonic substitution; it is unique, not only in Brahms' *oeuvre* but also for the century as a whole.

Brahms' sets of variations, whether movements of an instrumental cycle or independent compositions, are an important portion of his work. They derive more from J. S. Bach's "Goldberg" Variations and Beethoven's later variations than from the free variations of Schumann's *Symphonic Etudes,* and are generally called "character variations" in that each individual variation is an alteration of the "character" of the theme. To use a mathematical analogy, the "constants" are the structure of the theme (number of phrases, binary or ternary organization) and the harmony in the broadest sense, allowing for substitutions of chords especially in changes of mode; the variables are the other elements—melody, rhythm, pitch location, and texture. Figure 9-1 shows the organization of Brahms' most familiar set of variations, the Variations on a Theme by Haydn, Op. 56. This analysis may be regarded as a point of departure for an intensive study of the motivic development and harmonic substitution typical of the composer's other mature variations.

Brahms' achievement. It is generally thought today that Brahms' contemporaries viewed him as a pedantic musical reactionary who eschewed program music and music drama in favor of Classic-era forms; yet Wagner remarked, on hearing Brahms play his Handel Variations, that there was still life in the old forms when one knew how to handle them, and Liszt, though cool to most of Brahms' music, enjoyed his Hungarian finales. Actually, Brahms fused Baroque attitudes toward counterpoint and exploitation of all the possibilities of a musical idea and Classic techniques of musical craftsmanship with the Romantic views of musical expressiveness through harmonic and sonorous resources; he thus synthesized the best elements of the eighteenth and nineteenth centuries in music without creating stylistic incongruities or relying on antiquarian devices divorced from a living musical language. Brahms was the greatest composer of Protestant church music after J. S. Bach; his arrange-

VARIATION	TEMPO	METER	STRUCTURE	REMARKS
Theme	Andante	2/4	A 5+5, B 4+4, A 4, Coda (prolongs tonic) 7	
I	Poco più animato	2/4	The same	Essentially the same harmony.
II	Più vivace	2/4	The same	5-measure phrase of A 1 + 4. Essentially the same harmony but in minor.
III	Con moto	2/4	A 10+10, B 4+4, A Coda 4+7 (repeated)	Major. Written-out repeats with changes of orchestration and pitch-location.
IV	Andante con moto	3/8	A 5+5, B 4+4, A 5+5 Coda, A 4+7 (repeated)	Written-out repeats with second statement in invertible counterpoint at the twelfth. Minor.
V	Vivace	6/8	A 10+10, B+A 12+7, B+A 12+7	Diminution and distortion of theme, often using hemiola. Major.
VI	Vivace	2/4	A 5+5, B 4+4, A Coda 4 4+3	Reversion to original structure with repeats. Theme recognizable but changes in harmony, especially at cadences. Major.
VII	Grazioso	6/8	A 5+5, B A Coda 8+4+7	Richer harmony; oscillation between 6/8 and 3/4, especially in section B. Major.
VIII	Presto non troppo	3/4	A 10+5+5, B A Coda 4+4+4+7	Minor. Variation farthest removed from theme.
Finale	Andante	2/2	Five-measure ground bass derived from harmony of theme.	Bass pattern repeated 11 times; 12th time ornamented; 13th through 15th time in minor and in upper parts; 16th time as before. Concludes with statement of theme and coda.

FIGURE 9-1. Brahms: Variations on a Theme by Haydn, Op. 56.

ments of folk or popular music, either as solo songs, in choral settings, or for piano duet, provided models for future composers; and he revived the duet sonata, the independent set of variations, and chamber music as viable artistic forms. Especially in the variation form, Brahms' influence strongly affected such twentieth-century composers as Reger, Dohnányi, and Hindemith.

Composers in Brahms' Orbit. Perhaps the most neglected among all nineteenth-century composers are the German and Austrian representatives of the conservative wing of Late Romanticism in music. As conservatives, they have been referred to, if mentioned at all, as minor neoclassicists, academics (many were excellent teachers), epigones, and also-rans: composers whose music is too derivative from Mendelssohn or Schumann, or stylistically too close to Brahms, to have, at least by present-day standards, much individual identity. Yet among the works of these composers the conductor of the male or female chorus, the violist, the cellist, the flutist, and the clarinetist will find many compositions that are worthy additions to a rather limited repertoire.

Of all the composers in this group, Carl Reinecke (1824–1910) seems to have the best chance of having his music revived. A highly prolific composer with 288 opus numbers, he wrote in all media; of greatest possible interest today are his concertos for relatively neglected instruments (flute, harp, clarinet), his duet sonatas, and his chamber works that include wind instruments. If his music does not rise to the heights of Brahms, it is nevertheless idiomatic, euphonious, and skillfully written with considerable craftsmanship. Max Bruch (1838–1920) is best known today for violin works like his G minor Concerto and Scottish Fantasy; his "Kol Nidre" for cello and orchestra gave rise to the erroneous claim that he was Jewish. Although Bruch wrote symphonies and chamber music, his chief achievement lies in choral works written for Rhenish and other music festivals. Karl Goldmark (1830–1915), a Jewish composer who grew up in Hungary, was in his operas a neo-Wagnerian influenced by French *opéra lyrique,* but he was also an heir of the various German Romantic traditions in his instrumental compositions. His orchestral suite (not a symphony) *The Rustic Wedding* (1876), a simple and melodious work, is performed occasionally.

THE "FRENCH MUSICAL RENAISSANCE"

Berlioz died, broken and embittered, in 1869. In the following year Prussia crushingly defeated France, and in 1871, shortly before the victorious German armies paraded through Paris, the Société nationale de musique was founded with the slogan *Ars gallica*—French art; its establishment marked a rebirth of French instrumental composition that was soon to provide musical alternatives to German symphonic thought or music drama.

The superficial impression given by the term "French Musical Renaissance" is that instrumental music finally became appreciated by Parisian audiences. In reality, quartet societies and symphony orchestras had been founded between 1850 and 1870, but the dislocations of the Franco-Prussian War and the insurrection of the Paris Commune caused a temporary suspension of musical activities; after the war instrumental organizations found it easier to resume their schedules than did opera companies. Besides Berlioz, other though lesser instrumental composers were active in France before 1870: the expatriate Englishman George Onslow (1784–1853), for example, turned out a prodigious amount of chamber music in a style resembling second-rate Weber and Mendelssohn, and Gounod and Bizet, as well as Franck and Saint-Saëns, wrote instrumental music before 1870. Absolute music, furthermore, was only one facet of the activity of French composers after 1870, for all of them at least dabbled in opera, and in their instrumental compositions they were influenced not only by Beethoven and Schumann but also by the "new German school," especially Liszt. Wagner's influence on French composers, however, has been overstated, and the French cult of Wagner consisted of literary or even political figures rather than musicians.

The principal musical change in France after 1870 was the acceptance of French composers in more than one field of music. Although there was a significant school of French composers of symphonies, *symphonies concertantes*, and chamber music during the Classic period (including the first significant Negro composer, Joseph Boulogne, Chevalier de Saint-Georges, 1739–1799), between 1750 and 1870 foreign composers tended to dominate absolute music and serious opera in France, whether Germans like Schobert, Gluck, and Meyerbeer or Italians like Cherubini, Salieri, Spontini, and Rossini. Between 1780 and 1870 the proper province for the French composer was a certain kind of opera: the rescue opera, *opéra comique*, or *opéra lyrique*. After 1870, however, critics and audiences accepted the absolute music of French composers, showing them an appreciation which had only hesitantly been granted Berlioz. During the first stage (1870–1890) of the "French Musical Renaissance," influences from across the Rhine were strong, especially those of Beethoven, Schumann, and Liszt; furthermore, Franck was born in Belgium and Lalo was of Spanish descent.

César Franck (1822–1890) was not a prolific composer, and most of his major works date from the last decade of his life. The organ was his principal instrument: this accounts for his polyphonic writing; the improvisatory nature of much of his music, especially in its developments and transitions; the awkwardness of his piano music; and the "registration changes" of his orchestration. In contrast to his organist-contemporary Anton Bruckner, Franck's orchestra stresses the reed- or flue-pipe sounds of the oboe, English horn, and bass clarinet.

Chromaticism and cyclic form are usually cited as the two salient characteristics of Franck's style, but like most attempts to summarize a composer's style in a few words, such statements have resulted in over-simplified generalizations. Franck used chromaticism as a source of contrast to a diatonicism with modal undercurrents, best seen in the central movement of his *Prelude, Chorale, and Fugue* for piano; his chromaticism is often the result of melodic chromaticism in many parts rather than either a functional or coloristic harmony. Typical devices are sequences, either stepwise or by thirds; sinuous chromatic motion within a narrow melodic ambitus, often centered around the third degree of the scale; and an essentially tonal framework. Example 9-5 is a good illustration: note the third-related chords, the enharmonic use of augmented triads, and the irregular resolution of chords of the augmented sixth. Critics are seldom neutral about Franck's chromaticism; they consider it either as an expressive seasoning which compensates for bland melodies

EXAMPLE 9-5. Franck, Organ Chorale in B minor.

and sagging rhythms, or (especially in the Piano Quintet) as an irritating mannerism.

Although Franck gave hints of his future reliance on cyclic form in his F-sharp minor Trio (1841), he did not set his ideas definitely forth until his *Grande pièce symphonique* (1860–1862) for organ. His cyclic form consists of thematic transformation and the recapitulation of salient motives or even full themes in subsequent movements; it derives from Schumann and the "thematic transformation" of Liszt's Weimar works rather than from Wagner's treatment of leitmotives. Cyclic forms are most evident in *Le Chasseur maudit* (1882, his noisiest work), the Piano Quintet (1879), and the Symphony in D minor (1889), but are subtly stated in his *Prelude, Chorale, and Fugue*. Franck frequently used not one but two "germ-cells" to create a contrast and duality of expression, often with a mystic connotation of light opposed to darkness; the best examples of such usage are the Symphony and the *Variations symphoniques* (1885), in which he also contributed to the re-assessment of the solo piano as a participatory rather than the dominant instrument in a concerto. Cyclic form for Franck was an effective means of unifying an often loose, rhapsodic, and rambling musical structure, but it remained for his pupil Vincent d'Indy to carry this device to its most logical conclusion (see Example 11-8).

Though Franck's students called him "Pater Seraphicus," the line between the sacred and the secular elements in his music is most difficult to draw, and there are few more voluptuous compositions than the first movement of his Violin Sonata. Franck's church music stands midway between the unashamedly operatic expressiveness, sometimes bordering on sentimentality, of Gounod's *St. Cecilia Mass* and *The Seven Last Words* of the young Théodore Dubois (1837–1924) and the relative austerity of Fauré, d'Indy, and Dubois' twentieth-century works. Franck's church music, like that of his French and Victorian contemporaries, was also influenced by a kind of feminized Christianity, different from the sturdy piety of Bruckner, Brahms, and Dvořák or the rugged self-taught American "Sacred Harp" composers.[2]

Franck's highly individual style did not permit imitation, yet he taught a diverse group of composers, some of whom will be discussed in Chapter 11, and passed on to them a sense of high seriousness about music with patriotic and religious overtones, also an interpretation of chromatic harmony and musical structure which contributed to the breaking-down of nineteenth-century concepts of tonality and form.

Edouard Lalo (1823–1892) spent most of his life as a violinist in orchestras or chamber ensembles and was second violinist in a string quartet that introduced Wagner to Beethoven's late works in this genre. Strongly influenced by Schumann, Lalo wrote little music but it is of high quality, sound technique, and appropriate for its purpose. His Symphony in G minor (1889) is exceeded only by Brahms' C minor String Quartet as the most somber instrumental work of the century, but the soberness of the Cello Concerto (1877) is relieved in the second and third movements by delightful Spanish intermezzi, a vein Lalo had previously exploited in his best-known work, the *Symphonie espagnole* (1875) for violin and orchestra. Lalo was not successful as an operatic composer, but his best work, *Le Roi d'Ys* (1888), enjoys occasional performances and is among the midpoints between *opéra lyrique* and Debussy's *Pelléas et Mélisande*.

Camille Saint-Saëns (1835–1921) was the most prolific and universal among his contemporaries, for he wrote in virtually every musical medium. In 1871, when he was 36, he was considered the dean of French composers and became the most important founder of the Société nationale de musique. Though he wrote some significant works before 1870, especially the intimate *Oratorio de Noël* and G minor Piano Concerto, his reputation rests solely on his works of the 1870's since his later music was eclipsed by the new developments of the 1890's.

Among his instrumental works are four symphonic poems, modeled on Liszt's but with a much simpler structure: *Danse macabre* (1875) is the best known. His most admired chamber work is the Septet for strings, piano, and trumpet (1881); its movements, entitled "Préambule," "Minuet," "Intermède," and "Gavotte et final," hearken back in spirit to the chamber suites of Couperin and Rameau rather than to the instrumental cycles of the High Classic and Romantic period (see Ex-

---

[2] It is difficult for us properly to assess nineteenth-century church music, especially that of Catholic France, because our ideals of musical austerity as the most fitting expression of religious worship make this music sound operatic and saccharine, particularly to Protestant ears attuned to Schütz, J. S. Bach, and Vaughan Williams. The socio-cultural and theological connotations of church music are fertile fields for investigation.

ample 11-7b). His Third Symphony (1886) is from a technical standpoint the best synthesis of the expressive resources of the "music of the future" with the ethos and techniques of absolute instrumental music, for Saint-Saëns uses thematic transformation and reminiscence as effectively as Liszt and with more technical surety than Franck, and he links the sections together with thematically connecting material, often contrapuntally treated, with almost as much finesse as Brahms. The elegance, unpretentiousness, and skillful craftsmanship characteristic of his best work may be seen in his finest concertos: the A minor Cello Concerto (1873), C minor Piano Concerto (1875), and B minor Violin Concerto (1880).

Saint-Saëns strove for years to make a reputation as an opera composer but with little success. *La Princesse jaune* (1872) has a delightful overture replete with pentatonic exoticism. *Samson and Delilah* (completed 1877) was originally conceived as an oratorio and betrays many characteristics of this genre: considerable use of counterpoint (the canon in the final scene between Delilah and the Philistine priest, for example), the important position of the chorus, and the consistently static action. Yet the choral writing is extremely idiomatic if neo-Handelian, and the mezzo-soprano arias are as voluptuous as those for Massenet's heroines.

Saint-Saëns was one of the major forerunners of twentieth-century music. In Example 2-9, from his Fifth Piano Concerto, we have seen how his diatonic harmonizations, avoiding leading-tone or dominant-tonic tendencies, weakened the force of traditional tonality as much as the chromaticism of Liszt and Wagner or the empiricism of Musorgsky and led to the pan-diatonic writing which characterizes twentieth-century neo-classicism. Equally important was Saint-Saëns' attitude toward music in stating his credo of musical objectivity toward the end of his life: "He who does not feel wholly satisfied with elegant lines, harmonious colors, and a fine series of chords does not understand art."[3] The subjective approach to music which had continued from the Baroque through the *Sturm und Drang* and culminated in nineteenth-century Romanticism ended with Saint-Saëns far more than with Brahms, whose music is full-bloodedly Romantic despite its composer's technical mastery and reliance on what Baroque composers called "invention." Saint-Saëns' music is objective: an orderly, disciplined kaleidoscope of sonorities lacking both the cosmic message of Beethoven, Wagner, Franck, or d'Indy and the sublimated personal emotions of Schumann, Liszt, or Brahms. Saint-Saëns' use of musical parody, best seen in his *Carnival of the Animals* (completed in 1886 but suppressed during his lifetime lest it damage his reputation as a serious composer), stemmed from Rossini's "secret" piano compositions but (in contrast to Beethoven's "Romantic irony") is an im-

---

[3] *Les Idées de M. Vincent d'Indy* (Paris, 1919), cited in James Harding, *Saint-Saëns and His Circle* (London, 1965), p. 219.

portant transition to the anti-Romantic parody and caricature of Chabrier, Satie, Poulenc, and Milhaud. Saint-Saëns was a great admirer of earlier French music; he edited the music of Gluck, Rameau, and the *clavecinistes*, and incorporated their aesthetic into his works through his use of restraint and simplicity. He may be therefore considered the chief forerunner of the neoclassic revival transmitted by his pupil Fauré to Ravel, and ultimately to others like Stravinsky and Piston.

BIBLIOGRAPHICAL NOTES

The most satisfactory study of Bruckner's music in English is Erwin Doernberg's *The Life and Symphonies of Anton Bruckner* (London, 1960). Although the analyses resemble program notes, they are superior to the superficial and chatty examinations in Robert Simpson's *The Essence of Bruckner* (London, 1967), which contains, however, brief mentions of Bruckner's other compositions. A biography of Bruckner in English translation by Hans-Hubert Schönzeler has been announced for publication.

The best biography of Brahms in English is still Karl Geiringer's *Brahms: His Life and Work* (1947; reprint, New York, 1962). The standard biography is Max Kalbeck's monumental study in eight volumes (Leipzig, 1904–1911), in German. The bar-by-bar analyses of Brahms' compositions by Edwin Evans, Sr. (London, 1912–1936) can be disagreed with but should not be altogether ignored. William S. Newman's *The Sonata Since Beethoven* (Chapel Hill, 1969) gives an extremely comprehensive survey not only of the sonatas of Brahms and his major French contemporaries, but also of the numerous composers in Brahms' orbit, with several musical examples as illustrations.

Martin Cooper's *French Music from the Death of Berlioz to the Death of Fauré* (London, 1951) and the second volume of Paul Landormy's *La Musique française* (Paris, 1945) are the best surveys of French music under the Third Republic. Biographies of the major French composers discussed in this chapter include James Harding's *Saint-Saëns and His Circle* (London, 1965), more anecdotal than critical with little discussion of his music, and Laurence Davies' much better study, *César Franck and His Circle* (New York, 1970).

Brahms' music is contained in a fairly authoritative set of complete works, and a complete edition of Bruckner's music, which will include his various revisions, is in progress.

TEN

NINETEENTH-CENTURY NATIONALISM IN MUSIC

Nationalism is a concept better described than defined. It includes a feeling of political or cultural inferiority, a seeking for identity among the folk arts of the common people and especially the "unspoiled" peasants, and a search for particular national means of expression different from the cultural norms of the dominant group. Music played an important role in the cultural nationalism that swept Europe during the nineteenth century. The opposite side of musical nationalism was exoticism, a search for new effects from the folk music of other lands and peoples, generally those considered to be less spoiled by civilization; this even led to the phenomenon of Russian nationalists who proclaimed their musical independence from western European models by exploiting the exotica of the peoples of central Asia who had recently been conquered by the Tsarist imperium.

Nationalism in the nineteenth century is first evident in western Europe. The reaction against the French literary and Italian musical culture of the eighteenth-century German courts culminated in the temporary unification of the Germanic peoples at the "Battle of the Nations" near Leipzig in 1813 against Napoleon, whose downfall was celebrated by cantatas or battle pieces by Weber and Beethoven, who at this time began to use German tempo and expression markings rather than the customary Italian indications. The male chorus (Männerchor) movement played an important role in the drive for German unification, and Wagner's writings, with their anti-Semitism and mythologizing, reflect the souring of German liberalism into a perverse nationalism after 1848.

We have already seen the important roles played by Verdi in the Italian *Risorgimento,* which culminated in the unification of Italy in 1870, and by nationalism in French music after the Franco-Prussian War. Perhaps inspired by French colonial adventures in the Near East and North Africa, French composers turned to exoticism, as seen in the Near Eastern motives in *Le Désert* and *Lalla Roukh* by Félicien David (1810–1876) or Saint-Saëns' *Samson and Delilah, Suite algérienne,* and Fifth Piano Concerto. Imperialism is occasionally reflected in French operas such as Délibes' *Lakmé.* Spain was a favorite topic for French exoticism, from Auber's *Le Domino noir* (1839) to such masterpieces of local color as Bizet's *Carmen,* Chabrier's *España,* and Debussy's *Ibéria.* As we shall see, Hungary was a similar source of exotica for German composers. Yet nationalism was at its strongest in the countries east of Germany or in areas peripheral to the musical centers of the eighteenth century.

Not all the composers mentioned in this chapter were deliberate nationalists. Such composers as Anton Rubinstein and Horatio Parker wrote in an "international" Romantic style; Berwald, Chaikovsky, and MacDowell are unique musical figures, not locatable in convenient pigeonholes, who included musical materials or at least topical themes from their homelands in their works and can thereby be subsumed under the heading of musical nationalism.

By 1900 virtually every ethnic group in Europe had developed its own national art music; let us concentrate on only the principal cultural areas of musical nationalism: Russia, Bohemia, Scandinavia, Hungary, England, and the United States.

RUSSIA

Tsar Pyotr the Great (1672–1725) opened a "window on the West" with his conquest of the eastern shores of the Baltic and the construction of his new capital, St. Petersburg, by Western architects. Throughout the eighteenth century many foreign musicians and composers came there, among them Galuppi, Paisiello, and finally Boïeldieu and John Field. Catherine the Great (1729–1796) attempted to create a "national opera" by writing opera librettos in Russian and having them set by court composers. The opposition of East and West in Russian music is discernible at the end of the eighteenth century: Evstigeney Ipatovich Fomin (1761–1800) sought to incorporate Russian folk melodies into his operas, whereas Russia's principal composer of the time, Dmitri Bortniansky (1751–1825), wrote Italianate operas and keyboard music, although Russian elements are present in the church music by which he is best known today. Ventures were also made at this time by Western composers in utilizing Russian folk song in the context of Western tonal harmony; the best known specimens are the *thèmes russes* in Beethoven's Op. 59 Quartets (see Example 10-3a).

     In 1802 Spohr described the singing of Russian soldiers which he heard near Mitau:

> They howled frightfully, so that one would almost have to cover his ears. The songs are rehearsed by a cudgel-wielding noncom. The melodies of the songs were not bad, but were accompanied by nothing but false harmonies.[1]

Such views of their native music were shared by many of the Russian connoisseurs. It remained for Mikhail Ivanovich Glinka (1804–1857) to synthesize authentic Russian folk idioms with the heritage of Western music.

     A dilettante like most of his Russian successors, Glinka was influenced by Italian music, especially Bellini's, and loved the folk music of Spain. His output was not large; it consists chiefly of short orchestral pieces utilizing either Russian or Spanish folk and popular music, some piano pieces and songs, and two operas, the historical *A Life for the Tsar* (1836) and the fairy-tale *Ruslan and Lyudmila* (1842).

     Glinka's operas show, respectively, two of the three basic trends of east European opera during the nineteenth century (the third trend, the parody of the Meyerbeerian opera exemplified by Dargomÿzhsky's *Esmeralda* and Chaikovsky's *Orleanskaya Dieva*, need not detain us here). *A Life for the Tsar* is a historical opera calculated to arouse strong national or patriotic feelings, with the peasants or popular heroes as the central figures, their music in the style of folk song and folk harmony. This harmony utilizes a large number of secondary triads, especially in the minor mode, which has led many to refer to it as "modal"

---

[1] Louis Spohr, *Selbstbiographie (Kassel and Göttingen*, 1860–1861, 2 vols.), I, pp. 36–37.

harmony; Glinka often gives his folk-like melodies contrapuntal treatment, as Example 10-1 shows. The enemy are depicted by their own national music, Polish dances like the krakowiak, mazurka, and polonaise, and the opera concludes with the patriotic cannon-shots-*cum*-

EXAMPLE 10-1. Glinka, *A Life for the Tsar*, Act I.

Kremlin-bells finale epitomized in the conclusion of Chaikovsky's *1812 Overture*. *Ruslan and Lyudmila*, on the other hand, is a fairy-tale opera with brilliant orchestration and strange melodies and harmonies for fantastic episodes: Example 10-2 accompanies the cortege of the wicked magician Chernomor. Exoticism, through the use of Persian dances or

EXAMPLE 10-2. Glinka, *Ruslan and Lyudmila,* Act IV.

the Caucasian *lezginka,* plays an important role. (Glinka's version of the latter dance surprisingly anticipates Khachaturian's melody, harmony, and orchestration.) Noteworthy in both operas are the important role of the chorus, the exotic ballets, and the use of the alto and low bass voices for principal characters. Folk idioms and intonations appear most frequently in the choruses, less in the arias for male voices, and least of all in the soprano arias, which are strongly influenced by Bellini and Donizetti. Glinka's remarkable orchestration deserves comment for its extensive use of the "primary" or unmixed colors of the orchestral palette rather than the blended sounds of the Germanic composers.

Glinka's piano music, the most uneven corpus of his work, spans his entire creative lifetime from the mid-1820's to 1855. Variations on themes by Mozart, Cherubini, Donizetti, and Bellini; popular dances such as the waltz, contradanse, and polka; and characteristic pieces which sometimes contain folk elements (the "Tarantelle" is a good illustration) form the bulk of his work for the piano. Although almost all of these compositions are well-written salon pieces, the best of them share the sensitive and refined so-called *morbidezza* of Field, Bellini, and especially Chopin. The Barcarolle, the F Minor Nocturne, the later mazurkas, and especially the Valse-Fantaisie in B minor exemplify this *morbidezza* and embody a strain of pessimism and world-weariness that was to reach full flower in Chaikovsky's last three symphonies. To some extent this tendency is shown in Glinka's romance-like songs, with their predilection for the minor mode.

Glinka's treatment of folk song influenced composers throughout the century. He employed such techniques as changing the harmonies, placing the song in different voices, or contriving effective countermelodies, all of which gave variety to repeated melodic material. One of his favorite devices, the use of sinuous chromatic inner parts, is found also in Cherubini, Beethoven, and Auber but became even more of a hallmark of various "national" composers' treatment of folk-like melodies, as Example 10-3 shows.

EXAMPLE 10-3. (a) Beethoven, Quartet Op. 59, No. 2, third movement; (b) Glinka, *Kamarinskaya;* (c) Grieg, Ballade, Op. 24 (Copyright 1918 by G. Schirmer, Inc. Reproduced by permission); (d) Delius, *Appalachia* (Copyright 1906 by Harmonie, Berlin. Copyright 1927 by Universal Edition. Reproduced by permission).

(c) Andante espressivo

(d) Andante

Glinka's work was continued by Aleksandr Sergeyevich Dargomÿzhsky (1813–1869), whose music contains a vein of lyricism lacking in Glinka's works and leads directly to the soaring melodies of Chaikovsky (Example 10-4). In such "experimental" works, however, as the *Overture on Finnish Themes* and *The Stone Guest* (Pushkin's version of the Don Giovanni story), Dargomÿzhsky intensified Glinka's dissonances and linear writing; these and his experiments in musical declamation led to the speech-dominated vocal writing in Musorgsky's operas and songs.

Five quite dissimilar Russian composers—Cui, Borodin, Balakirev, Musorgsky, and Rimsky-Korsakov—have frequently been arbitrarily grouped together under the headings of "the New Russian School," "the

EXAMPLE 10-4. Dargomÿzhsky, *Rusalka*, Act III.

mighty little handful," or simply as "The Five." All of these composers were essentially self-taught and were frequently engaged in other than musical occupations: Musorgsky as an army officer and civil servant, Rimsky-Korsakov as a naval officer, Borodin as a research chemist, and Cui as a career army officer who eventually became a lieutenant general of engineers.

César Cui (Kyui, 1835–1918) is known today, if at all, only as a writer of good salon music (Example 10-6a). Aleksandr Porfirievich Borodin (1833–1887), the least productive composer of this group, is the most famous for his Oriental exoticisms in such works as the Polovetsian Dances from his unfinished opera *Prince Igor,* his symphonic sketch *In*

the Steppes of Central Asia, and his Second Symphony. Mily Aleksandro-
vich Balakirev (1837–1910), the mentor of this group, was the principal
generator of new musical ideas which, were, however, treated more
effectively by others in his circle. The Orientalia of his brilliant piano
fantasy *Islamey* (1869) were more strikingly exploited by Borodin in his
exotic works, and one need but compare Balakirev's symphonic poem
Tamar (1867–1882; Balakirev would often spend several years on one
composition) with Rimsky-Korsakov's *Scheherazade* (1888) to see that
Balakirev had the original ideas but that Rimsky-Korsakov could treat
them in a slicker and more popularly effective manner.

Balakirev's *Russia—1000 Years* (1869) was a seminal work not only
for his colleagues but also for Chaikovsky's symphonic developments and
for treatments of folk music by such disparate Western composers as
Gustav Holst and Henry F. Gilbert. Perhaps the most striking contrast
in Balakirev's music occurs in his *King Lear* overture (1859): a Schumannesque closing theme is followed by a storm scene in which the juxtaposition of two chords whose roots are an augmented fourth apart
anticipates a comparable harmonic progression in Musorgsky's *Boris
Godunov* (Example 10-5a; a similar progression occurs also in *Islamey*).
Almost all of Balakirev's later piano music, published during the opening
years of the twentieth century, is a nostalgic summing-up of the Romantic melancholy that we have previously seen in Field, Glinka, and

EXAMPLE 10-5. (a) Balakirev, Overture to *King Lear;* (b), (c). Musorgsky,
Boris Godunov, Prologue.

(c)

Chopin. The greatest composer of this group is Modest Petrovich Musorgsky (1839–1881), the composer of operas in various states of completion or revision (*Boris Godunov, Khovanchina*), some keyboard music, and a number of superb songs.

An army officer or civil servant during most of his life, Musorgsky deplored his lack of "polish" and "craftsmanship," yet it is precisely the lack of Western-oriented training that gives his music such an inhibited power and directness. His harmony is the most empirical of any composer since Monteverdi; one of his most interesting devices is the coloristic juxtaposition of chords unrelated by conventional standards but containing two common tones: note how his treatment of this device (Example 10-5b) is more brutal and direct than Balakirev's (Example 10-5a), and one need only compare Beethoven's (Example 10-3a) and Musorgsky's (Example 10-5c) harmonizations of the same melody to be aware of the basic differences between Western and Russian harmonic practices. In *Boris Godunov* Musorgsky contrasts Western and Eastern idioms in the third (Polish) act, added to provide a love interest to the opera, and in the powerful "Revolutionary" scene, where the tonal chant of the Jesuits is opposed to the Russian hymnody of the rascally monks Missail and Varlaam. Russian folk or ecclesiastical music dominates the choral scenes (as also in *Khovanchina*), and folk song idioms characterize the charming scene between Boris' son Fyodor and his nurse. The soloistic high points of the opera, written in Musorgsky's declamatory style, are Boris' soliloquies; the confrontation scene between Boris and Prince Shuisky, followed by the "Clock Scene" in which Boris imagines he sees the corpse of the murdered child Tsarevich (it is quite probable that Alban Berg had this scene in mind when he wrote his more brutal passages in *Wozzeck*); and Boris' death.

Musorgsky, building on Dargomÿzhsky's unsuccessful experiments, succeeded in creating a speech-dominated Slavic musical language much as Caccini, Schütz, Lully, and Purcell had done for Western European languages during the Baroque era. The Slavic countries had lagged in achieving this kind of declamation possibly because of the widespread performance of Western operas in translation, the reluctance of singers (especially female) to try anything new, and the pervasiveness of Western melodic idioms which could not readily be adapted to Slavic or Magyar languages; other Eastern countries did not develop their own speech-dominated musical languages until the time of Janáček and Bartók early in the twentieth century. Musorgsky succeeded because he combined realistic declamation with a compelling musical expression that is declamatory rather than lyric, interjectory rather than melodically continuous, motivic rather than phrase-dominated, variable rather than symmetrical; it often relies on irregular or complex musical meters, and it is often reinforced by empirical harmonies and snatches of folk or ecclesiastical motives.

In both his operas and songs Musorgsky achieves a realism comparable to Courbet's in painting or Zola's in literature. Like his contemporary Fyodor Dostoyevsky (1821–1881), Musogorsky excels in the psychological portrayal of character and thus anticipates twentieth-century realism and expressionism. Compare, as an illustration, a sentimental romance by Cui with an example of "slice-of-life" realism by Musorgsky, who wrote the text as well as the music for his song "Kozel" to describe a girl frightened by a dirty, hairy goat yet who has no qualms about marrying an old man with the same unattractive qualities (Example 10-6). The unprepared, dissonant augmented triads help communicate

EXAMPLE 10-6. (a) Cui, "Zhelanie" (Desire), Op. 57, No. 25; (b) Musorgsky, "Kozel" (The He-Goat).

the atmosphere of distaste and revulsion. In both text and music one can see the sharp contrast between Cui's (and Pushkin's) Romanticism and Musorgsky's brutal rejection of these conventions. Musorgsky's posthumous influence was strong not only on Janáček and Bartók but also on Debussy, who spent a brief time in Russia, and who continued Musorgsky's work in using coloristic harmonies, seemingly unrelated chords in succession, and declamatory expression.

Nikolai Andreyevich Rimsky-Korsakov (1844–1908), the most professionally trained musician of "The Five," arranged, orchestrated, reorchestrated, completed, and "improved" many of the works of his colleagues; his versions of Glinka's Valse-Fantaisie and Musorgsky's *Boris*

Godunov, for example, are better known than the original works. Although his own orchestral works have declined in popularity, new interest has been directed to his operas as the source of his best music. Rimsky-Korsakov excels in continuing Glinka's portrayals of the exotic, fantastic, and grotesque, often through the use of artificial scales; this is best shown in his last opera, *Le Coq d'Or* (1907). In his best and most varied opera, *Sadko* (1898), the composer juxtaposes fantasy with portraits of mediaeval Russia (including a chorus in rapid 11/4 meter), folk-like scenes to represent the "real" world, and some of the best musical portrayals of the ocean ever composed. Example 10-7 shows (a) the "real"

EXAMPLE 10-7. Rimsky-Korsakov, *Sadko.*

world of the clowns; (b) the free-floating chromatic harmony of the *russalky* (water-maidens), aquatic but hardly musical kin of Wagner's Rhinemaidens; and (c) an artificial scale used for the leitmotive of the sea-king's daughter.

Other Russian composers turned to the West for their models. Anton Grigorievich Rubinstein (1829–1894), a conservative and eclectic cosmopolitan whose D minor Concerto was once a staple of the pianist's

repertoire, did much to bring Western standards of musical education
to Russia. Pyotr Ilyich Chaikovsky (1840–1893) was far more oriented toward the West than the composers of "The Five," but incorporated Russian folk music within an essentially Western framework in the first two
of his six symphonies. His lyricism, inherited from Dargomÿzhsky, is best
seen in the slow movements of his symphonies, his operas (especially
Eugene Onegin, probably his finest work), and in his ballets; *Swan Lake*
is a direct successor of the underwater ballet in Act IV of Dargomÿzhsky's *Rusalka.* In his music Chaikovsky displayed a strong if not subtle
harmonic sense, obtaining his effects chiefly through oscillations around
the mediants or submediants (as in Example 10-8) or through clustered
non-harmonic tones.

EXAMPLE 10-8. Chaikovsky, *Eugene Onegin,* Act I.

Chaikovsky's best instrumental works are his ballets and his instrumental cycles based on Western forms of absolute music; in some of them one can even see a neo-classic influence. Chaikovsky admired Mozart above all other composers, and in contrast to the extreme subjectivity of his last three symphonies and the four-movement symphonic poem *Manfred,* he shows an almost Classic restraint and balance in such works as the Op. 11 String Quartet (the slow movement the famous "Andante Cantabile"), Third Symphony, Second Piano Concerto, and Serenade for Strings—these works, incidentally, being his principal instrumental cycles in the major mode, in contrast to the prevailing minor tonalities in most of his compositions.

Like Glinka, Raff, and Rimsky-Korsakov, Chaikovsky created brilliant settings of the folk or popular music of other nations, as in his *Capriccio Italien* or the musical travelogues in the ballets *Swan Lake* and *The Nutcracker.* Russian nationalism was only one of the many colors in his musical palette.

The principal continuer of Chaikovsky's idiom was Aleksandr Konstantinovich Glazunov (1865–1936), best known for his symphonies, violin concerto, and ballets (*The Seasons, Raymonda*), in which his scintillating orchestration and emphasis on the lyric over the dramatic are most pronounced.

To conclude this section, a brief mention should be made of Russian church music during the nineteenth century. Polyphonic settings of the Russian Orthodox liturgy had been made, under Polish influence, in the seventeenth century; Italianate styles, as seen in Bortniansky's church music, were dominant until about 1825. The harmonies of German Romanticism, even in Chaikovsky's settings of the Russian liturgy, prevailed during most of the nineteenth century. Balakirev's appointment as musical director of the Russian Imperial Chapel in 1883, with Rimsky-Korsakov as his assistant, resulted in a sharp change in the style of Russian church music; more emphasis was placed on the original sources, especially the old Znamenny chant and its proper harmonization, which emphasized modal rather than Western harmonies and avoided such Western contrapuntal techniques as imitative counterpoint. Russian church music is unaccompanied by instruments and thus depends exclusively on effective choral writing. Characteristic of this music during its period of efflorescence, from 1883 to 1917, are full and rich sonorities arising from division of the chorus into eight to sixteen voice parts, with doublings of melodic lines or moving inner parts in octaves or thirds; contrasts of male or female voices alone; free rhythm rather than strict meters; harmonizations that emphasize secondary triads and chords with open fifths in contrast to such Western practices as pervasive dominant-tonic relationships, secondary dominants, and coloristic chords; and the exceptionally low basses who sing an octave below the customary bass register. Rakhmaninov and Aleksandr Dmitrievich Kastalsky (1856–1926) were the leading composers of Russian church music in this idiom.

BOHEMIA

Bohemia, the westernmost of the Czech provinces, was musically dominant in this region during the nineteenth century. After the Thirty Years' War (1618–1648) the Austrians subjugated Bohemia and overlaid its culture with Germanic influences to which the natives had to adapt. During the eighteenth century there was a great efflorescence of musical education in Bohemia, for since the Slavs were to be servants, the Austrian authorities thought that music would be a useful trade for them, and the products of especially the instrumental music programs of the Jesuit schools were disseminated throughout Europe: one need but mention Jan Stamic (Johann Stamitz) in Mannheim or Koželuch, Tomašek, and Voríšek in Vienna. Bohemian music remained dominant during the nineteenth century, with that of the other West Slavic peoples (Moravians and Slovaks) regarded as exotic rather than national products; the reason may have been that the Austrian rule over Bohemia was less restrictive than the Hungarian dominance over Slovakia. Tuneful homophony was characteristic of both Baroque and Classic music in Bohemia; combined with a long tradition of instrumental, especially string, performance, this gave birth to the Mannheim school and was a strong influence on Viennese composers from Haydn to Schubert. Yet not until the nineteenth century could Bohemian composers obtain recognition at home and devote themselves to a particularly national style.

František Škroup (1801–1862), the founder of Bohemian musical nationalism, wrote operas to librettos in Czech which contain some of the most technically simple music ever written. His most famous work, *Fidlovačka* (1834), includes folk song, quotations from *Der Freischütz*, and the aria "Kde domoj muj" which later became the Czech national anthem. The models for this work were evidently Rousseau's *Le Devin du village* and the simpler *Singspiele*.

Bedřich Smetana (1824–1884) founded the most viable school of Bohemian national music. His musical development was late, and his first significant compositions date from the late 1850's—tone poems for Göteborg in Sweden, where he was musical director. One of them, *Wallenstein's Camp*, is based on a Bohemian subject and contains almost all of the composer's stylistic traits: passages in fast harmonic rhythm with considerable chromatic activity to create a sense of excitement; dance motives; and a triumphal conclusion. The apex of his orchestral achievement is the cycle of six symphonic poems *Má Vlast* (My Country), of which *The Moldau* is best known. His historical operas dealing with Czech topics (*The Brandenburgers in Bohemia, Dalibor, Libuše*) are virtually unknown outside of Czechoslovakia; they contain many striking passages and show the influence of German Romantic opera, especially in the prevailingly continuous texture and the important role given to the orchestra. On the other hand, his internationally popular *Bartered Bride*, essentially (like *Fidlovačka*) an *opéra comique* transferred to a Czech village, is one of the masterpieces of national opera, with its humorous intrigue, natural characters, tuneful and delightful music (in the opening chorus, authentic folk music). His best keyboard compositions, technically quite difficult, frequently utilize folk dances.

Antonín Dvořák (1841–1904) is the most important Bohemian composer of the nineteenth century. In many ways his career parallels Haydn's: humble peasant beginnings, struggling musical apprenticeship, the slow growth of an international reputation with great acclaim in later life, a deeply fervent religious faith, and a reputation among the mass audience based on only one creative period. Dvořák is one of the few truly "universal" composers of the century in the sense that he wrote in all existing genres; though known primarily as a symphonist, he was both active and skilled as a composer of operas, chamber music, songs, choral works, and piano music.

Though Dvořák's operas are popular in their native land, they have not travelled well; the only one habitually performed outside Czechoslovakia is *Rusalka* (1901). A triptych of overtures, including the popular *Carnival*, dates from 1891; the other symphonic poems were written after Dvořák's return from America and range from the prolix *Golden Spinning Wheel* to the concise *Midday Witch* (both 1896). Posthumous publication of four symphonies that Dvořák repudiated during his lifetime has resulted in a renumbering of the others: the old First, Second, Third, Fourth, and Fifth are now, respectively, the Sixth, Seventh, Fifth, Eighth, and Ninth. As a symphonist Dvořák was most influenced by his friend Brahms, chiefly in his choice of an intermezzo rather than a scherzo in his Fifth, Seventh (a quiet Furiant), and Eighth symphonies and in architectonic structure. Dvořák was not successful in making his Ninth, or "New World" symphony, a cyclic work, for his themes were not well adapted to such treatment, and the so-called Negro and Indian themes cannot be ascribed to indigenous American "intonations" since gapped scales and "Lombard" rhythms are also prominent characteristics of Czech folk music (Example 10-9).

The chamber works from Dvořák's "American" period, the F major Quartet (Op. 96) and the E-flat String Quintet (Op. 97), have been

EXAMPLE 10-9. (a) Dvořák, Symphony No. 9, first movement; (b) Czech folksong "Ja ne, to ty" from Jan Seidel (ed.), *Národ v Písni* (Prague, 1941), p. 175.

overplayed to the exclusion of his finest chamber works, the Op. 81 Piano Quintet and the magnificent late quartets in A-flat, Op. 105, and G, Op. 106. As a violist, Dvořák was a skilled performer of chamber music and showed great and sympathetic understanding of the true possibilities of this medium.

If Smetana's basic dance rhythm is the slow polka, Dvořák's is the furiant, a dance based on the use of hemiola rhythm. In many furiants, Dvořák gives the impression of alternating a pattern consisting of one measure of 3/2 meter with two measures of 3/4 meter, as in Example 10–10b, but sometimes entire sections in one of the two meters (sometimes with cross-rhythms between the two) occur, as in his Slavonic Dance, Op. 46, No. 1. The two collections of Slavonic Dances (Op. 46 and Op. 72), originally for piano four-hands but subsequently orchestrated, are the most popular of his dance pieces: in these he includes not only Bohemian but other Slavic dances.

EXAMPLE 10-10. (a) Smetana, *The Moldau;* (b) Dvořák, Symphony No. 6, third movement.

With the exception of his oratorio *St. Ludmila,* Dvořák was least nationalistic in his large choral works, especially those to sacred texts. In these the composer eschewed dance and folk song idioms and permitted his personal melodic and harmonic styles, the latter marked by a frequent use of secondary triads, to come to the fore. The kinds of musical expression range from the "severe," as in the "Inflammatus" of the *Stabat Mater,* to the soulfully lyric, as in Example 10-11.

EXAMPLE 10-11. Dvořák, "Recordare" from *Requiem,* Op. 89.

Dvořák's most important Czech contemporary was Zdeněk Fibich (1850–1900), chiefly remembered today as a composer of operas. His numerous works include extensive cycles of piano miniatures (the *Images, Impressions and Souvenirs*, Op. 41, being the best of these) which are seemingly a late Romantic counterpart to Mendelssohn's *Songs Without Words* but in reality are a very detailed account of his love affair with one of his students.[2] The important post-Romantic Czech composers are Dvořák's son-in-law, Josef Šuk (1874–1935), and an unjustly neglected composer in the larger orchestral and choral forms, J. B. Foerster (1859–1951). The musical development of the great Moravian composer Leoš Janáček (1854–1928) was late and belongs in a study of the music of the twentieth century rather than in this volume.

SCANDINAVIA

At the opening of the nineteenth century, the major musical figures in Scandinavian countries were German emigrants. The most important was Friedrich Kuhlau (1786–1832), who moved to Copenhagen in 1810 and became a Danish citizen in 1813. Although he is remembered today by his easy sonatinas, which have become favorite teaching pieces for beginning pianists, his sonatas for piano duet and his flute music, highly esteemed by players of that instrument, show Weber's brilliance.

The Swedish composer Franz Berwald (1796–1868) is one of the most original and interesting of the composers of the first half of the nineteenth century. Although he wrote chamber music and operas, his symphonies are the peak of his achievement. His style is highly original, especially in its harmonic and rhythmic aspects, and his use of rhythmic surprise and silence can be compared only with Berlioz'. As Example 10-12 shows, Berwald's music is very melodious, with a subtle and original use of harmonic colors, but the Stockholm audiences for which he wrote had to be educated even to Beethoven's style, and Berwald—too

---

[2] Gerald Abraham, "An Erotic Diary for Piano," *Slavonic and Romantic Music* (New York, 1968), pp. 70–82.

progressive for them—had to support himself chiefly as a maker of ortho-pedic appliances. It is quite probable that Sibelius was well acquainted with such passages in Berwald's music as the opening of the *Sinfonie singulière* and the conclusion of the *Sinfonie sérieuse*.

EXAMPLE 10-12. Berwald, *Sinfonie sérieuse,* second theme of fourth movement.

Although the Danish composer Niels Wilhelm Gade (1817–1890) is written about as the most important Scandinavian composer before Grieg, his music is seldom heard. A protegé of Mendelssohn whose music was popular in Germany and England as well as in his native Denmark, Gade devoted much of his life to developing Danish musical institutions. He is at his best in his miniatures, such as the *Aquarelles* for piano, and as a musical landscape painter, as in the opening movements of his choral work *The Erl-King's Daughter*. A preference for the minor mode, often in its natural form, and a certain austerity are the chief "Nordic" elements in his music.

Edvard Hagerup Grieg (1843–1907), the major figure of nineteenth-century Scandinavian music, insisted that he was a localized Norwegian rather than a generalized Scandinavian composer. In his early works, like the E minor Piano Sonata or the popular A minor Piano Concerto, the influence of Schumann is pronounced. The Ballade, Op. 24, a set of variations on a Norwegian folk melody, is Grieg's most extensive solo piano work and can be regarded as the first of his individual compositions, especially in its harmonic devices (see Example 10-3c). His most important works for piano are arrangements of Norwegian folk dances and ten books of *Lyric Pieces*, which range from simple teaching pieces to such novel "impressionistic" works as the polytonal "Klokkeklang," Op. 54, No. 6. Of his orchestral music, the two suites compiled from his incidental music to Ibsen's drama *Peer Gynt* (1874) are deservedly popular, but his fine choral music, especially his settings of psalms for baritone solo and male chorus, is virtually unknown today.

There are several facets to Grieg's musical personality: there is Grieg the "Mendelssohn of the trolls," evident in "The Hall of the Mountain King" from the *Peer Gynt* music and in the piano piece "Kobold" (Op. 71, No. 3); Grieg the lyricist, seen in the A minor Concerto and the violin sonatas; Grieg the elegiac singer, at his best in the slow movement of the G minor Violin Sonata; Grieg the harmonist, whose effective use of altered chords and non-harmonic tones so strongly influenced MacDowell, Delius, and Gilbert; and finally Grieg the folklorist, whose transcriptions of the *Slåtter* of the Hardanger fiddle—characterized by a major scale with a raised fourth degree, ornamentation, and drone strings —have a very "modern" sound (Example 10-13). Grieg is one of the most individual composers of the nineteenth century, and those whose knowledge of his music is based only on the song "Ich liebe dich," the *Peer*

EXAMPLE 10-13. Grieg, "Bridal March from Telemark," *Slåtter*, Op. 72 (1902). Compare this example with his popular "Wedding Day at Troldhaugen!"

Gynt suites, or his easier *Lyric Pieces* would do well to examine his song cycle *Haugtussa, Slåtter,* and other less hackneyed works.

HUNGARY

During the eighteenth and nineteenth centuries the Hungarians were the most culturally independent of the national groups of eastern Europe. Many Hungarian aristocratic families, of which the Esterházys are best known, were patrons of Viennese composers, who in turn reciprocated by using "Hungarian" motives in their works. The separation of Hungarian, Turkish, and gypsy elements in Hungarian music of the nineteenth century is an almost impossible task, inasmuch as Hungary was occupied by the Turks for nearly two centuries and gypsy musicians were the chief disseminators of what became known as the Hungarian style. As in most of eastern Europe, folk and popular music was transmitted by oral rather than written tradition, and those who wrote the music down or incorporated it into their compositions were often far removed from the origins of the oral tradition of this music. What Western composers wrote as "Turkish" music was characterized by tonal instability and a marked rhythmic emphasis, often helped by a lavish use of percussion. In example 10-14a, note the tonal instability of the introduction, the major scale with the raised fourth in the melody after the introduction, and the strongly percussive rhythm. The vogue for "Turk-

ish" music lasted until the early 1820's, when the general European revulsion against the Turkish atrocities in the Greek War of Independence
abruptly terminated its popularity.

EXAMPLE 10-14. "Turkish" (a) and Hungarian (b), (c) influences in Western
art music. (a) Mozart, *Die Entführung aus dem Serail,* Act I; (b) Beethoven,
"Eroica" Symphony, last movement; (c) Schubert, *Divertissement à l'hongroise,*
D. 818.

8th-note rhythm in bass, percussion

In the middle of the eighteenth century a new kind of Hungarian popular music appeared, the *verbunkos* or recruiting music, originally played by bands of gypsy string players which accompanied Austrian recruiting officers to peasant villages. This music, disseminated by gypsy orchestras and composers of light music, soon became the favorite music of the Hungarian bourgeoisie and lesser nobility and, through the works of Germanic composers from Haydn to Brahms, became known as "Hungarian" music in the West until Bartók's folk song researches in the early twentieth century. Highly ornamented slow passages, syncopations, a characteristic cadential pattern (Example 10-14c, 15a, 15b), and fast passages in a fiery duple meter with much instrumental fioritura are characteristic of this style.

Liszt's Hungarian works are chiefly utilizations of the *verbunkos* style by a highly cosmopolitan composer, and his Hungarian Rhapsodies and book *The Gypsy in Music,* as well as the continued exploitation of the *verbunkos* style by Raff and Brahms (Hungarian gypsy music had the same influence on German composers that Spanish gypsy music had on their French colleagues), gave the West a false picture of Hungarian music. Although the *verbunkos* style degenerated into the salon piece or "Csárdas Princess" operetta during the closing years of the nineteenth century, it won a new lease on life with Kodály's popular compositions like *Háry János* and the *Galanta Dances.*

As the Viennese school of composition declined in influence after 1820, French and Italian opera became popular in Hungary. Their influences were effectively combined with the *verbunkos* style by Ferenc Erkel (1810–1893), Hungary's most important composer of this period, whose principal achievements were grand operas based on Hungarian history. His best-known work, *Hunyádi László* (1844), utilizes a mixture of styles: the *verbunkos* in its slow aspects (the farewell duet cited as Example 10-15c) or in the coloratura fireworks of the "La Grange" aria of Act II for his sympathetic characters, and an "international" style,

EXAMPLE 10-15. The *verbunkos* style in popular and art music. (a) "Saltus Hungaricus" from the Martonfi MS. (late eighteenth century),[3] (b) Márk Rószavölgyi, "First Hungarian Social Dance," 1842; (c) Ferenc Erkel, *Hunyádi László,* Act IV.

(a)

(b) Allegretto

[3] Cited in P. P. Domokos, "Magyar Táncdallamok a XVIII, Századból" in B. Szabolcsi and D. Bartha (eds.), *Az Opera Történetéböl* (Budapest, 1961), p. 284.

largely based on Meyerbeer's, for such unsympathetic personages as King László V. In his later operas, like *Bánk Bán* (1860) and *Dósza György* (1867), Erkel's development surprisingly parallels Verdi's in its increasing musical depth and use of harmonic and orchestral resources.

ENGLAND

England's prosperity, which attracted many foreign musicians and composers during the nineteenth century, hampered the development of a native serious art music. William Sterndale Bennett (1816–1875), highly praised by Schumann, gave evidence of talent in early works like his Piano Concerto and the overture *The Naiads,* which resembles in many respects Mendelssohn's "Melusine" overture; but the choir loft, the hymnal, and the festival chorus provided the main opportunities for serious English composers during the bulk of the century. The cathedral music of Samuel Sebastian Wesley (1810–1876) and the anthems of John Goss (1800–1880) are solid and effective, the best examples of Victorian church music; the processional hymns of the time, e.g., "Holy, Holy, Holy" by John Bacchus Dykes (1821–1876), have no rivals. But compositions in the larger vocal forms by English composers were too strongly influenced by foreign models: first Spohr and Mendelssohn, then Gounod and Dvořák, whose choral works were extremely popular in England. Perhaps England's most noteworthy contributions during this period were its school of theorists, best represented by Ebenezer Prout (1835–1909) and Donald F. Tovey (1875–1940), and the deft operettas of Arthur Sullivan (1842–1900), who combined a fine sense of craftsmanship with the piquancy of Auber in the works he wrote in collaboration with W. S. Gilbert; the most characteristic elements are the "patter songs," which derived from the fast parlando of the comic baritone arias of Rossini, and the bouncy choruses accompanied by a thrumming accompaniment in 6/8 or 2/4 meter.

Edward Elgar (1857–1934) is remembered today chiefly through his *Pomp and Circumstance* marches, models for the ceremonial processional march at which subsequent English composers have excelled. Moods of placid contemplativeness or elegiac reflection also are present in many of his orchestral works, of which the "Enigma" Variations (1899) shows the most variety. As a composer of oratorios, of which *The Dream of Gerontius* (1900) is best known, Elgar excelled in the portrayal of a Christian heaven, musically the opposite pole from the diabolism of Berlioz and Liszt. Frederick Delius (1862–1934), another late-developing composer, spent most of his days in France and during his lifetime was most celebrated in Germany. His English nationalist music consists of genre pictures of the countryside (*Brigg Fair, On Hearing the First Cuckoo in Spring*) which can be compared with the landscape paintings of John Constable (1776–1837). His rich harmonic sense was influenced to some extent by Grieg (compare Examples 10-3c and 10-3d), but his characteristic blend of lush chromatic harmony and static harmonic rhythm repels some listeners. His *Appalachia* (1902), a fine musical portrait of the American South, was inspired by its composer's stay in Florida and Virginia during the mid-1880's.

UNITED STATES

In 1800 the concert life of the urban Eastern seaboard was a pale reflection of London's musical activities, but the opening of the continent, the rise of cities in the Midwest, and the streams of immigration provided an increased strength for American musical life. Not until the twentieth century, however, did the strains of American popular music—the "singing school" tune, the minstrel-show tune, the gospel hymn, and the martial or sentimental Civil War song—become incorporated into art music; most nineteenth-century American art music was based on European models by composers who had studied there, and American musical nationalism was based chiefly on exploring Afro-American and, to a lesser extent, Indian music.

Louis Moreau Gottschalk (1829–1869) expressed the Creole culture of the Gulf coast and the Caribbean islands rather than that of Anglo-Saxon Protestant America. His use of Louisianan (Example 10-16a), Cuban, and Puerto Rican tunes and rhythms, his unusual piano sonorities which exploit the extreme upper ranges of the instrument, and a certain piquancy of expression raise his best piano compositions above the level of the "salon piece," although his *The Dying Poet* is the epitome of Romantic sentimentality.

The most important American composer at the end of the century was Edward MacDowell (1861–1908), a pupil of Joachim Raff who was also influenced by Grieg, especially in his harmony and musical miniatures. MacDowell's "Indian" Suite for orchestra is directly in line of descent from Raff's Hungarian travelogues, and his sonatas exploit a certain vein of Celtic nationalism. MacDowell is at his best in his genre pictures of the northeastern countryside and his finely wrought songs.

When Dvořák came to America in the early 1890's he advised the local composers to turn to Negro melodies for inspiration. The chief utilizer of Afro-American melodies and rhythms was MacDowell's pupil Henry F. Gilbert (1868–1928), both in his larger orchestral works like the *Dance in Place Congo* and in his collections of piano miniatures like the *Negro Dances* or *A Rag Bag*, which show the influences of the cakewalk and the new dance craze of ragtime (Example 10-16b), which was being raised to a near-art form in the piano rags of the Negro composer, Scott Joplin (1868–1917). Although Gilbert's treatment of Negro material may seem patronizing today, he was serious and sincere in trying to reconcile these popular idioms with art music. In contrast, Horatio Parker (1863–1919) is the best of the "international" American composers; his oratorio *Hora Novissima* (1893) is one of the finest works written for the English choral festivals, but the eclecticism of his operas *Mona* and *Fairyland* prevented them from surviving. Mention should be made of the Irish-born Victor Herbert (1859–1924), whose successful operettas have overshadowed his fine serious compositions, particularly his magnificent Second Concerto for violoncello.[4]

EXAMPLE 10-16. Comparative treatments of Afro-American musical material by American composers: (a) Gottschalk, *Bamboula;* (b) Gilbert, "Br'er Rabbit" from *Three American Dances* (Copyright 1919 by The Boston Music Co. Reproduced by permission).

[4] The reader is referred for a much more comprehensive evaluation to H. Wiley Hitchcock's *Music in the United States: A Historical Introduction* (Prentice-Hall, 1969) in this series.

BIBLIOGRAPHICAL NOTES

Only the most selective bibliography can be given. Concerning Russian music, Boris Asafiev's *Russian Music since the Beginning of the 19th Century* (tr. Alfred Swan, Ann Arbor, 1953) is clumsily written and translated; more reliable are Gerald Abraham's *Studies in Russian Music* (London, 1935) and his successive volumes and articles on this topic and R. A. Leonard's *A History of Russian Music* (1956; reprint, New York, 1968), principally based on secondary sources. James Bakst's *A History of Russian-Soviet Music* (New York, 1966) is a Marxist-oriented survey of limited value. Gerald Seaman's *History of Russian Music* (New York, 1967; volume I through Dargomÿzhsky) has been assailed as having been cribbed from Russian secondary sources (see Malcolm Brown's review of this and Leonard's study in *Notes*, XXVI, 1969). Boris Schwarz' *Two Hundred Years of Russian Music, 1770–1970,* to appear in this series, is by a distinguished authority on Russian music and should be the definitive survey of this topic in English. Among the good translations of primary sources dealing with Russian music are Richard Mudge, *Mikhail Ivanovich Glinka: Memoirs* (Norman, 1963); Jan Leyda and Sergei Bertensson, *The Musorgsky Reader* (New York, 1952), Wladimir Lukend, *The Diaries of Tchaikovsky* (New York, 1945); J. A. Joffe, *Rimsky-Korsakov: My Musical Life* (New York, 1942); and Florence Jonas, *V. V. Stasov: Selected Essays on Music* (London, 1968), by the first champion of "The Five."

The best biographies of Russian composers are Serge Dianin's *Borodin* (London, 1963) and Edward Garden's *Balakirev* (New York, 1967), a fine study of this neglected composer. Biographies of Chaikovsky in Western languages have focused on his life rather than his music; a good recent example is the biography by Lawrence and Elisabeth Hanson (New York, 1966). Gerald Abraham's *Slavonic and Romantic Music* (New York, 1968) contains essays on Russian and Czech composers.

Rosa Newmarch's *The Music of Czechoslovakia* (London, 1942) is badly out of date; a new volume on this topic is needed. For the major Czech composers there is a highly informative biography of Smetana by Brian Large (London, 1970) and an excellent study of Dvořák by John Clapham (London, 1966).

John Horton's *Scandinavian Music: A Short Survey* (London, 1963) is an excellent introduction to this topic. More detail is provided by the biographies of Berwald by Robert Layton (London, 1959) and of Grieg by Monrad Johansen (Princeton, 1938) and Dag Schjeldrup-Ebbe (Oslo, 1964), which discusses this composer's career only to 1867. Bence Szabolcsi's *A Concise History of Hungarian Music* (English translation, London, 1964) is an excellent survey, accompanied by an anthology of recorded music. Earlier histories of English music are a reaction against the Victorian era, now corrected by Frank Howes' *The English Musical Renaissance* (London, 1966). Michael Kennedy's *Portrait of Elgar* (London and New York, 1968) is a fine full-length study; the best concise accounts of the music of Elgar and Delius are in William W. Austin's *Music in the 20th Century* (New York, 1966).

H. Wiley Hitchcock's *Music in the United States* (see footnote 4) is the best one-volume survey of American music, though Gilbert Chase's *America's Music* (2nd ed., 1966) is still valuable; Wilfred Mellers' *Music in a New Found Land* (New York, 1965) is an interesting view by an English critic. Hitchcock's bibliographies should be consulted for further studies of American composers.

Much of the music by nationalist composers discussed in this chapter is very difficult to obtain or to consult except at major research libraries. Kalmus has reprinted Pavel Lamm's authoritative edition of Musorgsky's works, and complete editions of the music of Dvořák, Chaikovsky, Fibich, Dargomÿzhsky, and Berwald are in progress. The complete works of Glinka and Rimsky-Korsakov have been published in the Soviet Union. At present only the piano works of Balakirev, Gottschalk, Grieg, and Smetana are being published in a "collected works." Cherepnin's *Russische Musik-Anthologie* (Bonn, 1966), is limited to Russian music before Glinka and contains mis-attributions and suspect editions among its sources. A reprint of the music published by the Wa-Wan Press in the early twentieth century (Arno Press, 1970) makes much post-Romantic American music available, and there are recordings of many compositions by nineteenth-century American composers issued by the Society for the Preservation of the American Musical Heritage. Da Capo Press has initiated a series of reprints of scores, many of them from the nineteenth century, under the general title *Earlier American Music* (ed. H. Wiley Hitchcock).

ELEVEN

THE TWILIGHT
OF ROMANTICISM

The term "post-Romanticism" is often used to describe the music of composers born between 1850 and 1880 who adhered neither to an overtly nationalistic school (although such "national" composers as Delius, Foerster, Gilbert, and Glazunov wrote some works in a post-Romantic idiom on "international" themes) nor to the musical revolution accomplished by Debussy during the 1890's. Yet there are two "post-Romanticisms," one occurring at the end of the nineteenth century and the other at the beginning of the twentieth, with the point of demarcation lying between 1898 and 1905.

The post-Romanticism of the nineteenth century is that of the twilight of a musical epoch and represents consolidations of musical trends initiated by earlier composers. On the other hand, twentieth-century post-Romanticism is a separate if small epoch in itself, a unique transitional period. An expression from art history, "mannerism," is appropriate for this period, as it is for describing the chansons of the late fourteenth century in France and the chromatic madrigals of Gesualdo; it indicates a period of transition, distortion, exaggeration, epigonism, and a running up musical blind alleys, although many splendid works were the result. A few composers worked in both kinds of post-Romantic idioms, especially Richard Strauss and Gustav Mahler; the dividing point for the former was his change in emphasis from the symphonic poem to opera, and for the latter the interval between his Fourth and Fifth symphonies.

Twentieth-century post-Romanticism, covered briefly in Eric Salzman's *Twentieth-Century Music* and in greater detail in William Austin's *Music in the 20th Century*, deserves more intensive investigation. However, this volume is not the place for it, for twentieth-century post-Romanticism, despite its epigonism and blind alleys, looked to the future: one need but cite the new paths for the symphony found by Carl Nielsen (1865–1931) and Jan Sibelius (1865–1957), the searches for ways of combining Baroque contrapuntal techniques and Classic formal structures with new expressive means made by Ferruccio Busoni (1866–1924) and Max Reger (1873–1916), or the logical progression from exaggerated hyper-Romanticism to serial music achieved by Arnold Schoenberg (1874–1951) and his disciples Anton Webern (1883–1945) and Alban Berg (1885–1935), whose early compositions were also post-Romantic.

The inescapable conclusion is that the 1890's saw not only the last works of Verdi and Brahms but also the first mature works of Debussy and Schoenberg, and it is therefore one of the more tangled decades of the history of music as well as one of the least explored. It is hoped that the remainder of this chapter will provide some incentive for further study of this period.

ITALIAN OPERA AFTER LA TRAVIATA

Verdi, after writing *La Traviata* in 1853, went through a creative hiatus shorter than Wagner's fallow spell between *Lohengrin* and *Das Rheingold,* for he was now writing operas for France and thus came under the influence of the best elements of Meyerbeer's style—harmonic richness and appreciation of the dramatic and gestic functions of the orchestra. Verdi's first opera in this vein, *The Sicilian Vespers* (1855), has vanished from the repertoire although its overture, one of Verdi's last full-scale works in this genre, is a magnificent example of the "old warhorse" overture once a staple of outdoor band concerts. *Un Ballo in maschera* (1859), based on the libretto Scribe wrote for Auber about the assassination of Gustav III of Sweden in 1792 but with the locale changed by censor's decree to colonial Massachusetts, looks back to the melodrama of *Rigoletto* but also ahead, in the Act II finale, to the comic genius of *Falstaff*. *Simone Boccanegra* (1857, revised 1881) is an opera reminiscent of Verdi's earlier works and is chiefly a psychological drama on the order of *Luisa Miller*. *La Forza del destino* (1862) and *Don Carlo* (1867) are the most representative operas of this "experimental" period, which closed in 1871 with the first two acts of *Aïda*.

Several features are common to these operas. Most of them were given their first performance outside of Italy. Except for *Un Ballo in maschera*, they are long and contain many divertissements, either unrelated to or tenuously connected with the plot, which are frequently omitted in performance (even the entire first act of *Don Carlo*). The musical inspiration of these operas is uneven, with *Don Carlo* the most consistently good, and they are appreciated more by singers and connoisseurs of opera than by the general public. Spectacle plays an important role in many of them, and in all the tenor-baritone duet is a climactic moment, especially in *Don Carlo* where the "reminiscence motive" of freedom is grandiloquently proclaimed. The conclusion of the grandest soprano arias is often a magnificent soaring melody, a kind first introduced in Act II of *La Traviata* and brought to its heights in *La Forza del destino* (Example 11-1), *Don Carlo*, and the first act of *Aida*; such melo-

EXAMPLE 11-1. Verdi, *La Forza del destino*, Act II.

dies are accompanied by string tremolos and effectively utilize non-harmonic tones. Also retained from the period of *La Traviata*, but abandoned by Verdi after *La Forza del destino*, is the set-number in a closed form, usually a duet, characterized by square construction and an even quarter-note rhythm in the style of Example 7-3d, from the third act of *La Traviata*. In these operas between 1855 and 1871 Verdi's harmony is much richer than formerly, his tonality is broader, and his orchestra plays an important part in the musical dramaturgy instead of being confined to ritornelli, fortissimo interjections, and strumming accompaniments.

Verdi's final creative period includes not only a delightful string quartet, written while *Aïda* was in rehearsal, and the magnificent *Requiem* (1874) and other sacred choral works, but also the last two acts of *Aïda* and the two glowing sunsets of Italian Romantic opera: *Otello* (1887) for the serious style and *Falstaff* (1893) for the comic. These two operas display the quintessence of Verdi's harmonic, orchestral, and psychological development; in them his enthusiastic vulgarity, which persisted as late as the Act II finale of *Aïda*, was finally purged; and the character portrayal in *Otello* is equaled in musico-psychological insight only by Musorgsky. *Falstaff* is actually the epitome of Wagner's theories of opera, for plot and music, orchestra and singers, are on an equal footing; the demarcations between set-numbers are dissolved; and the aria, except for Falstaff's declamatory soliloquies, is replaced by deft ensemble writing. One need but compare Falstaff's soliloquies or Iago's "Credo" in Act II of *Otello* with Example 7-4 to see the range of Verdi's development.

Verdi overshadowed his later contemporaries, who were chiefly "one-opera" composers. Arrigo Boito (1842–1918), the most musically imaginative of this group, made his best contributions to music by writing the librettos for *Otello* and *Falstaff;* his one major opera, *Mefistofele* (1868, revised 1875), is a grandiose and impressive work but, perhaps because it also contains too much music, is one of that triad of "magnificent failures" of nineteenth-century opera which includes also Berlioz' *Les Troyens* and Cornelius' *Barber of Bagdad*. The somberly bitter-sweet tone of the operas of Alfredo Catalani (1854–1893) has affected their popularity, though his music is the most important Italian influence on Puccini's style. The best Italianate opera by a contemporary of Verdi is *Il Guarany* (1870) by the Brazilian A. Carlos Gomes (1836–1896), where intonations of Amazonian Indian melodies are woven into an operatic canvas comparable to that of *Don Carlo*.

Verismo (realism) is the generic term for a short-lived operatic movement which attempted to combine the musical portrayal of raw emotions, seen best previously in *Il Trovatore*, with the literary realism of such authors as Emile Zola (1840–1902) and Giovanni Verga (1840–1922). Only two Italian successes resulted: *Cavalleria rusticana* (1890) by

Pietro Mascagni (1863–1945) and *I Pagliacci* (1892) by Ruggiero Leoncavallo (1858–1919). Neither composer was able to repeat his success and their other operas have sunk into oblivion, though there are many beautiful portions in Mascagni's *L'Amico Fritz* (1891). The best verist work is actually Czech: Janáček's *Jenufa* (completed 1903), one of the initial masterworks of twentieth-century opera.

Since the operas of Giacomo Puccini (1858–1924) span both the nineteenth and twentieth centuries and his two masterpieces, *Gianni Schicchi* (1918) and *Turandot* (incomplete at his death), are outside the chronological confines of this volume, attention need be paid only to the genesis of his style. Except for the memorable soaring melodies often sung by soprano and tenor in unison at the climax of a love duet, Puccini's Italian model was Catalani rather than Verdi, and he was principally influenced by French *opéra lyrique,* especially in his focusing of attention on the wayward heroine and in his use of understatement and restraint. Puccini's writing for the voice and his operatic orchestration deserve detailed study by today's opera composers. His harmony is a delicately pastel synthesis of all the effective devices from Liszt through Debussy, especially an employment of augmented triads and half-diminished-seventh chords; and his "modal" harmony, which he shares with Fauré, may well stem from the organ accompaniments to Gregorian chant which became increasingly used during the nineteenth century. The most memorable moments of his operas are often the arias and the love duets, usually containing an intense and climactic melody, subtly harmonized and closely bound to the orchestral accompaniment (Example 11-2). Whereas critics may disagree about the integrity of Puccini's music, no one can deny his fine sense for the theatre or his attention to subtle musical details.

EXAMPLE 11-2. Puccini, *La Bohème,* Act I.

CENTRAL EUROPE

During the closing years of the nineteenth century Vienna again became a musical capital. Brahms and Bruckner were still active, Wagner's music had gained impressive support despite the opposition of the critic Eduard Hanslick (1825–1904), and despite the decline of the Austro-Hungarian Empire Vienna was virtually the crossroads of Europe. On the other hand, the unification of Germany after 1870, though it resulted in centralizing political and financial power in Berlin, saw a qualitative decline in Germany's musical energies although an immense amount of music, now mostly forgotten, continued to be written and performed.

Hugo Wolf (1860–1903) came from a border province of the Austro-Hungarian Empire and is said to have been partially of Slavic (Slovene) descent. His reputation rests almost exclusively on his songs, though he made ventures into opera, the symphonic poem, and chamber music. His creative process consisted of short bursts of intense activity, during which he wrote as many as three songs in a single day, followed by extensive periods of fallowness. One writer has speculated that the works on which Wolf's reputation rests were the product of only eighteen months of effort spread over nine years: his first major songs date from 1888 and he became incurably insane in 1897.

To explain the frequently made claim that Wolf set the "inner meaning" of a poem to music is a difficult task. One writer has suggested the concept of "song as an extension into musical terms of the essence of the poem," with the central issue not the poem's literal meaning but "its connotations, its ambiguities, its paradoxes."[1] Frequently Wolf entitled his collections of songs "Poems for solo voice and piano," showing that the poem was paramount in his thinking. Wolf's ideal was as complete a synthesis as possible of word and tone, with the vocal declamation corresponding to the rhythm of the poem and the depiction of its imagery while the piano part (comparable to the way in which Wagner had treated his orchestra) was the source of the musical atmosphere, serving to create a background for the poem and to express emotions that the singing voice alone cannot suggest.

Wolf had the best literary taste of all the composers of nineteenth-century song, and his major works in this genre consist of a prodigious number of settings of poems by Mörike, Eichendorff, Goethe, and lesser poets or of translations of Spanish and Italian folk poetry; virtually all these are in collections designated by the name or nationality of the poet. The songs show a great variety of mood and emotional intensity, ranging from deep pathos to ironical humor; from placid contemplativeness, seen in the songs dealing with nature, to rollicking waltzes or songs in a popular style (on the evidence of "Auftrag," Wolf could have made a fortune as a composer of light music); from deeply mystical religious ecstasy, best seen in the *Spanish Songbook*, to a realism exceeding even Musorgsky's, as in "Zur Warnung," Mörike's description of a hangover, in setting which Wolf pushed nineteenth-century tonality to its limits.

Wolf's songs are frequently described as being piano-dominated and filled with chromatic harmony; like all generalizations, this one has its exceptions. One may profitably compare the songs "Peregrina I" and "Peregrina II" from the Mörike songs: the former contains one of Wolf's finest vocal melodies, supported by the piano, whereas the other is a piano-dominated song with the voice declaiming the text; both songs are linked by a common ritornello. Even as late as the *Italian Songbook* some of the songs, e.g., "Mein Liebster singt," are independent piano pieces with words attached. The most common kind of song has an ostinato-like accompaniment, often subtly varied in the course of the song. Many of the songs are declamatory with a chromatic substructure, but some are

[1] Jack M. Stein, "Poem and Music in Hugo Wolf's Mörike Songs," *Musical Quarterly*, LIII (1967), 22–23; see also his *Poetry and Music in the German Lied* (Cambridge, Mass., 1971), pp. 155–202.

quite diatonic, yet with the phrases extended to avoid square-cut writing, e.g., "Fussreise" from the Mörike songs.

Wolf's rich harmonic palette derives from that of Liszt and Wagner. His sharpest dissonance is the chord of the major seventh, chiefly associated with the more tortured aspects of religious mysticism, as in Example 11-3. Actually, most of Wolf's harmonic vocabulary and turns

EXAMPLE 11-3. Wolf, "Herr, was trägt der Boden hier" from the *Spanish Songbook* (1889–1890).

of expression may be found in the miniatures of MacDowell and Grieg. Although some of the songs, especially the narrative ballads, are rather long, almost all of the finest are extremely concentrated and show great restraint and economy of means; in structure they are through-composed but unified by the musical patterns of the accompaniment.

Wolf is a major forerunner of the twentieth-century Viennese school. The intense concentration of many of his songs inspired the similarly condensed instrumental compositions of Schoenberg and Webern; the "progressive tonality," with many changes of key, of several of his songs contributed in no small degree to the breakdown of traditional tonality;[2] and Wolf's realism anticipates the expressionism of Schoenberg's *Erwartung* or Berg's *Wozzeck* and *Lulu*.

Gustav Mahler (1860–1911), like Wolf, came from a border province of Austria. Except for an early oratorio, Mahler limited himself to two musical genres, the song and the symphony, and described himself as a "holiday composer" ·since so much of his life was spent in conducting. But whereas Wolf aimed toward an increasing condensation of musical space in his songs through economy of means and a corresponding heightening of intensity, Mahler endeavored to create the "symphonic song," not only through the use of orchestral accompaniments in the *Songs of a Wayfarer* (1883–1885) and several settings of folk poems from *Des Knaben Wunderhorn* (his chief source of texts) but also in expanding the scale of the song and elaborating its accompaniment. Certain topics appealed to him: the ironic and sardonic ("St. Anthony's Sermon to the Fish," later used as the third movement of the Second Symphony), the macabre ("Reveille," 1899), or the child's pictures of heaven in the Third and Fourth Symphonies. The culmination of Mahler's symphonic songs came in the first decade of the twentieth century with his songs to Rückert's texts, especially the moving *Kindertotenlieder*, and the most massive and symphonic of song cycles, *Das Lied von der Erde* (1907–1908), to German translations of pessimistic Chinese poems. Mahler led the art-song on a grand scale (as opposed to the ballad), originally exemplified by Schubert's "Der Zwerg" and "Ganymed," to a point from which further development was impossible.

Mahler's first four symphonies belong chronologically as well as aesthetically to the nineteenth century. They are all on a massive time-scale, though the intimacy and light orchestration of the Fourth Symphony make it seem like a chamber work in comparison with the others. Only the First Symphony is purely orchestral; the others use voices in at least one movement. Except in the Fourth Symphony, Mahler uses a

---

[2] One might go so far as to say that Wolf's modulations within a four-page song are as extensive, far-reaching, and significant as those within an entire act of one of Wagner's operas.

large orchestra, with quadrupled woodwinds (many doubling on piccolo, English horn, E-flat or bass clarinet), eight horns, occasional offstage brass choirs, and the heaviest artillery of the brass and percussion to emphasize his climaxes. Added woodwind color is used for doubling melodic lines in high registers to provide a "military band" effect. The scores are liberally sprinkled with explicit directions to performers and the conductor and are an excellent source for the study of orchestral performance practice around 1900. Far more than Schubert or Brahms, Mahler relied on songs to provide movements for his instrumental cycles, either pre-existing songs expanded as instrumental symphonic movements or newly composed, orchestrally accompanied solo songs. To Mahler the symphony was a kaleidoscopic world, calling for a mixture of a variety of styles and often incongruous musical elements and moods; the immense Third Symphony (1893–1896) in six movements, originally conceived as a series of fantastic dream-episodes during a summer noonday, is the epitome of this idea.

Though Bruckner taught and befriended the young Mahler, the principal similarities between them are not their long symphonies with apocalyptic climaxes but certain harmonic devices, especially the use of shifting tonal planes (but for different reasons) and certain effects like the slow march, which Bruckner used in his Fourth Symphony and which Mahler adopted even more extensively. Mahler's symphonies are really continuations of the symphonic ideal established by Liszt in his *Dante* and *Faust* Symphonies, with reliance on thematic transformations, sharp contrasts between diatonic and chromatic writing, an expanded time-scale, rhetorical and even sensational passages for dramatic effect, and sardonically diabolic distortion of melodic materials—the last-named deriving from the finale of Berlioz' *Symphonie fantastique* and fully established in Liszt's *Totentanz* and the third movement of his *Faust Symphony*. Liszt's funeral marches, especially that of *Héroïde funèbre*, also influenced Mahler, and the climactic apotheoses of Liszt's symphonies and tone poems were further intensified by Mahler through expanded orchestration and sudden shifting of tonal planes, as in Example 11-4. As a harmonist, Mahler was more conservative than such contemporaries of his as Wolf, Grieg, or Fauré; his chromaticism consists chiefly of melodic non-harmonic tones, often accented, with delayed resolutions imparting an intense yearning to his lyrical melodies. He relied heavily on wide melodic leaps, especially in violin melodies, and on sudden changes of tonal plane for effect (as in Example 11-4 or in several places in the chorale finale of the Second Symphony) rather than for architectonic reasons in the manner of Bruckner.

Mahler's symphonies are the culmination of the tradition of the expanded symphony with more or less programmatic content, extending

EXAMPLE 11-4. Mahler, Symphony No. 1, finale (string and most woodwind parts omitted) [Copyright assigned 1952 to Universal Edition (London), Ltd. Reproduced by permission].

from the Third and Ninth Symphonies of Beethoven through the program symphonies of Berlioz and Liszt and Bruckner's Fourth and Sixth Symphonies. With his Fifth Symphony (1901–1902), however, Mahler stepped from nineteenth-century to twentieth-century post- if not hyper-Romanticism. His time-scales became more massive; he oscillated between the huge resources demanded for his Eighth Symphony and the extremely restricted scoring (strings and harp) of the adagietto of the Fifth Symphony or the delicate opening of the Ninth Symphony; his sardonic diabolisms became more and more distorted, especially in his scherzos; and his climaxes, though even more apocalyptic, soon petered out to be succeeded by moods of deep pessimism. He brought the expanded programmatic symphony to its fullest possible development and, as with the art-song, concluded a chapter in the history of this genre.

The early development of Richard Strauss (1864–1949) is almost as astounding as those of the young Mozart or Mendelssohn. Among the magnificent works of this early period (1881–1888) are the Cello Sonata, Op. 5; the Serenade for wind instruments, Op. 7; the First Concerto for horn; the *Burleske* for piano and orchestra; some of his finest songs; and the concluding work of this period, the Violin Sonata, Op. 18. These works have erroneously been called "classical"; they are really in the tradition of Romantic neoclassicism as exemplified by the duet sonatas of Schumann, Brahms, and other German composers of absolute music, and it is significant that Strauss wrote these compositions before Brahms' "late" period, which began in 1891. They all contain a virile and sturdy expression, strong and forceful harmonies, and fine construction leavened with a vein of piquant humor, most evident in the *Burleske* and the finale of the Cello Sonata.

Strauss is said to have changed his musical style under the influence of Alexander Ritter, who introduced the young composer to the works of Liszt and Wagner. In the first works where this change is evident, the symphonic fantasy *Aus Italien* (1886) and the first version of the symphonic poem *Macbeth* (1888, revised 1890), the influences seem also to include, respectively, Raff's musical travelogues and Chaikovsky's tone poems. *Aus Italien* particularly contains harbingers of Strauss' later styles: soaring, fortissimo string melodies, brass fanfares, bubbling horns in the first movement, and intimations of *Der Rosenkavalier* in the third movement. In the finale, the popular song "Funiculì-funiculà" (in using which Strauss had some trouble with copyright laws) is contrasted with a *Meistersinger*-like second theme. *Macbeth,* on the other hand, is too much influenced by Liszt's and Chaikovsky's tone poems, too experimental, and often too gloomy and lacking in contrast and variety to be popular.

The pivotal year for Strauss was 1888, for during it he not only completed the Violin Sonata but also *Don Juan,* his first successful symphonic poem; *Death and Transfiguration* was finished in the following year. Both works owe much to Liszt and something to Raff, but the influence of two other composers is evident: the organist-composer Josef Rheinberger (1839–1901), best known as the teacher of many American composers of the nineteenth-century "New England" school, and Moritz Moszkowski (1854–1925), best known for his "Spanish dances" and salon music but who also wrote in the larger forms. *Don Juan* is written in a free but recognizable sonata form with its most striking theme (initially stated by the horns) first appearing in the development; its recapitulation is truncated and its coda is wry, a direct contrast to Liszt's optimistic conclusions. *Death and Transfiguration,* influenced by Moszkowski even to its title, is a sonata-form movement with long introduction and coda, and represents a fine continuation of Liszt's best ideas of thematic transformation (see Example 11-5) as well as Liszt's tendency to anticipate his

EXAMPLE 11-5. Thematic transformation in Strauss' *Death and Transfiguration.*

apotheoses.[3] *Till Eulenspiegel's Merry Pranks* (1895), a "scherzo in rondeau form," is a later work but in its spirit and brevity belongs with Strauss' earlier tone poems. Its structure is akin not to the High Classic rondo of Haydn and Mozart but to the rondos of C. P. E. Bach in which the theme itself undergoes transformations and statements outside the tonic.

Example 11-5 illustrates an important ingredient of Strauss' thematic transformation, his use of the original theme as a counterpoint to new melodic ideas which have a strong programmatic significance. The theme cited in this example follows the protagonist of the tone poem from his childhood (Example 11-5b) to his deathbed reveries (Example 11-5a); it is part of the theme of his young manhood (Example 11-5c) but is subsequently combined with the motives of his mature manhood (Example 11-5d), his struggle against death (Example 11-5e), and the apotheosis theme of transfiguration (Example 11-5f).

Don Juan, Death and Transfiguration, and *Till Eulenspiegel's Merry Pranks* represent the peak of Strauss' career during the nineteenth century. The next group of tone poems, from *Also sprach Zarathustra* (1896) to the *Sinfonia Domestica* (1903), shows a decline in his creative powers and especially a marked lessening of the feeling of freshness and spontaneity that characterizes his earlier compositions; this new group of tone poems also shows Strauss' shift from late to post-Romanticism.

[3] See my study "Schiller, Moszkowski, and Strauss: Joan of Arc's 'Death and Transfiguration,' " *Music Review,* XXVIII (1967), 209–217.

Although each of these new works is triple the length of the earlier tone poems, they do not have an equivalent amount of the earlier verve, élan, and dash, which appear only occasionally. Strauss at this time also began a kind of "role-playing," like Berlioz more than sixty years previously, in setting himself up as a "bad boy of music." He provoked indignation by imitating, in muted brass, the bleating of sheep and even calling for a real wind machine in *Don Quixote* (1897), a free set of variations analogous to Franck's *Variations symphoniques* in its use of a double theme; and he aroused critical wrath with *Ein Heldenleben* (1898), an autobiographical tone poem of large dimensions in which he utilized several quotations from his earlier works to make the hero's identity clear, with the carpingly chattering woodwinds unmistakably setting forth Strauss' opinion of his critics.

Comparisons have been made between Strauss' expansion of his musical and orchestral dimensions and the ethos of Germany after the accession of Kaiser Wilhelm II in 1888 and the subsequent transformation of German life into emphasis on armaments and imperialist adventures. It is more appropriate to compare Strauss' change of style and his attitude toward the orchestra with the industrialization of Germany and its concentration not only on armaments but also on precision machinery, for Strauss' orchestra relies not so much on the heavy artillery of brass and percussion, which he uses with much more restraint than Mahler, as on efficient, meticulous precision, best seen in the difficult string passages which entire sections must execute cleanly (Example 2-2b). Strauss' orchestra became a precision instrument like a Siemens dynamo or Zeiss camera, with a corresponding loss of status for the individual musician, who became a cog in a remarkably efficient mechanism. It should be added that Strauss' orchestral music must be heard in live performance to be fully appreciated.

The active inner parts in Strauss' music have been attacked as a cluttering of the texture, but this is true only in a few passages such as the introduction to *Don Quixote*, in which the composer tried to create an atmosphere of confusion for deliberate effect. The function of these inner parts is either to sustain a mood of drive and excitement, through intricate string passages of a sort derived from Wagner, or to give a restful or propulsive effect, through countermelodies or active accompaniment patterns, often in involved rhythms. In the middle of *Don Juan*, for example, the quiet pattern which accompanies the yearning oboe solo is transformed into the driving transition to the exuberant horn melody. When Strauss used genuine counterpoint it was to create a mood of archaism or "learnedness," as in the fugue "Science" in *Also sprach Zarathustra*. Strauss' melodies, for the most part, are motives rather than themes, but there are many memorable examples of the latter, like the horn themes in *Don Juan* or *Till Eulenspiegel,* the apotheosis of *Death and Transfiguration,* or the conclusion of *Also sprach Zarathustra,* accompanied with parallel thirds, which can be considered a poignant farewell to the nineteenth century. Strauss' harmony seldom goes beyond that of his contemporaries; one of the most striking exceptions is the conflict, at the end of *Zarathustra,* between the triads of B major and C major (with an added F-sharp).

Strauss' abandonment of nineteenth-century post-Romanticism is shown in his change of emphasis from the symphonic poem to opera. He had begun this shift of interest with *Guntram* (1887–1893), but his successes in this medium did not occur until the first decade of the twentieth century with *Salome* and *Elektra,* with their monster orchestras and Grand Guignol effects; these actually are an aberration in his stylistic development (his songs, for instance, show little change in style throughout his career), for he later found the vein of a post-Romantic nostalgia in *Der Rosenkavalier* and *Ariadne auf Naxos* most congenial to his muse.

FRANCE

French music during the closing years of the nineteenth century presents a complex picture of overlapping styles. The pioneers of the "French Musical Renaissance" continued their activity—Franck until 1890 and Saint-Saëns until 1920—Fauré's first major works date from the late 1870's, and Franck's best pupils, Chausson and d'Indy, wrote their first major compositions during the 1880's. The music by all these composers except Franck overlapped to some extent Debussy's revolutionary works of the 1890's; hence chronology alone is no guide to this period, for French music after 1880 moved along several different paths.

Many of the composers in France had made a pilgrimage to Bayreuth or Munich to hear Wagner's operas, and almost all found the program of instruction at the Paris Conservatoire to be musically stultifying since it centered around operatic composition and the acquisition of mere technical skills in performance; this did not change until Fauré became director in 1905. A number of composers sought alternate means of instruction: private lessons with Franck; study at the École Niedermeyer (originally a school to train organists and church musicians), which included Saint-Saëns on its faculty and Gounod and Fauré among its distinguished alumni; and even, in the case of d'Indy and his friends, the founding of a new school of music, the Schola Cantorum, which placed considerable emphasis on the history of music in its curriculum. All four of the major French post-Romantic composers discussed in this chapter were outside the prevailing musical "Establishment," which stressed opera as the highest form of musical expression; all followed different paths; and all had significant influence on twentieth-century French music.

Emmanuel Chabrier (1841–1894) was a minor bureaucrat who heard a performance of *Tristan* when he was 38 and decided to devote himself to composition. Though his reputation today rests largely on a single orchestral work, *España* (1883), an exciting musical travelogue, his genius is best revealed in his light, unpretentious compositions, with the *opéra comique Le Roi malgré lui* (1887) his masterpiece in this genre. As a musical parodist, he was a significant forerunner of Satie, Milhaud, and Poulenc; one of the best of his parodies, a milestone in the French rejection of the more turgid aspects of Wagnerian Romanticism, is the *Souvenirs de Munich* (1886) in which he arranged a series of quadrille dances based on motives from Wagner's *Tristan und Isolde*. Chabrier has erroneously been called a Wagnerian because of his opera *Gwendoline* (1886), but Wagner's influence is felt more in the libretto than in the music, which contains much modal writing or emphasizes the tritone. Chabrier's rhythm is quite free and supple, as *España* or the parodistic *Trois valses romantiques* for two pianos will show; his phrases are often irregular in length and avoid the square-cut four-measure symmetry so common during the century. An anticipator of twentieth-century pan-diatonicism, he uses lush harmonies generally in a parodistic context. In Example 11-6, quite representative of his style, he delays the tonic

EXAMPLE 11-6. Chabrier, "Idylle" from *Pièces pittoresques* (1881).

chord until the end of the phrase. Chabrier's musical innovations have been frequently overlooked or misunderstood because they occurred within the context of "light" music rather than within the more "serious" frameworks of symphony, sonata, or neo-Wagnerian opera.

Gabriel Fauré (1845–1924), Saint-Saëns' pupil, strayed the farthest of all these composers from the musical language of Romanticism, and to many writers he is no Romantic at all. He excelled in works on an intimate scale, like piano pieces, chamber music, and songs; friends or pupils scored most of his few orchestral works. As a composer of absolute instrument music, he followed the leadership of Schumann as transmitted through Saint-Saëns, but in a very original manner, as can be seen in his two most important early works, the Violin Sonata in A major, Op. 13 (1876), and the First Piano Quartet, Op. 15 (1879); it is interesting to note that his Violin Sonata precedes Franck's by a decade and that the Piano Quartet stems from the same year as Franck's Piano Quintet. Fauré's melodic lines are as long, unsymmetrical, and unpredictable as those of Berlioz; his slow movements are derived from song, but from the French *mélodie* rather than from the German Lied; and his music has a grace, elegance, and lightness which is often mistaken for lack of depth by those oriented toward German music.

Fauré's piano writing, deriving from Chopin's, is centered around expansions of small forms with such noncommittal titles as "Barcarolle" or "Nocturne," with melodies floating above or within arpeggiated accompaniments. Among his most delightful works for piano is the suite *Dolly*, Op. 56 (1894), for piano four-hands, in which the composer showed himself as adept in portraying the child's world as Schumann, Bizet (*Jeux d'enfants*), Musorgsky (*The Nursery*), or Debussy.

Fauré's chief achievements are his songs, and in them the contrast between the German Lied and the French song is most evident. Only in the late years of the nineteenth century did France enjoy a school of poets comparable to those between 1770 and 1850 in Germany; their poetry was evocative, hinting, suggesting, hesitant, and restrained in its declarations. Similar are Fauré's settings of these poems; they lack the exuberance of Schubert or Schumann, the idealized, sublimated sensuality of Brahms, or Wolf's musical "close reading" of a poem. Typical of Fauré's songs is an active yet subordinate piano accompaniment over which floats a vocal melody that sedulously avoids any suggestion of the square-cut popular song or of the strophic style; sometimes the piano participates with the voice in dialogue. The nearest German equivalents are Schumann's "Der Nussbaum" and his *Frauenliebe und Leben* songs. The French song melody is neither wholly tuneful nor wholly declamatory; it characteristically moves within a fairly limited ambitus and is principally devoted to bringing out the limited vocal sonority of the

French language with its diphthongs and mute "e" sounds. Not until Debussy's *Pelléas et Mélisande* was the technique of French song transferred to opera.

Fauré's restrained musical language is the antithesis of German
Romanticism. Fauré eschewed *Sturm und Drang* tempestuousness (note
the opening of the First Piano Quartet), unbridled exuberance, or obvious wrestling with knotty compositional problems, though his secure
contrapuntal technique is evident in such disparate works as the *Requiem*
(1887) and *Dolly*. Fauré's supple and flexible rhythm, like that of most
French composers at the end of the nineteenth century, is quite different
from that of Schumann or Brahms, for the latter two composers wrote
"bar-line" music even though the impression of the bar-line is different
from that which appears on the printed page, and the idea of a four-
measure phrase in the background, to be extended or elided, was in-
grained in their thinking. However, the suppleness of the rhythm and
phrase-structure of the second acts of *Tristan* and *Parsifal* contributed,
as did Berlioz' rhythmic flexibility, to the freedom of French rhythm and
phrasing. One may contrast Example 11-7 with Example 9-3 to see the
difference between sophisticated French and German rhythm and
phrase-structure.

EXAMPLE 11-7. (a) Fauré, Piano Quartet, Op. 15, second movement; (b)
Chausson, Symphony in B-flat major, Op. 20, first movement.

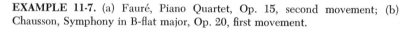

Fauré was one of the most revolutionary harmonists of the century, a fact which may be surprising because of his constant understatement which avoids the rhetorical gestures, attempts at surprise and pathos,
or dramatic contrasts so characteristic of both German and nationalist
composers. A major ingredient of Fauré's harmony, its modality, stems
from his study of Gregorian chant accompaniment at the École Niedermeyer and his years as organist in Parisian churches; this style of chant
accompaniment, though frowned on by the purists of Solesmes, con-

formed to the inherent modality of the chant through using many
secondary triads, especially in minor, rather than forcing it into a major-
minor straitjacket. Especially in minor, Fauré's melodies are also modal,
with much use of the lowered leading tone, with excellent illustrations in
the C minor Piano Quartet or the *Requiem*.

As did Puccini to a lesser extent, Fauré discovered the effectiveness of two chords of the seventh which had been neglected during the
century, perhaps because of their lack of tonal directive properties: the
minor seventh (C–E-flat–G–B-flat) and the major seventh (C–E–G–B-
natural). These differ from what Suckling has called the "straightjacket
of leading-note diatonicism" characteristic of German music and evident
in the chords of the dominant seventh, augmented sixth, and the juicier
"altered" chords in which "tendency" tones, resolved (or seeming to demand to be resolved) as if they were leading tones or dominant sevenths,
are prominent. With Fauré the major seventh chord is not a tortured dissonance as in Wolf's music (see Example 11-3) but a passing dissonance,
generally in an inversion, and the minor seventh, either in root position
or inverted, is flexibly used not only as a harmonization of modal melodies but also as a pivot to or from remote key centers since it lacks the
"pull" of a dominant harmony with a leading tone. Fauré's tonality is
very clear, but he subtly avoids strong emphases on dominant harmonies
and delicately blurs the "directional" pull of individual chords. The following cadences illustrate Fauré's harmonic subtlety: note the replacement of the dominant by a chord of the flat submediant with a dominant
seventh which does not resolve in Example 11-8a (a perfect support for
the text's " 'Tis the night of ecstasy"); the "conventional" way to treat
such a cadence in Example 11-8b; and the quasi-modality and tonal ambiguity of the preparations of the dominant seventh-tonic cadence in Examples 11-8c and 11-8d.

EXAMPLE 11-8. Fauré's cadences: (a) *La bonne chanson*, Op. 61, No. 3; (b)
"Traditional" resolution of the cadential augmented-sixth chord; (c) Sixth
Barcarolle, Op. 70; (d) "Kitty-Valse" from *Dolly*, Op. 56.

(b)

(c)

(d)

A love for Fauré's music is an acquired taste and is generally found among those with a conspicuous lack of enthusiasm for Wagner and Brahms. Although Maurice Ravel (1875–1937) was the only one of Fauré's pupils to become a major composer, his influence was transmitted well into the twentieth century by the teacher Nadia Boulanger (born 1887), another of his pupils, and he can be considered one of the principal sources of French neoclassicism with its emphasis on restraint, long melodic lines, and modal-sounding harmonies.

Ernest Chausson (1855–1899) is both one of the most derivative and one of the most progressive of this group of composers. Independently wealthy, he was not a professional composer, and his music suffers from a certain amateurishness. He is at his most derivative in such Franckian works as the *Poème* for violin and orchestra (1896), the first movement of the curiously hybrid Concerto for piano, violin, and string quartet (1889–1891), and in the cyclic structure of his best composition, the Symphony in B-flat major (1889–1890), the finale of which recapitulates material from the previous two movements in the manner of his mentor Franck's D minor Symphony. Chausson constantly wrestled with what he called "the red spectre of Wagner which does not let go of me" (see Example 8-5d). The Wagnerian influence was the evocative, atmospheric mood of most of the second act of *Tristan,* the last act of *Parsifal,* and the *Siegfried Idyl;* and it is chiefly evident in the symphonic poem *Vivianne* (1882, revised 1887), the extended song-cycle, *Poème de l'amour et de la mer* (1882–1892), and the posthumously performed opera *Le Roi Arthus.*

Chausson's most progressive ideas are to be seen in his use of a neoclassic style, most evident in the delightful Sicilienne of his Violin Concerto or the *Quelques danses* (1896) for piano, of which the Sarabande (Example 11-9c) is cited as an illustration. Note, in Example 11-9, the difference between Raff's diatonically oriented harmony, Saint-Saëns' extensive use of secondary triads, and Chausson's free modality. Chausson seemed to be on the verge of creating a highly individual style when he was killed in a bicycling accident at the age of 44.

EXAMPLE 11-9. (a) Raff, Sarabande from Suite, Op. 207 (*ca.* 1880); (b) Saint-Saëns, trio of minuet from Septuor, Op. 65 (1881); (c) Chausson, Sarabande from *Quelques danses,* Op. 26 (1896).

Vincent d'Indy (1851–1931) made the best synthesis of French and Germanic musical styles in creating works of strong originality and masterly workmanship. Though in his later music he used such Debussy-esque devices as whole-tone scales and unrelated parallel fifths or triads, chiefly for coloristic effects (as in his *Sept chants de terroir* of 1918), in spirit he was of all French composers the most antithetical to Debussy's music and the newer French trends; yet his influence extended into the twentieth century in the larger works of Albert Roussel (1869–1937) and Arthur Honegger (1892–1955) as well as in the French version of *Gebrauchsmusik*, the Paris Conservatoire contest solo. An ardent and contentious polemicist not only for his musical ideas but also for a conservatively ultramontane Catholicism and a chauvinistic nationalism, his ideas may be compared with Wagner's. D'Indy's logical, systematic, intellectual view of music was expressed not only in his compositions but also in his work as a teacher and in his monumental *Cours de composition musicale* (1903–1933, the last part published posthumously).

One of the few "universal" composers of the century, d'Indy wrote in many different media. His atmospherically Wagnerian operas belong to the twentieth century, and his choral works include not only much church music (which increased in austerity during the course of his career) but also an early statement of his artistic credo in *Le Chant de la cloche* (1885), in which he overlaid Schiller's poem with a sturdy uncompromising Catholicism and the artistic ideas expressed by Wagner in *Die Meistersinger*. D'Indy's absolute instrumental music was strongly influenced by the architectonic principles of cyclic form and the melodic styles of Gregorian chant and French folk song; his chamber music includes not only string quartets (the E major Quartet is based on a chant motive) but also chamber music with winds.

D'Indy began his career as an orchestral composer with symphonic poems, of which the best known is the trilogy based on Schiller's *Wallenstein* (1874–1880). The *Symphony on a French Mountain Air* (1887), his most frequently performed work, follows the example of Franck's *Variations symphoniques* in having the solo piano prominent yet subordinate to the orchestra and contains ingenious thematic transformation. *Istar* (1897), based on an Assyrian legend in which Istar is gradually unclothed as she passes through the various portals of the temple, is a reversal of the standard variation form in that the theme, in a most effective orchestral unison, is stated toward the end of the composition.

D'Indy's crowning orchestral achievement was his Second Symphony in B-flat (1904); as Example 11-10 illustrates, the composer de-

EXAMPLE 11-10. Selected cyclic interrelationships in d'Indy's Symphony No. 2 in B-flat, Op. 57: (a) First movement, introduction; (b) First movement, second theme; (c) Coda of first movement: combination of motive A with (1) transitional theme between first and second theme-groups and (2) transformation of first theme; (d) Second movement, second theme with oboe countermelody; (e) Fourth movement, fugue subject; (f) Fourth movement, chorale in coda (inner voices omitted). (Permission for reprint granted by Durand et Cie.; Copyright Owners of Paris, France; Elkan-Vogel Co., Inc., Philadelphia, Pa., Sole Agents.)

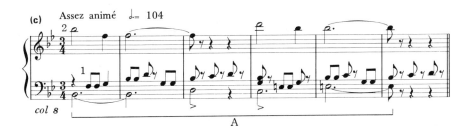

clined to add the term "major" or "minor" because of the ambiguity of the opening germ-motive. This symphony represents the culmination of the art of thematic transformation, for the germ motives, especially motive "A," permeate each movement, especially in transitional passages, and many of the themes that do not derive from the germ-motives can nevertheless be combined with them. With this work, the greatest French symphony since Berlioz' *Symphonie Fantastique,* the chronological discussion of the music of nineteenth-century Romanticism can be concluded.

BIBLIOGRAPHICAL NOTES

Grout's *Short History of Opera* (2nd ed., New York, 1965) is the best survey of the Italian operas of this period. The Verdi studies cited in the bibliographical notes for Chapter 7 should be consulted by the reader desiring more information about his career after 1851. Little has been written about Catalani; the best available studies of this composer in English are by John W. Klein, "Alfredo Catalani," *Musical Quarterly,* XXIII (1937) 287–294, and "Toscanini and Catalani," *Music and Letters,* XLVIII (1967), 213–228. Mosco Carner's *Puccini: A Critical Biography* (London, 1958) is an excellent study of Puccini's life and works; the operas are systematically covered in William Ashbrook's *The Operas of Puccini* (London, 1969). The rise of instrumental composition in late nineteenth-century Italy is excellently described in Bea Friedland's "Italy's Ottocento: Notes from the Musical Underground," *Musical Quarterly,* LVI (1970), 27–53.

The musical period from the death of Wagner to the outbreak of World War I has not been explored in the detail it deserves. Martin Cooper's two essays on "The Romantic Agony in Music" in his *Ideas and Music* (London, 1965) are stimulating introductions to this topic. A desirable addition to the scanty literature on post-Romanticism would be a translation of Israel Nestyev's *Na rubezhe dvukh stoletii (Bridging the Two Centuries,* Moscow, 1967), a series of essays on late nineteenth- and early twentieth-century music.

Frank Walker has written an excellent biography of Hugo Wolf (2nd ed., New York, 1968); the individual songs receive a detailed investigation in Eric Sams' *The Songs of Hugo Wolf* (London, 1961). Mahler is presently served by two large-scale, but at present incomplete, studies in English by Donald Mitchell (London, 1958) and Neville Cardus (London, 1965). Parks Grant's "Bruckner and Mahler," *Music Review,* XXXII (1971), 36–55, effectively shows the dissimilarity of styles of these two composers. Alma Mahler Werfel's *Gustav Mahler: Memories and Letters* (London, 1968) is a collection of letters and reminiscences edited by Mahler's widow. The definitive biography of Richard Strauss in English is Norman Del Mar's *Richard Strauss: A Critical Commentary on His Life and Works,* two volumes of which have appeared (London, 1961 and 1969), with the final volume in preparation. Ernst Krause's serviceable one-volume biography of Strauss (English translation, London, 1964; new German edition, Leipzig, 1970), from a Marxist standpoint, is nevertheless superior to George Marek's prejudiced *Richard Strauss: The Life of a Non-Hero* (New York, 1967). There are several published collections of Strauss' correspondence.

The books by Cooper and Landormy cited in the bibliographical notes for Chapter 9 give the best brief overview of late nineteenth-century French music. Excellent studies of individual composers include Jean-Pierre Barricelli and Leo Weinstein, *Ernest Chausson* (Norman, 1955); Rollo Myers, *Emmanuel Chabrier and His Circle* (London, 1969); and Norman Suckling, *Fauré* (London, 1951), which also points out many interesting contrasts between French and German music. D'Indy, unfortunately, is not well served either by the appreciation of his American pupil Daniel Gregory Mason in *Contemporary Composers* (New York, 1929) or by Norman Demuth's defensive biography (London, 1951).

Scholarly complete editions of Wolf and Mahler are in progress, and for Strauss' centennial year (1964) Boosey and Hawkes published his complete songs in four volumes. The fragile and crumbly paper used by most music publishers in the latter part of the nineteenth century is now rapidly deteriorating, making republication of the works of the other composers discussed in this chapter imperative.

TWELVE

NINETEENTH-CENTURY
MUSICAL ROMANTICISM
AND ITS AUDIENCE

At no time in history has music existed in a vacuum. Even during the individualistic nineteenth century, music and the relationship of composer and performer to their audience were affected by extra-artistic trends. These should be at least briefly examined if the music of this period is to be understood in its context. This chapter is also the best place to discuss the performance practices of Romantic music in hope that more detailed investigations of this neglected topic will be made.

SOCIOLOGY OF MUSICAL ROMANTICISM

One of the most striking differences between the Classic and Romantic periods is the change in the social function of the musician and his music. Most eighteenth-century composers were under some form of patronage, sometimes ecclesiastical but usually courtly, but the growing secularization of society and the increasing demands by the bourgeois classes for a constitutional government that would limit the arbitrary expenditure of revenues caused a sharp decline in the private patronage of music. The few composers of the nineteenth century who were under some form of courtly patronage during their careers, like Hummel, Spohr, or Wagner, bitterly resented it as demeaning.[1]

Composers and musicians became free artists, much as Handel was in eighteenth-century London. A few, like Mozart and Schubert, suffered from this new social arrangement. Much has been written about the exploitation of composers by unscrupulous publishers, but one must remember that copyright laws were not really enforced until the closing years of the century, that publishers had to depend for their income on exclusive relationships with composers and on rentals of performing materials, and that the less than scrupulous dealings of Beethoven or Wagner with publishers would not be tolerated today.

The musician, no longer under patronage, enjoyed a rise in social status but suffered from a corresponding drop in security. Whereas in the eighteenth century most musicians outside of Italy were trained under a system of apprenticeship, with the neophyte taken into a court orchestra under the watchful eye of his teacher, nineteenth-century musicians were generally trained in conservatories, institutions which were originally begun in Italy to teach orphans a trade but which received universal impetus after the founding of the Paris Conservatoire in 1795. These newer conservatories accepted children at an early age and their administration was characterized by frequent examinations, low tuition charges, governmental or philanthropic support, and a vocational kind of instruction. A large number of positions were available for trained instrumentalists or singers, from military bands and light music ensembles to symphony orchestras and opera companies; rewards for leading singers and virtuosos were great, but many opportunities (more than at present!) existed for the humble musician. As in previous centuries, music was an effective means for achieving upward social mobility; though a musician's duties were arduous and he was more subject to exploitation than at present, his life was considerably better than that of a coal miner or factory hand. The century also saw the rise of the musical entrepreneur, often a promoter in the manner of P. T. Barnum; though many of them were not exactly savory characters, we must acknowledge their

---

[1] For a study of the effects of the breakdown of the patronage system in Germany, see my "Musical Portraits in 'Sturm und Drang' Drama," *Music and Letters* XLVI (1965), 39–49. I discuss musical instruction as a means of achieving social mobility in "Music at the 'Hohe Karlsschule,' 1770–1794," *Journal of Research in Music Education* XII (1964), 123–133.

importance in bringing music to a much wider audience. Composers and singers of opera, and touring virtuosos, were the chief beneficiaries of— or sufferers from—these entrepreneurs.

Composers were writing for a new audience. The Industrial Revolution and the improved transportation of the steamboat and railroad brought about a rapid growth of cities and distributed wealth among a wider segment of the population. Art music became an urban phenomenon, for mass audiences were needed to support resident opera companies and symphony orchestras or to attend the concerts of the virtuosos. Books on how to understand music, musical journalism and criticism, and private musical instruction to provide an "accomplishment" for the daughters of the bourgeoisie flourished. The creation of salon and "entertainment" music became an industry in itself, with such specialists as Johann Strauss, Jr., and the Dane Hans Christian Lumbye (1810–1874) creating its masterpieces; analogous are the simple, sentimental, and beloved songs of Friedrich Silcher (1789–1860) in Germany, Stephen Collins Foster (1826–1864) in America, and Paolo Tosti (1846–1916) in Italy.

Kitsch, the degenerate side of light and salon music and of art music as well, developed along with musical Romanticism; its best concise definition is "triviality with pretentiousness." Among its essential ingredients are regular phrasing and rhythms, square-cut melodies, rich altered harmonies often appearing unexpectedly in diatonic contexts, delayed resolutions of non-harmonic tones, and descriptive titles intended to arouse religious, erotic, familial, or patriotic feelings; in short, the debasement of the musical idioms particularly of Weber, Schumann, and Liszt (Example 2-7c). Pictorial counterparts of kitsch are the grand battle scenes painted by German artists after the Franco-Prussian War or varnished segments of tree trunks adorned with garishly colored religious paintings.[2]

More people than before participated in the making of music. Under the influence of such pedagogical reformers as Rousseau, Johann Heinrich Pestalozzi (1746–1827), and Lowell Mason (1792–1872), musical education was no longer limited to future professionals but spread through those segments of society fortunate enough to attend school. Tonic sol-fa, a form of solfège based on "movable *do*," made choral music easier to sing and, with the price of music constantly decreasing thanks to innovations in printing, brought about an efflorescence of choral societies

---

[2] Carl Dahlhaus analyses the ingredients of *kitsch* in the second movement of Chaikovsky's Fifth Symphony (Example 2–2d) in "Über musikalischen Kitsch," *Studien zur Trivialmusik im 19. Jahrhundert* (Regensburg, 1967), p. 21. E. D. Mackerness analyzes an epigonously post-Romantic specimen of *kitsch*, Addinsell's *Warsaw Concerto* (1944), in *A Social History of English Music* (London, 1964), pp. 271–272.

and musical festivals. Through the improvements in technology and metallurgy brought about by the Industrial Revolution, musical instruments became both easier to make and less expensive, thus accessible to more people. The development of the concert grand and upright pianos and the addition of valves to brass instruments, more keys to woodwind instruments, and chin-rests or end-pins to stringed instruments made them easier to play although it significantly altered their timbres. Composers were not unduly hesitant to take advantage of these innovations.

The resultant growth in both orchestras and choral groups meant that by 1900 an essential manifestation of civic and national pride was the support of a resident symphony orchestra, choral society, or music festival, and even of such luxuries as an opera company or musicological investigation and publication of the works of important bygone composers, often from public funds. This replaced the princely support of music, especially in continental Europe, though it often meant that the frustrations of Wagner with courtly protocol were replaced by Berlioz' impatience with bureaucratic delay, and often such privately sponsored groups as the Société nationale de musique, École Niedermeyer, or Schola Cantorum were needed to create alternatives to officially controlled musical establishments.

Romantically or politically inclined biographers have emphasized the alienation of the artist from society during the nineteenth century. Most composers at some time felt a conflict between the demands of a Philistine public and the ideas, originally fostered by Goethe and Schiller and continued by Beethoven and Wagner, of art as equal to religion and of the composer as a superior being. Yet the composer willing to come to terms with the lowest common tastes of his public, like Meyerbeer and Puccini, was lavishly rewarded, and some were able to enjoy both general acclaim and a large measure of artistic integrity, like Mendelssohn, Verdi, and Richard Strauss. It is true that a few composers, like Schubert and Berwald, were grossly neglected or abused during their lifetimes; and Nicolas Slonimsky's *Lexicon of Musical Invective* (New York, 1953) is a fascinating chrestomathy of attacks on famous composers and their music, but the whole concept of the general lack of public or critical appreciation for the major composers of the century has been exaggerated.[3] The gap between composer and audience was not to become a yawning chasm until the twentieth century, and the blame for this does not rest exclusively on the musically inclined public.

[3] John H. Mueller's "The Aesthetic Gap Between Consumer and Composer," *Journal of Research in Music Education*, XV (1967), 151–158, effectively explodes the legend of Beethoven's being "unappreciated" during his lifetime and establishes a methodology whereby similar studies of the reception of other composers' works can be made.

ROMANTIC PERFORMANCE PRACTICES

The study of the performance practices of nineteenth-century music has been neglected, since priority has been given to examining the manifold problems of the correct interpretation of even earlier musics; "tradition," it has been felt, is a sufficient guide to today's performers of the "standard repertoire." Yet much needs to be done to obtain reasonably correct interpretation of the musical literature between Beethoven and Fauré.

One salient problem is the existence of so many corrupt musical texts. Although almost all of the errors consist of erroneous dynamic, phrasing, and interpretative markings or inconsistent reproductions of variant versions of given passages, even wrong notes have crept in, and the policies of several publishing houses have led to the repeated reissuing of defective scores.[4] It is further noteworthy that although among the once-definitive complete editions being redone are those of Schubert's and Berlioz' music, nevertheless the eighteenth and nineteenth centuries suffer most from the absence of scholarly complete collected editions of the works of many major composers, from C. P. E. Bach to Fauré.

The changes in instrumental and orchestral sonorities between Beethoven's time and the present have seldom been considered, especially by conductors. Of the instruments that Beethoven used in his Ninth Symphony, the trombones and cymbals are the only ones whose tone colors have not undergone radical changes. Techniques of performance have undergone alterations of similar scope. The addition of chinrests to violins and violas or end-pins to cellos and basses enabled the performer to produce a wider and more constant vibrato without tiring; the addition of valves to brass instruments and more keys to woodwind instruments made these instruments easier to play and more secure in intonation, but much of the original tone color was lost, especially with the French horn. Characteristic of most nineteenth-century string playing was a frequent use of audible shifts of position on the string, heard at its most exaggerated in the glissandos of the gypsy fiddle and at its best in the old 78 rpm recordings of the Lener, Pro Arte, and original Budapest quartets. However, the Russian-Jewish school of violin playing headed by Leopold Auer (1845–1930), dominant in the twentieth century,

---

[4] See, for example, Eva Badura-Skoda, "Textual Problems in Masterpieces of the 18th and 19th Centuries," *Musical Quarterly*, LI (1965), 301–317, and "In Verdi Veritas," *Newsweek*, XXXI (December 1962), 54; Emmanuel Winternitz, *Musical Autographs from Monteverdi to Hindemith* (Princeton, 1955, 2 vols.). In recent years text-criticism of musical sources has become one of the frontiers of research in nineteenth-century music.

emphasizes a continuous bowstroke which conceals the difference between up-bow and down-bow and suppresses audible shifts of position.

National schools of playing woodwind and brass instruments developed as early as the eighteenth century. One can cite as illustrations the wide vibratos of French bassoonists and hornists; the Italian technique of clarinet performance, prevalent past 1900, with the reed above the mouthpiece, providing more facile articulation but a much shriller tone with less dynamic shading; the opposite German technique of clarinet playing with the reed below the mouthpiece which almost universally supplanted the Italian school; or the veiled tone of the Viennese "Pumphorn," a single horn with piston rather than rotary valves, and described as the original valved *Waldhorn* of the early Romantic period.[5] Conductors who are concerned about the proper oboe for Bach's works would do well to consider performances of the clarinet solos in Rossini's overtures or the E-flat clarinet solo in Berlioz' *Symphonie fantastique* to be played with the reed above the mouthpiece, or the horn solos in the orchestral works of Wagner, Brahms, Mahler, and Richard Strauss to be played on the *Wiener Pumphorn*.

Orchestral seating plans of the nineteenth century varied, but Spontini's dictum "My left eye, first violins; my right eye, second violins" was prevalent through this period, and antiphonal writing for the two violin sections occurs as late as Bruckner and Chaikovsky; the effect is lost if, as is now customary, all the violins are grouped together. Cellos and basses should face the audience, and the brass and percussion should be grouped together, not spatially separated. It is possible to secure reasonable approximation of the sound of a nineteenth-century orchestral performance by following these suggestions—and no one would miss the sloppy technical execution, insecure intonation, and almost hysterically subjective "interpretations" by conductors or soloists that were the negative features of much nineteenth-century playing.

The topic of Romantic ornamentation is still not wholly clear, yet many of the rules for eighteenth-century performance, particularly the playing of ornaments on instead of before the beat, hold true, even in the case of the compound appoggiaturas of Hummel and Chopin. Whether the trills are to begin with the main note or to follow the earlier practice of starting on the beat with the upper auxiliary is subject to dispute; Beethoven was as careless as Chopin was meticulous in indicating preparations for his trills, but it is most likely that chains of trills, such as those typical of Beethoven's last sonatas and quartets, were begun on the main note.

[5] Horace Fitzpatrick, "Notes on the Vienna Horn," *Galpin Society Journal*, XIV (1961), 49–51.

BIBLIOGRAPHICAL NOTES

Most studies of the social history of music are written from a left-wing viewpoint; this is most evident in Knepler's nineteenth-century history cited in the bibliography of Chapter 2 and to some extent in Wilfred Mellers' *Music in Society* (New York, 1950). Marcel Brion's *Daily Life in the Vienna of Mozart and Schubert* (New York, 1962) and E. D. Mackerness' *A Social History of English Music* (London, 1964) avoid sociopolitical value judgments and can be considered more objective studies. The autobiographies and memoirs by Spohr, Glinka, Berlioz, Wagner, and others are invaluable primary sources, as are literary works with musicians as prominent characters, like Schiller's *Kabale und Liebe* and Balzac's *Le Cousin Pons*. George Schoolfield's *The Figure of the Musician in German Literature* (Chapel Hill, 1956) is an excellent point of departure for further studies which can contribute to a sociological history of music. The musical periodicals of the nineteenth century are the best sources for items of the social history of music, performance practice, and depictions of the musical audience. The social psychology of the nineteenth-century composer or musician is extremely difficult to reconstruct: the discussions of Vladimir Fédorov's essay "Čajkovsky, musicien-type du XIXe siècle?" *Acta Musicologica*, XLII (1970), 59–70, and XLIII (1971), 205–35, show the insufficiency of the measurements at our disposal today. Albert Lavignac's *Musical Education* (English translation, New York, 1902) is a good survey of trends in the education of the nineteenth-century professional musician, but even an elementary history of general musical education remains to be written.

Romantic performance practice has received but a fraction of the attention given to that of music of earlier periods, although Thurston Dart's *The Interpretation of Music* (London, 1954) and Robert Donington's *The Interpretation of Early Music* (2nd. ed., New York, 1966) touch briefly at various points on this topic. Several articles in the *Galpin Society Journal* and *The Brass and Woodwind Quarterly* deal with problems of instrumental performance in the nineteenth century. William S. Newman's *Performance Practice in Beethoven's Piano Sonatas* (New York, 1971) is an excellent study. Much work with primary sources such as articles in contemporaneous musical periodicals, tutors, methods, virtuoso solos, and early phonograph records needs to be done in reconstructing near-authentic Romantic performance practice.

Carl Dahlaus (ed.), *Studien zur Trivialmusik*, in the *19. Jahrhundert* series (Regensburg, 1967), contains essays on light, trivial, salon, and church music as well as *kitsch*. The musical essays in Gillo Dorfles (ed.), *Kitsch* (English translation, London, 1969) are unsatisfactory treatments of this topic.

Excellent pictorial illustrations of Romantic music making are contained in two volumes of the series *Musikgeschichte in Bildern:* Walter Salmen's *Haus- und Kammermusik* (Leipzig, 1969) and Hellmuth Christian Wolff's *Oper* (Leipzig, 1968).

INDEX